# SECRETS

*of the*

# ROYALS

# SECRETS

*of the*

# ROYALS

———

*Gordon Winter*

*and*

*Wendy Kochman*

ST. MARTIN'S PRESS    NEW YORK

*Design by Judith A. Stagnitto*

**Library of Congress Cataloging-in-Publication Data**

Winter, Gordon.
　　Secrets of the royals / Gordon Winter & Wendy Kochman.
　　　　p.　　cm.
　　"A Thomas Dunne book."
　　ISBN 0-312-04415-1
　　1. Great Britain—Kings and rulers—Anecdotes. 2. Great Britain—History—Anecdotes. I. Kochman, Wendy. II. Title.
DA28.1. W526　1990
941'.008'621—dc20　　　　　　　89-77821
　　　　　　　　　　　　　　　CIP

First Edition
10 9 8 7 6 5 4 3 2 1

*This book is dedicated to*
*Kate Winter, age nine.*

# Contents

# Thanks to You All

## By Gordon Winter

$M$any people helped with this book in various ways, but the most important foundation-layer was Mr. Lavender, the former royal employee who (illegally!) allowed me to live at St. James's Palace for one year in the early fifties.

I shared his home after his wife died and might have lasted there longer if I had not climbed up to sunbathe on a flat roof overlooking the grounds of Marlborough House, the home of Queen Mary. This ended in high embarrassment when one of the elderly ladies-in-waiting (who must have been using binoculars) saw me lying naked on that roof and called the police.

Three burly Special Branch men dragged me down, shouting "lunatic" and other unfriendly terms, but I was saved from certain arrest as a "flasher" by Mr. Lavender. Being a delightfully eccentric character brimming over with tolerance and kindness, he untruthfully told them that I was his nephew from the north of England, spending a week's holiday with him.

It was a close shave for Mr. Lavender, who could easily have lost his job. So I reluctantly packed my bags and went to stay with one of his friends who rented me her attic in London's rather less socially acceptable area, the Elephant and Castle. What a comedown for one accustomed to better things!

Mr. Lavender did not actively help with this book, but several other royal insiders did. For obvious reasons, we have agreed not to contact each other after this book is published. They are D.C. and David; "Tio Pepe," the royal maid; "Douglas"; "Arnold," the butler (now retired); "Joe," the bodyguard; and "John," the chef (now working in France).

Several people who admire the royal family also gave me honorable assistance in various ways. They are:

Dr. Fraser Anderson of Tangier, who gave me most of his royal library; Matthew D, who taught me far more than he knows; Rex Nankerville, the former London art dealer (who introduced me to Sir Anthony Blunt); "Kitty" Murdoch of Savile Row; Sefton Delmer of the *Daily Express* (and British Intelligence); Alec Waugh, the author and former British Intelligence operative; Rupert Croft-Cooke, another author and former intelligence officer; and my favorite secret agent, the Australian-born journalist George Greaves, who, in the 1950s, taught me what information-gathering was all about. News-wise and otherwise.

For valuable information regarding H.M.'s spies and agents of other kinds (including judges, professors, journalists, and authors), I thank Stephen Dorril and Robin Ramsey, who bravely continue to publish their astonishing antispy magazine *Lobster* from 214 Westbourne Avenue, Hull, Yorkshire.

For introducing me to the mysteries of the British Museum's Reading Room, I thank Eric Partridge, the prolific author who labored in that room for six hours every weekday for over forty years.

Another man who helped in a roundabout way was John T, a rich English property developer in Spain. On hearing I was writing this book, he sent me this message: "For God's sake don't do it. They will send a British Intelligence doctor to kill you, or a British Intelligence judge will sentence you to life." I still don't know whether he was joking or not.

Other debts of gratitude are owed to Tommie Gorman, Ceara

Roche, Kate Carter, Noreen Egan, Pat Kelly, Gill Bell, Charles Cooper, Robert Barnette, and Anne Dunn-Foster of Connecticut, who all acted as invaluable copy-tasters and reassuring backslappers during the birth (hard labor) of the book.

Above all, a big hug to my wife, Wendy, who not only inserted that all-important female point of view, but also managed to cancel out just a little of the male conceit.

Without me, she couldn't have done it.

# Introduction

When we were impressionable kids at school, teachers and their government-approved history books gave us a one-sided story about kings and queens through the ages.

Most of the villainy and weaknesses were ignored. We were taught that monarchs were wonderfully brave and honorable—and that we should admire and respect them. So much so that, should we ever be fortunate enough to meet a royal personage, we should bow or curtsey before them.

It came as something of a shock when, in later years, we discovered that "they eat and excrete, and are often on heat" (as an irreverent poet once quipped)—just like the rest of us mere mortals.

Uncovering the nitty gritty about kings and queens is not easy, however, because the royals have long been past masters of the great cover up—usually by bribing, terrorizing or censoring the leading writers of their day.

When a monarch was so bad, mad, or oversexed that the facts started to leak out, friendly scribes were recruited to disguise the truth by bending it a little. If that didn't work, they introduced so many denials and convoluted side issues that the confused public decided it was all a load of nonsense anyway, and lost interest.

Even when documentary proof of villainy exists, there is always some historian or favored journalist who will leap into print in an effort to persuade the general public that it's a forgery. Better still, the relevant documents can "go missing"—like the death certificate of King George the Fifth, who was murdered by his royal doctors in 1936.

All this means that the history of the known royal rogues is a mass of loose ends and conflicting clues which take a long time to untangle and piece together again. One has to apply the triple-think because the monarchists have never been backward in the art of the double-think.

After starting in journalism as a gossip columnist in Tangier, Morocco, during the fifties, I was a crime reporter in Johannesburg, a foot-in-the door Sunday newsman in London, and, for sixteen years—under cover of being a writer on African affairs—a full-time intelligence operative.

During the madness of all that, as a mentally relaxing hobby, I started collecting unusual royal snippets in 1972 and began writing this book in 1987 with my wife, who was also a hard news journalist. Our aim was to provoke reflection as well as a wry smile and to give readers something to muse on while being amused.

More important, we realized that we could tell the truth, without fear or favor, because, as retired journalists living in peaceful, rural Ireland, we have no masters to answer to, no jobs to be fired from, and no place in society to lose.

The biggest problem was selecting our royal rascals. There have been so many that we had enough material for five books. They were incredible, larger-than-life characters. Some of them were hateful, some lovable, and some just the victims of deliberate character assassination—usually for religious or political reasons.

We have tried to give a general view of the tricks and villainy of monarchy, lightening the horror with humor, and writing in a relaxed, breezy style because we felt that an informative, easy to read guide to this complex subject was sorely needed. The professional apologists for royalty will definitely accuse us of "digging the dirt," but—as this book proves—there was plenty of it to dig.

As backup for every chapter we have hundreds of slips of paper bearing clues and proof drawn from documents, letters, newspapers, private archives, and ancient or out-of-print books. Although we give most of the major sources in the text, it would take another book to list all the minor ones. Yet serious scholars needing any of these can write to us care of the publisher (enclosing a stamped, addressed envelope). All letters, friendly or otherwise, will be answered. Politely or otherwise.

While every effort has been made to avoid causing unnecessary embarrassment to innocent descendants of aristocrats long dead, it is impossible for anyone to have full knowledge of every twig on a family tree. And so, fair's fair; any passage which might cause distress to relatives will be reworded in any future reprint if good cause is provided. It is not our intention to be unkind to any living person. As for the dead, they can wait until we join them.

This raises an important question of etiquette. If we meet any of their royal highnesses in the hereafter—whether heaven or hell—will we still have to bow or curtsey to them?

—Gordon Winter and Wendy Kochman
Ireland, January 1990

# 1

## The Sexy Old Royals
### (The Modern Ones Come Later)

When it comes to sex, history proves that the royals have always had more than their fair share. The most titillating period of English sexual history is from the Georges to the present day—though to use the word English in any way when discussing the Georges is ridiculous. They were 100 percent German.

Whatever they might tell you, KING GEORGE THE FIRST hated England and its people so much that he hardly spoke English. He spent much of his time in Germany and left Britain to be ruled by his favorite politicians. He was stupid, selfish, sly, and deceitful.

He had a gaggle of mistresses mostly built like mountains, and, when he was brought over from Deutschland in 1714, he was escorted by two who were so fat and atrocious to behold that the British public thought they were his pet bears.

Although George was known as "the blockhead," he was wise enough not to trust royal doctors. When his son and heir George Augustus had wanted to marry the sexy-looking Caroline of Anspach in 1705, Dad insisted that he must see, with his own eyes, whether the girl was a virgin or not. On being brought before him, Caroline was told to lie down on a couch and lift her skirt and many petticoats over her face (to save her embarrassment, one must presume). With the aid of a bright light, George satisfied himself that the honorable lady was, in fact, a lady with honor intact.

King George insisted on making that examination because, apart from not trusting royal doctors, he also distrusted all women ever since his German wife (and cousin) Dorothea, after bearing him two children, had rebelled against his long line of incredibly ugly mistresses and had taken the dashingly handsome Swedish army officer, Count von Konigsmark, as a lover.

When George found out about this illicit affair, the count was quietly murdered. George was far more lenient with his unfaithful wife. After divorcing her in 1694 and refusing to let her see her children ever again, he had her locked away in a castle in Germany. When George came to the English throne, nobody asked: "Where's the wife?" They knew. And she stayed in that castle until she died in 1726—after thirty-two years of imprisonment.

When dear German George died of a coronary in 1727, his son took the throne as GEORGE THE SECOND, and his wife, Caroline (no longer a virgin), became queen. Although he was of pure German stock and born in Germany, George Two was desperately keen to be a typical English gentleman. If anyone referred to his German background, he would haughtily retort: "I hef not vun drop of blud in my weins zat ist not Englisch."

He could not hide the renowned German efficiency in his blood, however. In fact, he was something of a time-and-motion freak. At one minute to nine every night he was to be seen standing outside his mistress's bedroom, holding a fob watch in the palm of his hand. At exactly nine he entered, pulled down his breeches, and got straight down to business—often not bothering to take off his hat. That snide little detail about the hat comes from his wife's diary, so it might or might not be true.

Another bittersweet anecdote about his wife is that when she lay dying in 1737, she urged George to marry again. When he looked shocked and said: "Nein, I vill haff mistresses," Caroline stabbed back with: "Oh, Mein Gott, that should not hamper you."

When George died in 1760, his elder son's eldest son took the throne as GEORGE THE THIRD. We are told that he was a good husband with a happy marriage, fifteen children, and "a blameless private life." Well, that's not quite true, because he definitely made hay with Lady Sarah Lennox—although, to be fair, she was a naughty little minx who deliberately seduced him in a hayfield.

They say George Three was "a truly pious" king, yet he still dallied with Hannah Lightfoot, a devout Quaker by whom he is alleged to have sired a daughter, although to cleanse this stain from his religious image, some historians will tell you that George had actually married Hannah (illegally) five years before he married his queen, Charlotte Sophia. So that makes it all right then, doesn't it?

George Three is remembered because he lost his mind and also his American colonies. Less famous are the scandals surrounding some of his oddball sons.

Oddball number one was the brave one-eyed warrior, ERNEST AUGUSTUS, Duke of Cumberland. Born in 1771, he was a nutcase who was said to have murdered his valet. Not guilty, my Lord. His Royal Highness had been innocently lying in bed when his crazed, knife-wielding valet had viciously attacked him without any provocation whatsoever. He had regrettably been forced to slash the valet's throat from ear to ear in self-defense. Case dismissed. Don't waste the court's time. Next case please.

Yes, your honor. This involves two former palace employees who, before taking an afternoon off to go and look at the crown jewels in the Tower of London (and mysteriously failing to return), told their workmates that His Royal Highness Ernest Augustus had fathered a child by Sophia, his fifteen-year-old sister. Sorry, hearsay evidence is not admissible in this or any other royal court, and in any case, the royal family says Princess Sophia's illegitimate child was fathered by a courtier named General Garth and he's an officer and a gentleman, so case dismissed.

In 1815 Ernest married the twice-widowed German princess Frederika. Reliable history books say she most probably poisoned both her previous husbands, but Ernest did not mind. She suited him perfectly. In 1837 Ernest went to Germany to become the king of Hanover—which pleased the English because he was "the most hated man in England" at the time. In 1840 Ernest was widely rumored to have been behind a a plot to assassinate Queen Victoria, but a massive cover-up was mounted to keep his name out of it.

King George the Third's oddball son number two was GEORGE, who was born in 1762. Most history books style him as "the First Gentleman of Europe" and "one of Britain's most cultured monarchs." The truth, however, is that he was a bad son, a bigamist, a liar, a gambler, a spendthrift, and a full-time fornicator. Pro-royal historians often play down these aspects by giving us the disarming throwaway line that he "enjoyed a checkered career."

At the age of seventeen, he met the actress Mary "Perdita" Robinson and promised to give her £20,000 if she would become his mistress. She agreed but, after giving birth to his baby daughter, Perdita suddenly realized she had not been paid. When George said he had no recollection of such an arrangement, the angry lady blackmailed him with some love letters he had written to her. This forced George's mad dad, George the Third, to pay her an annual pension of £500, and not a pfennig more, in return for the letters. The pension was later cancelled and Perdita died in poverty.

At the age of twenty, George entered into an illegal marriage with a widow named Mrs. Maria Fitzherbert. As she was a

Catholic this caused a rumpus and looked as if it would cost George Junior the throne when Dad died. To make amends, George Junior promised to marry, sight unseen, his first cousin, the German-born Caroline of Brunswick-Wolfenbuttel.

Ahead of her time fashion-wise, Caroline wore a miniskirt, which was rather unfortunate. She not only had tree-trunk legs but, weighing in at 224 pounds, she closely resembled a zeppelin. When George set eyes on this monster for the very first time—just before the wedding in 1795—he staggered back and uttered the immortal words: "I am not well, pray get me a glass of brandy."

On his wedding day he drank so much that he was only half conscious during the marriage ceremony. Unable to cope with the prospect of watching Caroline undress that night, he got so sloshed that he fell on the floor, totally drunk, by the fireplace. Caroline was so appalled by this first-night performance that she left him there snoring. When he woke in the morning, Caroline called him into her bed where he stayed for what is euphemistically called "a short time." It was the one and only time he shared a bed with her, and he obviously disliked the experience because he then told her to find another lover in another land. Please, I beg of you.

Being an obedient wife, she did. But when George ascended to the throne as GEORGE THE FOURTH in 1820, Caroline rushed back to England to claim her rightful role as queen. Disgusted, George offered her a huge pension if she would disappear. When she refused he mounted a divorce case against her on the grounds of the adultery he had earlier urged.

Heard in the House of Lords, it was the most sensational divorce hearing in British royal history. Caroline was accused of sleeping with an Italian named Bartolomeo Pergami. During the incredibly sexy hearing, a witness gave evidence that although Caroline claimed to sleep alone, she always had two chamberpots under her bed and, in the morning, both were nearly full. The strangest part of all this, added the witness, was that the urine in each chamberpot was always a different color. (Gosh!)

A maid told the court that she had seen Queen Caroline in Mr. Pergami's bedroom. (Golly!) And she had been sitting on Pergami's bed wearing a nightdress. (Gasp!) And his arms were around her. (Gadzooks!) The comments in parentheses, by the way, are not ours. They appeared in one of the illegal scandal sheets that sold like hotcakes after every hearing.

The maid added that when she had made Pergami's bed the next morning, she had noticed "various stains on his sheets." (Omigod!) The trial lasted three months, and the detailed reports of it (some even more sordid than those we have given) gave great delight to the workers but brought total contempt for the British monarchy from the middle and upper classes. So much so that the government forced King George to drop the case and pay Caroline £50,000 a year.

Although the mass of public opinion was behind Caroline, she had little time to savor her victory. Just nineteen days after her husband's coronation ceremony—to which she was actually refused admittance even though she ran around banging on all the doors wearing her designer-made coronation dress—Caroline died of what was described as "a bowel obstruction." There is evidence, however, that she died of an overdose of magnesia. Perhaps suicide, but then again, remembering King George's hatred of her, perhaps not.

George Four loved his breakfasts. A good example is the one he swallowed on the morning of April 9, 1830. It consisted of three beefsteaks, two whole pigeons, three-quarters of a bottle of Moselle wine, one glass of champagne, one glass of brandy, and two glasses of port. Four hours after enjoying a similar dinner just before midnight on June 25, George's repast caught up with him. His stomach blew a fuse and he died screaming: "Oh, Mein Gott, this must be death." The official cause was rupture of the stomach blood vessels and alcoholic cirrhosis.

Nobody mourned him. Even that normally respectful British newspaper *The Times* wrote in its lead column: "There was never an individual less regretted by his fellow creatures than this deceased King. What heart has heaved one sob of unmercenary sorrow?"

During his sordid sixty-eight years of life, King George the Fourth fornicated with more than 7,000 women. This is known because he had a strange kink. Every time he had sex with a woman, he clipped off a tiny lock of her hair and placed it in an envelope as a sentimental (or sexy) reminder. Some 7,100 of those envelopes were found in his bedroom cupboards after he died. Each bore a woman's name: Lady Hertford, Lady Melbourne, Lady Conyngham, Lady Jersey, Annie, the scullery maid, and so on.

As George failed to leave a legitimate heir, his eldest surviving brother, William Henry (he being the third oddball son of the mad King George the Third) took the throne as WILLIAM THE FOURTH. Born in 1765, he entered the royal navy at the age of fourteen and, not surprisingly, ended up admiral of the fleet.

While sailing around the West Indies, he contracted VD from a dusky young woman not of the blue blood, which cooled his ardor somewhat and made him realize it was unwise to sleep around with foreigners. So, after returning to England, he settled down with the Irish-born actress Mrs. Dorothea Jordan in 1790. She bore him ten illegitimate children. It was a good relationship but, tiring of her services in 1811, he paid her off and she died in poverty five years later.

Shortly after this, William's family said he must try to provide a (legal) heir, so he married the German princess Adelaide of Saxe-Meiningen. But the two daughters she produced both died in infancy, and when King William died of alcoholic cirrhosis in 1837, the English crown passed to his niece, Victoria. But, before we deal with that sexy old lady, let's take a look at her father EDWARD, the Duke of Kent—who was mad King George the Third's fourth oddball son.

Born in 1767, Edward was a brave soldier but, having received his military training in Germany, he was a very strict disciplinarian who believed that a good beating solved any problem. The sight of men being whipped apparently excited him. When, as a colonel in the British army, he was sent to command Gibraltar in 1790, he quickly became notorious as "The Beast" by decreeing that scores of English troops should be flogged without mercy.

Gibraltar's famous cobbled barrack square echoed with the anguished screams of men being given one hundred lashes just because their boots weren't highly polished. The average punishment for other offenses, such as being drunk, was about four hundred lashes. The duke loved to watch as the blood spurted from their bare backs.

It couldn't last. Within a year, after the troops repeatedly deserted or mutinied, London pulled him out and packed him off to Canada, where he continued to flog his troops with such "bestial severity" that they also mutinied and he was recalled again. So where did the Whitehall mandarins send him? Back to Gibraltar—as its governor.

To celebrate his promotion, the duke handed out punishment of up to seven hundred lashes. When a soldier named Rose tried to desert by escaping to Spain, the duke imposed the maximum whipping allowed under the law. This was 999 lashes, and he stood counting them very carefully in case one was missed. A few weeks later in 1803, a soldier named Ben Armstrong died while being flogged and the entire company of troops on the Rock of Gibraltar, including many officers, mounted a mass revolt. They warned Whitehall that if "the Royal Sadist" was not posted away from Gib, the troops would definitely kill him.

The duke was immediately recalled to London in disgrace. But a member of the British royal family cannot possibly be humiliated by being seen to be sacked, so he was quickly promoted to field marshal. He also retained the official title of governor of Gibraltar until he died seventeen years later— although he was never allowed to set foot on the Rock again during all those years.

This Prince Charming lived with his mistress, Julie de St.

Laurent, for twenty-seven years. She also seems to have been a great character. Royal legend would have you believe she was an aristocratic refugee from the French Revolution, but the Canadian writer Mollie Gillen in her book *The Prince and His Lady* (Sidgwick & Jackson, 1970) rather convincingly identifies her as a civil engineer's daughter who was previously the mistress of two French aristocrats.

Some people in the Canadian city of Quebec insist to this day that Julie married the Duke of Kent, that she had children by him and that their descendants are the rightful sovereigns of Great Britain. But royalist historians say this cannot possibly be true because, even if he was married to her (which they strenuously and most emphatically deny), that marriage would have been illegal in terms of the Royal Marriages Act of 1772. Whether royally "illegal" or not, poor Julie could not prove she had been married to the duke anyway because two masked Watergate-type burglars (alleged to have been British Intelligence officers sent over by the royal family) stole her marriage certificate from files in Quebec.

As for the children Julie is said to have produced, royal apologists claim that if the duke *did* sire a couple of bastard sons, he must have had them by other women. This was a clever escape clause, which barred the duke's alleged sons from being heirs to the British throne even if it could have been proved that Julie and the duke were married.

Whatever the truth about these allegations and smears, history tries to assure us that the duke was a perfect gentleman and that his love for Julie was so genuine it was "out of this world." But in 1817, when he was broke and in debt, his family told him of a wonderful way to improve his bank balance. So the duke decided, "most unhappily," to throw Julie out of his world and stick her in a French nunnery.

Explaining that heirs to the English throne were short on the ground, his family had told the duke that Parliament would have to grant him a substantial annual income if he married someone suitable and worked hard at producing a legal child to be in line for the succession. The duke thought this a great idea. Right, they said. We have a suitable woman lined up for you.

This was a German princess named Victoire Mary Louisa, a widow with two young children. Her lack of virginity and two ready-made kids did not worry the duke. He badly needed the money and married her in 1818. One year later she presented him with a baby daughter named VICTORIA who, when King William the Fourth died seventeen years later, took the throne as the Queen of England.

Standing less than five feet small, this colossus of a woman gave her name to an age that produced a British Empire covering some 40 million square kilometers. Her 387 million subjects in that great empire were led to believe that Her Royal Highness was the classic Victorian prude. Not true. She was an extremely randy lady.

Her marriage to the German prince ALBERT of Saxe-Coburg-Gotha in 1840 is said to have been "one of the great royal love stories of all time." This could be a slight exaggeration considering that as soon as Albert was born in August 1819, it was proposed that he would eventually marry Victoria (his cousin) who was then just three months old.

According to the book *Victoria R.I.* (Weidenfeld & Nicolson, 1964), written by the outstanding British historian Lady Elizabeth Longford, there was a strong rumor "believed by many of her court" that Victoria's prince consort was illegitimate, probably with a Jewish father. The mention of his father's religion is somewhat puzzling, but far more fascinating is the fact that dear Albert was rather effeminate and that he was definitely a virgin when he married Victoria! When asked why he had never sown his wild oats with women, he rather oddly replied: "That species of vice disgusts me."

Poor Albert. It is no secret that he complained bitterly about Victoria wanting her conjugal rights just about every night. He would cower behind his deliberately locked bedroom door while she hammered on it from the outside screaming (in German): "Open the door, I'm the Queen!" And even when he did allow her in his bed, he was the passive lover. Yet, in her diary, the rampant queen wrote that she still enjoyed the "heavenly lovemaking."

On arriving at Buckingham Palace, German Albert was a smashing-looking fellow with fabulous legs who wore very sexy skin-tight breeches. Within ten years however, the good life made him fat, bald, and prematurely middle aged. When the tired old fellow died at age forty-two in 1861 after siring nine children, Victoria entered into her famous years of deep mourning, which bored the public so much that everybody suspected she was using her grief as an excuse for not carrying out her public duties.

For those ardent royalists who think this is a disgraceful suggestion, it is necessary to point out that even the top people's newspaper *The Times* stated in a lead column that a bit of work would help to cure Victoria's "great grief."

When Albert died, a bishop told Victoria that it would be unseemly for her to consider taking another man and that she should consider herself as "now being married only to Christ." Looking at him as if he were totally insane, the queen replied: "Now that's what I call twaddle!"

Her Majesty's long days of mourning certainly did not extend into her nights. She is known to have taken several lovers, the most famous being her Scots gillie, John Brown, who was officially called Her Majesty's "Highland Servant"—which is hardly accurate because he also serviced her in the lowlands of London, and other places.

All the courtiers at Buckingham Palace hated John Brown because he was coarse, arrogant, and a heavy drinker (although he could handle it) and had become the queen's "blatant favorite." When rumors of this started to spread into the public domain, Buckingham Palace cunningly leaked a disinformation rumor that stated Queen Victoria was a keen spiritualist and was actually friendly with John Brown only because he was her medium.

This might have conned some of the lower classes but not the smart society hostesses. When they referred to Victoria as

"Mrs. Brown" during their cocktail parties, everyone giggled knowingly. The *Lausanne Gazette* even published a story claiming Victoria was secretly married to Brown, but anyone with the slightest knowledge of the British class system will realize that this was a most ludicrous suggestion. An English queen may sleep with a servant, but she would never let the side down by marrying one.

Whatever they say about the well-endowed John Brown, his relationship with Victoria was definitely not platonic. This subject is no great secret to historians. Many of them have hinted at it—though always delicately, without any reference whatsoever to that awfully common word, sex. Until December 1986, that is, when that fabulously cantankerous *Sunday Express* columnist, Sir John Junor, told his millions of readers that when Queen Victoria knew she was dying, she arranged to be buried with a photograph of John Brown in her left hand. Commenting on this, Sir John wrote: "Which would suggest that during the 34 years he served her, he did more than help her mount her cuddy." (Our dictionary says a cuddy can be a stupid fellow, a closet, or a donkey. Sir John left it for us to decide which he meant.) After mentioning that Queen Victoria had also known an "Indian gentleman," Sir John asked: "Does it matter that she was so highly sexed? Not a damn!"

Many readers of the staunchly conservative *Sunday Express* must have wondered why such things should suddenly be unearthed about dear old long-dead Victoria. But canny Sir John knew what he was about. His brief mention of Her Majesty's libido was almost certainly a deliberate "shock absorber" aimed at preparing his true-blue readers for worse things to come. Sir John had advance knowledge that an upcoming book would throw new light on Victoria's sex life.

Entitled *Victoria: An Intimate Biography*, it was published in the United States three months later. This was not one of those quickly written, slick and superficial books. It was dangerous because the author was Professor Stanley Weintraub, the eminently respectable director of the Institute for Arts and Humanistic Studies at Pennsylvania State University.

To make matters worse (from the English point of view), the book was not just a one-shot deal. The professor had spent thirty-one years researching and writing about the Victorian period. It's not easy to trash a man of that caliber, but when the paperback edition was brought out in Britain, the normally up-market newspaper *The Observer* had a nice little bash at it.

In their issue of September 11, 1988, they dismissed the book with a thirty-two word (small-print) mention that started: "Makes too many mistakes and is too concerned with dubious speculation about the Queen's sexual state." Having solved the problem of not offending the royals, the critic then continued with the balancing-act comment: "but this is a bright and re- freshing Life, wafted briskly along by gusts of transatlantic ir- reverence." In journalism, this is known as playing it both ways down the middle. Yet, whether by "mistake" or not, *The Ob- server* selectively failed to tell its readers that the author was a professor.

A rather different example of our renowned English fair play came when the British publisher of the book (Unwin Hyman) deleted that rather suggestive word "Intimate" from the title and brought it out under the more sedate: *Victoria: Biography of a Queen*. Jolly good show, old chaps.

When a British journalist interviewed Professor Weintraub and asked him how he had managed to unearth the infor- mation about Queen Victoria's love life, the professor said he had experienced no trouble at all in digging it out of British archives. He added: "Much of the material was available to British biographers, but maybe they felt it might not be quite right to use it. I thought it was astonishing."

Queen Victoria's taste in men was certainly astonishing. Apart from the crude and drunken peasant John Brown, who died in 1883, she had another strange favorite. This was the low-caste, stupid, uneducated but cunning Indian named Abdul "the Munshi" Karim who started working at the palace by serving the queen at her table (as a waiter, of course). She quickly recognized his special talents and promoted him to the position of her "Indian Secretary."

Just like John Brown, the common-born "Munshi" was hated by the courtiers at Buckingham Palace, but the queen was so besotted by him that she gave him three homes: a cottage at Windsor, a bungalow on the Isle of Wight, and a lovely house at Balmoral, which he filled with his poor Indian relatives at the British taxpayer's expense.

# 2

## *Noblesse Oblige*

*I*f you like a royal love story with a massive dollop of mystery, sex, and confusing double-talk, here's a classic.

In 1327 a fifteen-year-old boy came to the English throne as EDWARD THE THIRD. School history books usually say he was utterly adored by his public because he conquered a quarter of France and "gave England back her pride." But this brilliant brainwashing for kids needs to be translated into adult language so that it can be better understood.

King Edward was *not* adored by his public. They hated him because he taxed them heavily in order to finance his never-ending war games in Scotland and France. King Edward *was* utterly adored by his aristocratic knights because while fighting with him in France, they grabbed lots and lots of lovely loot, which they brought home on the backs of thousands of donkeys.

On arriving back in England, the king and his super-rich knights didn't give any taxes back to the poor public. Instead they said: "Look. By conquering a quarter of France, we have given England her pride back." It worked. The gullibles rushed around the taverns and marketplaces slapping each other on the back and telling each other how wonderful it was to be English and to have pockets bursting with pride.

Yet, for all his great victories in foreign parts, King Edward the Third never realized his ambitions, and even before he lapsed into senility, his public finances drifted into ruin and he was intensely disliked by both public and Parliament. He was also a notorious lustpot but, by a superb masterstroke, his image was brilliantly cleansed, whiter than white, through the shrewd manipulation of what was actually a decidedly dodgy story.

Many British children's history books—and even some of the adult ones—state that King Edward was dancing in a crowded ballroom when a lady's garter fell to the floor. To stop anyone spreading the despicable rumor that he had been sliding his hand up her leg, the quick-thinking monarch picked up the blue garter and placed it around his knee. Glaring at some of the loudly sniggering noblemen, Edward then mumbled what might have been "You dirty-minded bastards!"

But that, not sounding quite right to the mythmakers, was quite rightly translated into "Shame on him who thinks evil of it," which, in the posher-sounding French—*"Honi soit qui mal y pense"*—became the motto of England's highest honor, the Most Noble Order of the Garter, which symbolizes the "Triumph of Chastity and Chivalry over Temptation."

It all sounds extremely virtuous but the truth is that King Edward, although allegedly chivalrous, was certainly not chaste and he was definitely not above temptation. Closer investigation of that alleged ballroom incident discloses some very strange facts—and incredible confusion in the royal records. And whenever one finds confusion in the royal diaries, journals, or official pronouncements, they are usually hiding something. The confusion is introduced to muddy the waters and cloud the issue to the point that people will become bored with argument and counterargument and walk away. We don't think you will walk away from this humdinger, though.

First of all, who was the lady whose garter snapped while dancing? Some history books tell you she was Catherine, the beautiful countess of Salisbury. But if the Most Noble Order of the Garter was in any way connected with Catherine, here's a very ignoble snippet of information: King Edward the Third fancied Countess Catherine like crazy and when she refused to go to bed with him in 1342, he is alleged to have gagged her mouth so that she was unable to scream and then to have raped her.

The countess is said to have been so badly affected by this dastardly deed that she told her husband (William, the First Earl of Salisbury) she was no longer interested in sex. Being a gentle fellow, William sat on the edge of the bed and treated her kindly until she tearfully disclosed what had happened. The angry William went to King Edward and told him: "You have villainously dishonored me and thrown me in the dung." So saying, he sold all his lands, left the country, and died brokenhearted two years later.

That terrible story was suppressed at the time, though two eminent foreign chroniclers, one of them a churchman, placed it all on record for nosy people like us to find. Yet, according to various historians (mostly English), those two learned men of letters made "a terrible mistake." They claim that the two chroniclers confused Countess Catherine with Joan, "the Fair Maid of Kent"—as it was actually Joan's garter that King Edward picked up.

Is that so? All right then, let's take a closer look at Joan: The daughter of the earl of Kent, she was born in 1328. At the age of eleven she entered into a marriage with a one-eyed knight named Sir Thomas Holland, who then went off to war in France. Some historians claim that this was only a contract to marry, but others insist it was a full marriage.

Whatever the truth, one year later, while Sir Thomas was still away, twelve-year-old Joan entered into another marriage. This was with William de Montacute, the *second* earl of Salisbury, the eldest son of the Countess of Salisbury (who was allegedly raped by Edward the Third).

Four years later, when Joan was sixteen and said to be the most beautiful (and the "most amorous") girl in England, her first husband, Sir Thomas, returned from fighting in France and, taking strong exception to Joan's infidelity, sent a petition to the pope requesting that his rights to Joan's divine body be restored to him. The pope agreed and Joan's marriage to William was finally annulled on November 13, 1349, when Joan was twenty-one.

Joan then became the full-time wife of Sir Thomas, who was not quite the dog in the manger he appears because it has been recorded that Joan, the Fair Maiden, also became the mistress of King Edward III. She must have pleased the king because he granted her the value of eight hundred ounces of silver as an annual "pension" for the rest of her life.

In December 1360, when Joan was thirty-two, her husband (Sir Thomas, the one-eyed one) died and King Edward immediately told Joan to marry his eldest son, Edward, "the Black Prince." In an effort to distance King Edward from any suggestion that he had passed on his mistress to his son, some historians claim that Joan's love match with the Black Prince was made "without the knowledge of King Edward III," but this contradicts the recorded fact that King Edward's wife, Philippa, was "opposed to the marriage."

The Black Prince was so determined to marry Joan, however, that he applied to the pope for special permission. The pope replied that the marriage would be okay by him if the prince would finance a new chantry chapel in Canterbury Cathedral. The Black Prince agreed to this deal and so, at the age of thirty-three, Joan the "Fair Maiden" became the very first PRINCESS OF WALES.

It was at this stage that they started to cleanse Joan's public image. We are told the lovely blonde Princess of Wales was such a goody-goody that she employed three full-time priests whose only job was to say daily prayers for her dead husband (the one-eyed one). She apparently didn't have the time to say the prayers herself, probably because she was too busy keeping track of the hundreds of servants she employed at the twenty-six mansions she owned in various parts of England.

Another suspicious little story about Joan is that in 1381, during the peasant revolt, she was caught by rebels as she drove by coach from Canterbury to London. We are told that the luscious lady persuaded the disgustingly common rebels to release her by agreeing to reward them "with a few kisses." There's something decidedly fishy about this yarn. Could those common roughnecks have forced her (against her will, of course) to reward them with something more?

The history books tell us that Joan was a good wife to the Black Prince—even though he kept dashing off to fight valiantly in battles overseas. This did not stop him from siring several bastards—two of them being Sir John Sounder and Sir Roger Clarendon. Yet when it came to creating titled babies, Joan went one better in 1367 by producing a baby who became England's KING RICHARD THE SECOND when he was ten years old.

Is *this* the reason they went to all that trouble to cleanse Joan's image—because she was the mother of a king? Most probably. But during their cleanout they threw away too many royal documents. As a result nobody in the British royal family (or the royal archives at Windsor) can today tell you *why* the Most Noble Order of the Garter was founded or even exactly *when*. Ask them when the first formal Garter ceremony was held and even then they flim-flam by suggesting it was "perhaps" on April 23, 1348. This really is incredible when you consider how fastidious the royals usually are when it comes to filing away every tiny detail about their illustrious past.

From all of this, it is clear that King Edward the Third and his family had quite an eventful life. But we haven't quite finished with King Edward yet. In 1366, when he was fifty-four, he lost sexual interest in his queen, Philippa (who had churned out twelve children for him), and took up with a tough little cookie named Alice Perrers. There is also a little confusion about this woman in the royal records. Royalists claim Alice

Perrers was an aristocrat, "perhaps" the daughter of Sir Richard Perrers. Others say she was quite definitely of low birth and a former kitchen scrubber.

Some historians have tried to condone the king's bad taste in women by claiming he was suffering from advanced senility at the time he chose Alice as his mistress. That's a pretty weak excuse as it's rather unusual for a man to go totally senile at the age of fifty-four. Other historians say the truth is that King Edward became "mentally unbalanced" as a result of his notorious sexual excesses.

The truth is that Alice Perrers was an awful bitch. She sucked the king dry of money during the last mad eleven years of his life and enjoyed so much power that when any of her many criminal pals got into trouble, she went down to the law courts and sat alongside the judges—to make sure that not guilty verdicts were delivered. On three occasions a judge refused to obey her, so Alice took the law into her own hands by physically persuading dotty old King Edward to pardon the three convicted crooks. In one scandalous case she protected one of her friends who had murdered a sailor—allegedly at her request.

In a desperate attempt to cleanse King Edward's image, some royal apologists claim that Alice Perrers was never his mistress—just a nurse who was hired to tend him on his sickbed. That cover-up failed abysmally when authenticated documents later disclosed the embarrassing snippet that King Edward the Third, the man who founded the Most Noble Order of the Garter, died insane in 1377 at the age of sixty-five—after catching syphilis from Alice.

We know that the Most Noble Order of the Garter symbolizes the "Triumph of Chastity and Chivalry over Temptation." The men upon whom the order is bestowed are supposed to epitomize all that kind of thing but, in several cases, somebody failed to do his homework—because some very doubtful characters have been given the Garter.

Way back in 1540, KING HENRY THE EIGHTH had a problem. Several of the knights given the order had been executed for high treason, but their names remained on the official roll of honor. What to do? Black their names out and make the document look terribly untidy—or leave the swines in? King Henry said their names should be left in, but told his scribes to write alongside that they were "Traitors."

In May 1915, ten months after Britain declared war on Germany, eight Knights of the Garter were stripped of the great English honor—because they were Germans or German sympathizers who couldn't wait to see Britain conquered by the kaiser.

Another recipient of the most noble order was that chivalrous Japanese gentleman EMPEROR HIROHITO, who was granted it in 1929. But in 1941, when Japan took Hitler's side in World War II, Britain snatched it back from him, saying he was an utter bounder and a cad who was totally unfit to wear England's greatest honor. This proved to be true; during that war, Hirohito's soldiers committed unbelievable atrocities against thousands of Allied prisoners of war in the emperor's name.

But time heals all wounds (except those of the prisoners who were tortured, beaten, starved, or worked to death), and the Most Noble Order of the Garter was restored to the "rehabilitated" Hirohito when he stayed at Buckingham Palace as the honored guest of QUEEN ELIZABETH in 1971.

One of the sexiest rogues to be given the Garter was the undoubtedly brilliant politician Lord Palmerston who, at various stages in his most illustrious career, was Queen Victoria's foreign secretary, home secretary, and prime minister.

Lord Palmerston was of the Irish peerage, and long before he was given the fabled Garter, everyone at Buckingham Palace called him "Cupid" because of his many adulterous escapades. Even that staid newspaper *The Times* tagged him "Lord Cupid," so it was hardly a secret that he was a right old ram.

Queen Victoria certainly knew. In her huge journal of a diary she described him as "an old sinner." Why? Because while he was Her Majesty's guest at Windsor Castle one weekend, Lord P, feeling full of life, slipped into the bedroom of one of Victoria's attractive ladies-in-waiting in the dead of night.

The lady's name was Mrs. Brand, and after barricading the door so that she could not escape, the chivalrous Lord P made "a violent and brutal" sexual attack on her. Her piercing screams were heard by half the inmates at Windsor Castle, and she was rescued in the nick of time just as her knickers were being torn off.

It was not the first time Lord P had burst into a lady's boudoir and attempted to get his leg over without being invited. He had done much the same some months earlier, but the lady in question had managed to run out quickly before there could be any question of damage being done to her reputation.

Apart from all this, while his wife was away in 1833, the old rascal had enjoyed a quick love affair with Lady Stanley. Quick is the operative word because the Irish peer's idea of foreplay was "Brace yourself, Bridget." No, that is not an unkind remark. It was confirmed by Lady Stanley herself who said he had made love to her "in his impudent, brusque way."

Now comes the best part of the story. Lord Palmerston's death, at 10:45 A.M. on October 18, 1865, was caused by overdoing it. Doing what? Deflowering a pretty young parlor maid. Where? On the billiard table in his baronial mansion, Brocket Hall.

The cause of his death was not disclosed to the public. But one basically honest historian couldn't resist stating, tongue in cheek, that a half-finished letter, found in Lord P's study, "showed he had died in harness."

Lord Palmerston, Britain's prime minister and the proud holder of the Most Noble Order of the Garter, was given a state funeral and buried in Westminister Abbey.

# 3

## Gay Royals
### (And Their Mates)

*D*eciding that history was riddled with hypocrisy when it came to homosexuality, London's Haringey Council thought it would be a good idea if local schoolchildren were given lessons on the subject.

So, in 1988, they issued a manual containing guidelines for lessons that would help children to "develop an awareness of the problems suffered by great gays in history and also to help remove the gay stigma."

This caused high-pitched screams of outrage from several British newspapers. They described the idea as "trendy twaddle." *Sunday People* columnist John Smith wrote that while it might well be true that Britain's nursing heroine Florence Nightingale was "a raving dyke," he did not see why the youngsters of Haringey should have homosexuality added to the curriculum "just to pander to a load of poofs."

Strong stuff. But Haringey Council have a good answer. Schoolchildren eventually find out about the adulterous relationships King Charles the Second, King George the Fourth, and King Edward the Seventh, and so on, enjoyed with dozens of mistresses, so why the double standards when it comes to gays?

The whole subject really is riddled with hypocrisy. Most senior journalists in London are fully aware that hundreds of the very top people in Britain are gay, particularly in Parliament, the House of Lords, and the various security services. The wrists of one recent tall, handsome, and plummy-voiced prime minister were so limp that some people thought he was hanging them out to dry.

The homosexuality of these top people is ignored as long as they toe the Establishment line. But just let them take one step outside it and the "queer" label is quickly slapped on them.

Good examples of this were the high-level British Intelligence operatives Guy Burgess, Donald Maclean, and Sir Anthony Blunt, the queen's art advisor. Although it was well known that all three were rampant homosexuals, nobody at top level in British Intelligence seemed to notice any possible "security risk." Yet when it was discovered that they were actually double agents for the KGB, they suddenly became "disgusting queers."

There is nothing new about this. The best royal example is WILLIAM "RUFUS," the son of William the Conqueror. He was crowned king of England in 1087 when about thirty-two. Most schoolbooks smear Rufus by saying his reign was "worthless, despotic, and tyrannical," but the truth is that he was actually recommended for the throne by his father, who described him as "a good and dutiful son."

He never broke his word. He treated prisoners of war with fairness because he was brainy enough to work out that any captured enemy was some mother's son. He was also an effective ruler, but most history books describe how Rufus "extorted money from his poor subjects with the claws of a harpy because his avarice was unbounded." Translated, this means he imposed taxes just like any other greedy, luxury-loving monarch.

Rufus claimed that the church was a "big business" setup that should be taxed like everyone else. The churchmen didn't mind Rufus milking the public of taxes, but they took strong exception when he grabbed their monies as well. So, when he died, church scribes gave him "bad press" by writing in their chronicles that he was an evil king and a homosexual who did not believe in God. The smear worked so well that Rufus became one of the big royal ogres of history.

It is untrue to say he did not believe in God. He believed in Him all right, but hated Him for giving him a rugged, thickset masculine appearance but the sensitivity of a female. This was probably why he grabbed church monies—to get his revenge on God. Officially, Rufus gave another reason. He said he needed the money to finance England's role in the first "crusade" against the "heathen" Turks who worshipped Allah and had occupied Palestine. He claimed it was quite valid to grab the English bishoprics and sell them off to pay for what was, after all, a holy war.

Rufus further angered the men of God when he fell seriously ill in February 1093 and, believing he was dying, told them he was willing to do a deal with God: if he was spared, he would promise to live a more "normal" life, stop being horrid to the church, and desist from grabbing at its mountains of money and lands. Thinking this was a fair deal, the churchmen shook hands on it. But, instead of keeping his side of the bargain when he enjoyed a miraculous recovery, Rufus told God he could go to hell.

No wonder the church scribes denigrated Rufus after his death. We are told he died while hunting in the New Forest after his close friend, Sir Walter Tyrell, accidentally shot an arrow into the back of his head. It is strongly suspected, however, that Rufus was murdered on the orders of his younger brother, Henry, who then took the throne as HENRY THE FIRST.

This fits because Henry never bothered to institute an inquiry into Rufus's death, as one normally does when one's king dies in an accident. Also, after Rufus was hit by that arrow, his men "dispersed at once," which is very suspect. Even odder, they left his "profusely bleeding body" to be wrapped up by local peasants who trundled it on the back of an unregal old cart to Winchester.

Poor old Rufus. His body was refused religious rites by those wronged men of the cloth, and he was buried in Winchester Cathedral with hardly anyone being told, not even the bells. Why? Because, the churchmen said he was: "Loathsome to his people, abominable to God and unworthy of his own manhood." You can translate "unworthy of his own manhood" whichever way you like. Unworthy because he loved men— or unworthy because he never took out a marriage license.

Yet, while it is true that Rufus was a lifelong bachelor, he was not a woman-hater. On the contrary, he was clearly bisexual as he had affairs with several women and produced half a dozen illegitimate children. This, however, was not given page one treatment by the church chroniclers because it did not fit in neatly with the "queer" image they wished to convey.

The most intellectual king to rule England was a Scot and he was also bisexual though, when given the choice, he opted for the boys. This was James, the only son of Mary Queen of Scots. He was proclaimed King James the Sixth of Scotland in 1567 at the age of thirteen months and took the English throne as JAMES THE FIRST in 1603 when Queen Elizabeth the First died.

While the Scots say he was one of the best kings they had, the English didn't like him at all. The English elite, that is. They claimed he was "conceited." He said this was mainly because he found it difficult to talk down to their "limited intelligence and stupid arrogance." They said he was "a slovenly eater," but the truth is that he was born with an abnormally large tongue, which caused him great difficulty when chewing.

The English complained that he wore clothes to scare a crow, and they were also appalled by his "coarse language and vulgar wit." In this they did not lie. James was decidedly coarse and definitely vulgar, particularly when he wished to prick pomposity and pretension. Once, when alighting from his coach in Whitehall, the crowd rushed forward and started pushing each other. Turning to his aide-de-camp, James asked why the crowd was so badly behaved. The fawning aide gushed: "Because they only want to get closer for a better look at Your Royal Majesty, sire," to which the king retorted: "Then I will let down my breeches and they shall also see my arse."

On another occasion when sitting in church, the minister droned on in a long and boring mealy-mouthed sermon without any real meat or meaning. The exasperated king shocked all the blue bloods present by shouting from his front-row pew: "I give not one turd for your preaching." This should not be taken to mean James was opposed to the word of God. Actually, he was a learned theologian who wrote fourteen pamphlets and books about the church, monarchy, and even a treatise on witchcraft.

Proving himself a man ahead of his time, King James also wrote a short book entitled *A Counterblaste to Tobacco*, in which he stated that cigarette smoking was: "A custom loathsome to the eye, hateful to the nose, harmful to the brain [and] dangerous to the lungs . . ."

In 1611 King James gave each of the English families settling in the colony of Virginia free plots of land for the planting of hemp (cannabis), and the settlers named their site Jamestown in his honor. Some historians claim he wanted the cannabis grown after hearing that American Indians used the resin to cure syphilis. This however, is another nasty smear. At the time, the British Parliament encouraged hemp growing to meet the enormous demand for hemp fiber used to rig the English fleets.

Being a Scot, King James was cynical about the English class system and alleged that the practice of bestowing titles on those loyal to the Establishment was a reward verging on bribery. Well, that was the excuse he used when he was caught giving titles to anyone who would pay him. In one single day (July

23, 1603) he dubbed no less than 432 knights in the Royal Garden at Whitehall and in so doing made his mark in the Guinness Book of Records. As if that was not enough, just forty-eight hours later he appointed sixty-two other knights.

From then on, until 1609, he created scores of other knight-hoods. He also sold baronetcies at prices starting from $2,000. When they discovered this, the English nobles attacked the king for making a mockery of the Honours System and forced him to apologize to Parliament in March 1610. They also made him promise that he would not do that kind of thing again. But he did. He also gave titles away. Often to his boyfriends. Once, when James fell madly in love with a handsome but smelly pirate, he made him an earl.

In 1589 James married Princess Anne of Denmark, who bore him three sons and four daughters. The couple had obviously done one of those usual royal deals: "You take your lovers and I'll take mine, but let nobody come between us." Before taking any male lover, James always asked his wife to approve his choice. If she said no, the boy had to go—which indicates that King James was astute enough to know that queens always have impeccable taste.

Another reason was given by George Abbot, who was the archbishop of Canterbury from 1611 to 1633. He knew King James well and in his celebrated *Biographia Britannica*, he wrote that King James shrewdly insisted on Queen Anne choosing his lovers so that if anything went wrong, he might answer: "It is long of yourself: for you were the party that commended him unto me." All wives will recognize this as meaning: "Yes, dear, but it's your fault."

There is written evidence that King James, that great lover of the arts, was overwhelmingly gay. This comes in a love letter he wrote to George Villiers, the duke of Buckingham, who was one of his lovers. The letter is a classic in royal history as it states, in part: "I desire only to live in this world for your sake, and I [would] rather live banished in any part of the world with you than live a sorrowful widow's life without you my sweet child and wife, and grant that ye may ever be a comfort to your dear dad and husband."

King James may have been highly intelligent, but in affairs of the heart it's obvious that he didn't know whether he was Arthur or Martha when it came to being a widow(er).

In 1622, three years before he died of a stroke, King James appointed a privy council to investigate the setting up of a government department that would concern itself with the various aspects of commerce. It was a great idea and, when finally set up in 1786, was named the board of trade—a delicious epitaph for King James.

Another great lover of the arts was the gay Scots King JAMES THE THIRD. Having a "refined and cultivated mind," he spent most of his time with painters and musicians and showered them with gifts. Although he preferred his witty favorites to the business of government, James did not neglect his duties when it came to providing heirs to the throne. In 1469 he married Margaret of Denmark when she was about thirteen, and she presented him with three sons. King James was also a valiant warrior, but he was murdered in 1488 after losing a battle near Bannockburn.

Another warrior was RICHARD THE LION HEART who became king of England in 1189. He is usually presented to schoolchildren as that tall, strong, handsome, blue-eyed blond, a gallant and splendid soldier, poet and musician who fought valiantly in the Third Crusade. Not quite true. He was cruel, haughty, vindictive, and an anti-Semite. His mother, the beautiful Eleanor of Aquitane, spoiled him silly, yet he was a bad son to her. When he was thirty, he had an argument with his father, King Henry the Second, and in a fit of pique took himself off to Paris where he ate and slept with his father's greatest enemy, Philip Augustus, the king of France.

Four years later, in 1191, Richard the Lion Heart married Berengaria of Navarre, not for romantic reasons as legend claims, but for purely political purposes. He was a bad husband who neglected her in and out of bed, which probably explains why they were childless. He was also a bad king of England who never bothered to learn English and spent only six months in his English realm—which he regarded merely as a cow to be milked of money.

When this delightful king was crowned, he issued a public notice forbidding any Jews from attending the ceremony or the coronation banquet held afterward. In spite of this snub, the leaders of London's Jewish community arrived with gifts of gold as proof of their loyalty to the new king. They wasted their time. The courtiers welcomed them by tearing off their clothing and flogging them mercilessly. Some died during the beating and the rest were thrown out suffering serious wounds—which clearly signaled to the king's subjects that, as far as he was concerned, Jews were not the chosen people. This led to the nationwide robbing and killing of Jews.

In York alone five hundred Jews who realized that they were doomed killed their wives and children mercifully (probably with poison) and then locked themselves in a castle. Rather than surrender to a lynch mob gathered outside, they set fire to the castle and are said to have committed mass suicide by deliberately breathing in the noxious smoke and fumes, which rendered them unconscious before the fire burned their bodies to ashes.

British schoolchildren, however, know Richard the Lion Heart by the far more charming and acceptable (when the gay angle is not stressed) tale of his French-born minstrel friend, Blondel. This famous legend of one man's great (brotherly) love for another tells how, in 1193, while returning from his crusade, King Richard was captured and later imprisoned in Austria. The heartbroken Blondel trudged the length and breadth of that country, going from castle to castle, playing a lyre and singing a song he and Richard had composed at a picnic during a camping holiday in happier days.

His great devotion was rewarded one day as he sang the first lines of the song outside a castle overlooking the Danube. From deep within its thick walls he heard the melodious voice of his adored king sing out the rest of the song. Not being your butch James Bond type who would have effected a dramatic one-man rescue, Blondel sang and danced all the way home to tell Mother England—who got her beloved son released after paying a ransom worth about $12 million in modern currency.

If cruelty distresses you, perhaps you should not read how England's unluckiest gay monarch, KING EDWARD THE SECOND, was murdered. You might think you can cope and then, after reading it, find yourself nauseated. If that happens, don't ask for your money back. We gave you fair warning. However, just to be on the safe side, we will give you another warning when the tasteless, though historically important, part begins.

Edward was born in the famous Welsh castle of Caernarvon in 1284 at a time when his mother and father (Edward the First) were enjoying a break from London. As the rebellious Welsh had long been complaining that they wanted a prince of their own, rather than a London-based Englishman, Edward's father called in the Welsh chieftains and asked them if they would accept a handsome young prince who was born in Wales, could not speak one word of English, and could be proved to have led a completely blameless life. Not believing this could be true, the Welsh chiefs said they most definitely would—without asking any further questions. Legend has it that the cunning king then triumphantly produced his Caernarvon-born baby Edward, who thus became the first English PRINCE OF WALES to be thrust upon them.

Baby Edward grew up to be a tall, handsome, and highly intelligent fellow. But instead of mixing with his own upper-crusters, he spent most of his spare time with grooms, blacksmiths, foresters, and other men of rough trade. Although he was a brave warrior, he hated war—thinking it much more fun to sleep with men than fight with them. His first big love was Piers Gaveston, his French foster brother whom he loved so much that he gave him duchies, riches, and his royal ring. When Edward became king in 1307, he left Gaveston in charge of England while he went on a trip to France. Disliking this intensely, the powerful barons of England eventually had Gaveston executed.

In 1308 King Edward married Isabella, the "she-wolf" daughter of the French king, Philip the Fourth. Not that Edward loved Isabella. It was a political marriage arranged several years earlier by Pope Boniface VIII who, perhaps not coincidentally, also happened to be gay. Edward slept with Isabella because he was supposed to produce an heir to the throne. Although his heart wasn't in it, he managed to sire two sons and two daughters. But he still continued to sleep with men for pleasure.

Isabella also liked sex to be fun and, disliking the idea of only being used for royal breeding purposes, took herself a real lover named Roger Mortimer. Edward also took another lover. This was Hugh de Spenser, who was twenty-two years older and had a son, also named Hugh, who was equally handsome. So Edward said "I love you" to both of them. Both met a nasty end when Isabella and her lover Roger Mortimer raised an army and took over England in 1326. Hugh de Spenser was executed in Bristol after his private parts were chopped off and Hugh Junior was executed in Hereford. Isabella then had her husband imprisoned, and he was deposed as king in January 1327.

Now comes the tasteless part of the story: Eight months later, in the third week of September, three assassins silently entered Berkeley Castle where Edward was being held prisoner. Using keys, they opened the door of his cell and crept in silently as he lay sleeping. Then they carried out a murder which had been rehearsed with great care.

Grabbing Edward, they swung his body to the floor, face down. Man number one quickly placed a heavy upturned table on Edward's back and stood on it so that his body was pinned down. Man number two held Edward by the throat and hair as man number three pushed a long, open-topped deer's horn up Edward's backside. Once this was firmly in position, he inserted the red-hot tip of a long-handled poker through the deer's horn and deep into Edward's bowels.

Edward's screams echoed through the castle and were heard by villagers living outside the castle walls. The tip of the poker was withdrawn, reheated, and then reinserted at least one more time, causing Edward to suffer excruciating agony before he died. Next day the body was placed on show to prove to the public that he had died of natural causes during the night. Nobody believed one word of it as news of the terrible screams had already swept the neighborhood. But there was no proof. The body bore no marks (although the face was contorted in agony) and Edward was given a spectacular funeral. His fifteen-year-old son took the throne as KING EDWARD THE THIRD and later became famous for picking up and giving away garters.

Now that we have buried poor Edward the Second, it is a good time to resurrect his most astonishing love affair. That was with—wait for it—none other than an outlaw named Robin Hood. This is an extremely tricky subject because the good people of Nottingham will go to great lengths to shoot down any suggestion that their outstanding and upstanding hero could be linked with homosexuality.

Yet it is all something of an "open secret" because Professor James Clarke Holt, Master of Fitzwilliam College, Cambridge, has spelled it all out in the most learned and unbiased fashion in his book *Robin Hood*. Published by Thames and Hudson in 1982, this book is the product of some twenty years of research in which the professor was helped by various experts—and his wife.

The shocking disclosures in the professor's book were never given front-page treatment by any newspaper, so the "open secret" remained secret to most of the general public—until early 1988, that is, when Nottingham's Tourism Committee decided to issue a special souvenir brochure entitled "Robin Hood and His Times." They made this decision because, of course, Nottingham's Sherwood Forest has long been famous as Robin's traditional camping site and the city earns some $43 *million* each year from tourists fascinated by the outlaw and his legend.

They asked the curator of Nottingham Castle's Museum to compile all the facts necessary for the brochure. Being a bright fellow, the curator obtained special permission to take all the facts he needed from that book written by the acknowledged expert, Professor Holt. The curator then typed out a scholarly report and left it to the men of Nottingham to decide which sections they wished to use or leave out. But someone failed to do his homework and check the curator's manuscript for "suitability" content.

The hilarious result was that when the brochure was published, it contained some unpalatable, though quite factual, statements about Robin Hood. One was that Friar Tuck and Maid Marian—two of the most important characters in the Robin Hood legend—did not appear in the earlier tales.

Shock horror! This meant Robin had never had that famous girlfriend Maid Marian—which suggests he was a bachelor boy, which, in fact, he was. In the first published, and best known, accounts of Robin Hood, the outlaw did not have any girlfriends. None at all. He was a religious fellow who gave himself only to the Virgin Mother.

The fact that Robin had not enjoyed any romantic or physical involvement with girls was not such an awkward thing. But then the diabolical brochure went on to link Robin Hood directly with Edward the Second of red-hot poker fame by stating that the two had met in a forest and, after being pardoned, Robin Hood had gone to work for His Highness in London.

Although all this spicy stuff had been mentioned in Professor Holt's scholarly book, the press instantly saw the irony of Nottingham Council giving its famous hero Robin such doubtful publicity. Gleefully seizing on the obvious homosexual angle, the British *Daily Mail* of March 11, 1988, published a large cartoon in which Robin Hood was portrayed as a gay, sitting on a log in Sherwood Forest with his arms around a limp-wristed and weeping camp follower and saying: "Aw, don't sulk, sweetie. The scribe feels that it would look better in the history books if you changed your name to Maid Marian."

So what is the background to those gay claims about Robin? Well, one of the first stories to be published about him was "A Gest Of Robyn Hode." This was produced in the form of a lengthy poem by the London printer Wynken de Worde in the late 1400s, though it was probably written about eighty years earlier.

"Gest" tells us that Robyn Hode was the leader of an outlaw band and that Edward, "the comely King," once went hunting in the north of England and was puzzled by the lack of deer. When told they were being poached (and roasted) by the outlaw Robyn Hode, the king entered the forest disguised as an abbot, found Robyn, liked him, pardoned him, and gave him a job at his London court. Robin's "straight" admirers hate this because it is very suggestive indeed.

But the person who wrote that poem, certainly knew something, because some five hundred years later proof was unearthed, in the form of official royal records, that King Edward the Second actually did go on a hunting trip to Yorkshire and Nottingham between April and November 1323. And he did employ a Robyn Hode at his London Court at about that time.

There is no doubt about this. A "payslip" note in the official Royal Household Accounts, discovered in 1852, shows that on June 27, 1323 a Robyn Hode was paid his salary for the fortnight from June 5 to June 18, 1323. (London Public Record Office, reference number E101/379/6.) Other pay notes show that Robyn Hode worked at the court until November 1324 when he was paid five shillings severance pay and then returned to the north of England.

The records describe Robyn's job as a porter in King Edward's royal bedchamber. What does a porter do in the royal bedchamber? Carry chamberpots in and out? No, it would appear that in this context, a porter was a posher kind of fellow who made beds and set the breakfast tray or table. Making beds? That would be a bit of a comedown (or send-up) for our famous outlaw leader, wouldn't it? Yes, but some historians say Robyn wasn't really a porter. They claim he was actually a gentleman of the royal bedchamber. Ah yes, that sounds better, doesn't it?

Wait a minute though, what does a gentleman of the royal bedchamber do? Well, he could help the king to dress, rub his back down as he stepped out of the bath, and do for the king generally. Do? Do what? Oh, forget it! Nobody actually knows what Robyn did or did not do and, in any case, there is an added complication. According to Yorkshire historian Joseph Hunter (1783 to 1861), there was another Robyn Hood.

Authenticated documents show that this man lived at a house in Wakefield, near Leeds in the county of Yorkshire. He was a soldier for the earl of Lancaster, who had raised a rebellion against King Edward the Second. Lancaster was executed after the battle of Boroughbridge in 1322 and all his followers had their homes and possessions confiscated.

For that reason, this Robyn Hood had fled into the nearby forests of Barnsdale where he led a band of outlaws. He is said to have met King Edward the Second in that forest one year later in 1323, was pardoned by the king, and went to work for him in London. As a trained soldier, this man fits the skilled bowman image of Robin Hood perfectly, and he is also in exactly the right time slot.

Perhaps, by some fantastic coincidence, there were two hoods named Robin? Robyn Hode and Robyn Hood. And both led bands of robbers in forests at about the same time and within less than 150 miles of each other? If that is the case, which Robyn ended up becoming the boyfriend of gay King Edward in London?

The good (business) men of Nottingham, who don't want to spoil that $43 million a year they earn from tourists in love with Robin (or his legend), will tell you it was the Yorkshire Robyn, insisting that their poor little Robin of Sherwood Forest was unfairly accused of doing you-know-what with the king.

But we still can't get away from the nasty historical fact that

Wynken de Worde's Gest of Robyn Hode (that's the Nottingham Robin Hood) tells us that "Edward the comely King" met the outlaw Robyn Hood in the forest. In answer, the men of Nottingham claim this was a mistake on Mr. de Worde's part. They say he must have got his facts mixed up and insist it was King Richard the Lion Heart, not the gay King Edward, who pardoned Robin.

How strange. They don't complain about another wordsmith who definitely made "mistakes" and got his facts all mixed up—on purpose. This was in 1601 when a brilliant Establishment propagandist decided that such a handsome, intelligent, articulate, witty, caring, charming and brave outlaw could not possibly have been a low-born peasant. So he invented a suitable new background for Robin Hood.

Suddenly he became the earl of Huntingdon who, after being "cruelly and wrongfully dispossessed of his inheritance," became the leader of a very gentlemanly outlaw band dedicated to combating evil by robbing the rich to feed the poor. This band of men was given a righteous air by having a priest (Friar Tuck) as one of its leaders. And to completely distance Robin from being a gay bachelor, Maid Marian was brought into the act. She was Lady Marian—a royal ward, no less!—whom Robin eventually married on being pardoned by King Richard the Lion Heart when he returned from his crusade.

Those good men of Nottingham are obviously unaware of one little thing. As we have already seen, Richard the Lion Heart was clearly bisexual—if not totally gay—when he slept with the king of France or went camping with his minstrel Blondel.

History is littered with rulers who were gay, bisexual, or even trisexual (try anything once). For those readers who might think the last category is rather flippant, we hasten to mention that SIGEFROI, the first ruler of Luxembourg (936 to 998), is listed in history books as having married a mermaid.

Back to the more conventional gays and bisexuals:

FREDERICK THE GREAT is the king who quipped that a crown was "merely a hat that lets in the rain" (rather than just to reign in, he should have added). In his teens, Frederick's first big love was a handsome lieutenant, Hans von Katte, who could not keep his hands off Frederick. When Fred's father discovered this he had Von Katte's head chopped off—in front of Frederick. At twenty-one, Fred was forced to marry Princess Elizabeth of Brunswick-Wolfenbuttel. Although she was pretty and only eighteen, he neglected her and spent most of his time fondling his valet and his flute. But he went on to become a great king. Under him Prussia was governed as one huge camp in which freedom of conscience was encouraged and the press was given much liberty until he died in 1786.

The campest royal in French history was PHILIPPE, DUKE OF ORLEANS, the son of the gay KING LOUIS THE THIR-TEENTH. Born in 1640, Philippe was definitely a boy, but his mother had wanted a daughter, so she clothed him in pretty dresses and gave him dolls to play with. Not surprisingly, Philippe grew up to be so effeminate that he rouged his cheeks, wore oodles of perfume, and tottered around in high-heeled shoes. For mainly political reasons he married twice, but his wives never heard him when he pouted his lips and called them to his royal bedchamber at night—which may have been due to the fact that his voice was so high-pitched that only a dog could hear it.

One ruler who was a great lover of the arts, but did not ignore his wife sexually, was Queen Victoria's grandson, KAI-SER WILHELM THE SECOND. A talented painter, poet, and composer, he still found time to help his plain and boring wife to have six sons and a daughter, but he enjoyed the company of men much more. His favorite was his "beloved friend" Philip, Count Eulenburg, until the count was charged with interfering with young boys in 1907. That's when the kaiser dropped his beloved like a hot brick and cut him dead socially.

Queen Victoria knew about the kaiser's partiality for men but, by dying in 1901, she was spared the bigger shock of him allowing his German generals to fight against Britain in World War I and the ignominy of his being deposed at the end of that war and having to flee to Holland. The British made rather weak attempts to have him extradited so that he could stand trial in London as a war criminal but, by some magnificent manipulation behind the diplomatic scenes, Holland refused to part with him. This was wonderful for the British royals— who would have died a thousand deaths at the embarrassment of seeing Queen Victoria's grandson standing in a public dock as a common criminal.

And so, the kaiser remained in Holland, living the life of a country squire and reading P. G. Wodehouse's "Jeeves" novels while his valet made him numerous pots of English-packed Earl Grey tea, until his death in 1941.

Queen Victoria's death also spared her the deep embarrassment of seeing another great man's career ruined. This was Major-General Sir Hector Archibald Macdonald, who had once been Her Majesty's trusted friend and personal aide-de-camp. Sir Hector's life story would normally have been made into one of those stirringly patriotic "for queen and country" war books—and even a film. But as he was not "normal," it didn't.

This truly gallant gay joined the British army at the age of eighteen and won the rare distinction of rising from the ranks to major-general. He served so brilliantly in the Sudan campaign of 1898 that he became a national hero in England and was officially thanked by Parliament.

He also fought against the Boer farmers in South Africa where he was wounded in action and twice mentioned in despatches. But in 1902, after he was appointed commander of the British troops in Ceylon, the lifelong bachelor, Sir Hector Archibald Macdonald KCB, DSO, was accused of sexually molesting several young non-white boys. And when he was ordered to appear before a court-martial, Sir Hector decided that as a national hero he definitely could not embarrass Britain's new king, Edward the Seventh—for whom he had also worked as an aide-de-camp—so he took the "honorable" way out by taking a gun and blowing out his brains.

It is clear that Queen Victoria knew all about male homosexuals but she knew nothing about lesbians. When an anti-homosexual bill was passed by Parliament, she refused to sign the document until all mentions of sexual acts between women were removed, saying: "I don't believe it."

If Victoria was telling the truth when she said she did not believe women made love to each other, it means she was surprisingly ill-informed about her royal history. It is no secret to historians that QUEEN ANNE (1702 to 1714) was a closet lesbian. Petite, shy, and rather plain, Anne had a long affair with Princess Di's ancestor, Sarah Jennings (Duchess of Marlborough), who was witty, attractive, and ambitious.

Lord Macauley, in his *History of England* (London, 1848) tells us that the two ladies wrote extremely intimate letters to each other for many years but, in typical secrecy, signed them with false names just in case. Queen Anne was "Mrs. Morley" and Sarah, being the dominant, masculine type, used the name "Mrs. Freeman." Although both women were married, their husbands apparently did not recognize their secret love.

Sarah was married to the Duke of Marlborough and Queen Anne was married to Prince George of Denmark. Poor Anne, she produced eighteen babies but, whether for physical or psychological reasons, seventeen of them died and the eighteenth survived until he was aged eleven. Queen Anne remained in love with Sarah for more than twenty years.

The queen's next lover was her maid of the bedchamber, Abigail Hill, who was later rewarded with the title Lady Masham. Anne's love affair with this maid was an "open secret" until the top society hostess Lady Mary Cowper let both cats out of the bag by writing and singing the following cunningly worded ballad:

*When as Queen Anne of great renown,*
*Great Britain's sceptre swayed,*
*Besides the Church she dearly loved*
*A dirty Chamber-Maid.*

*Oh, Abigail, that was her name,*
*She starched and stitched full well.*
*But how she pierced this Royal heart*
*No mortal man can tell.*

History plays strange tricks. The queen who sat on the English throne prior to Anne was MARY THE SECOND, and she too had strong lesbian tendencies. Passionately romantic letters from Mary to her beloved friend, Lady Frances Apsley, are still in existence. In them, Mary describes herself as the dutiful and faithful wife of Lady Frances. It is most probable that Queen Mary turned to the tomboys because her husband, KING WILLIAM THE THIRD, not only had a couple of mistresses but was also a bisexual who spent most of his time hunting in the fields and forests for young farm laborers.

KING GEORGE THE FIFTH, who reigned from 1910 to 1936, was definitely not the other way. In fact, he was one of those unobservant "straights" who was totally unable to recognize whether anyone was gay or not. When he was told that one of his friends was a homosexual he looked astonished and snapped: "I thought men like that shot themselves." And he refused to knight any man who admitted being, or was proven to be, gay. Perhaps it was a good thing for King George that he was deliberately murdered by his Royal doctors (as we shall see later) because he would probably have shot himself if he had lived to see some of the gay goings-on in royal circles later.

His own son, PRINCE GEORGE, the Duke of Kent, had a homosexual scene with a boy in Paris who blackmailed him—according to the *Diaries* of former British Intelligence officer Sir Robert Bruce Lockhart (Macmillan, 1973). However, Prince George was lucky enough to find an excellent wife,

Princess Marina of Greece, who gave him a happy marriage and some splendid children. During World War II, he served in British Naval Intelligence and was killed in a mysterious air crash in 1942.

In 1936, when King George the Fifth was sent to heaven, his first-born son took the throne as EDWARD THE EIGHTH. Later, when he was the DUKE OF WINDSOR, he saw no shame in being a house guest of the talented homosexual author (and British Intelligence agent) Somerset Maugham. Interestingly, several books have alleged that the Duke of Windsor was involved in homosexual experiences during his early youth and even that the Duke had enjoyed an affair with Noel Coward, the po-faced showbiz genius—who worked for British Intelligence as a gatherer of society gossip (usually of a sexual nature) which the British could use for political blackmail purposes.

King George must have turned in his tomb in the late forties when Buckingham Palace chose Sir Harold Nicolson to write his official life story (*King George V, His Life and Reign*, Constable: 1952), because Sir Harold was a delightfully eccentric homosexual. Not only that. He was quite happily married to the talented poet and novelist Vita Sackville-West, who rocked the marital boat somewhat and caused a society scandal by enjoying a passionate lesbian affair with the writer Violet Trefusis. Violet, just by the way, was the daughter of Alice Keppel, the mistress of King George's super sexy father, King Edward the Seventh.

In 1958 Gordon Langley-Hall, after writing a biography of PRINCESS MARGARET, underwent a sex-change operation and legally became a woman. Then, in November 1968, as Dawn Pepita Langley-Hall, she married her black butler.

In 1969 PRINCESS MARGARET'S ex-footman, David Payne, had a series of sex-change operations in Cannes, France, and also became a woman.

In 1974 James Pope-Hennessey, the gay biographer of QUEEN MARY, who spent most of his money on "disastrous sexual liaisons," was killed in his London home by younger male friends who thought he had a large amount of money hidden in his bedroom.

In 1980 a scandal erupted when the British press discovered that homosexuality was rampant among the all-male crew of the royal yacht *Britannia*. Nothing seems to have changed in this regard because a friend of ours, a senior steward on the yacht for many years, tells us that even today, "at least 80 percent of the white-collar crew are gay."

In 1983 PRINCE CHARLES' former valet, Stephen Barry, wrote about his life as a royal servant in *Royal Service* (Macmillan, New York: 1983), from which he earned well over $1 million. Commenting on this, Sir John Junor wrote in the Sunday Express that Mr. Barry was "a creepy little poofter." Undismayed, Mr. Barry increased his bank balance by writing another book, *Royal Secrets* (Villard/Random, New York: 1985).

Also in 1983, the news broke that the Queen's personal bodyguard was a practicing homosexual. Commander Michael Trestrail, an elegant bowler-hatted Scotland Yard man, had started work at the palace in 1966 and became the Queen's bodyguard in 1973. Not that he was ever really needed to protect the Queen's body—apart from covering her knees with a mohair car rug on cold days. His public duties consisted mainly of carrying her umbrella, her handbag, and all the flowers she was given when she descended among her adoring public.

Disaster struck for Trestrail when his discarded and poverty-stricken lover Michael Rauch offered the British tabloid newspaper *The Sun* some love letters the Queen's bodyguard had written to him. Declining to buy, *The Sun* tipped off Buckingham Palace, and they alerted Scotland Yard. When Trestrail was pulled in for quizzing, he shocked his senior officers by admitting that Michael Rauch had been his lover. He also admitted writing the letters. Although it was clear he had to go, the Queen was admirably loyal and is said to have suggested that he be allowed to resign "for health reasons" as a face-saving exercise (for both sides) because he had been an "excellent servant." But Scotland Yard explained that this was impossible as *The Sun* knew all about the affair and was poised to strike—particularly if Trestrail was not fired.

When Commander Trestrail left Her Majesty's service, he was surprisingly well treated. He was described by most of the press as "a broken man" with his "whole life in ruins" as a result of his "casual relationship" with the little nobody Mr. Rauch who was, on the other hand portrayed as "a filthy black-mailing male prostitute."

In 1985 yet another royal policeman bit the dust. This was Inspector M, who was the full-time bodyguard to Prince Charles. The Inspector was forced out of his job after he allegedly formed an "eyebrow-raising" relationship with another male servant. Prince Charles fought hard to keep this valued policeman on his staff but was forced to submit to heavy pressure from Scotland Yard chiefs. The whole thing was kept secret until 1988 when *The News of the World* devoted its front page to an exclusive story that the inspector had been ordered to resign from the police force altogether after he was allegedly caught "acting suspiciously" in a public lavatory.

The newspaper published a photograph of the inspector—and his full name—but we have decided not to name him in this book because our palace mole tells us that there was something decidedly suspicious about the whole case. While the inspector is quite definitely gay, we are assured that at no stage was he ever disloyal toward his master Prince Charles and that, in effect, he was "framed" by narrow-minded hypocrites at Scotland Yard who were allegedly in league with a certain lady based at Kensington Palace.

In 1986 Prince Charles's ex-valet, Stephen Barry, brought more embarrassing publicity for the royals when he died of AIDS. *The Sun* then disclosed in a front page article that several gays working at Buckingham Palace, who had enjoyed sex with Mr. Barry, were worried that they might have caught AIDS from him. This story also disclosed that gay parties had often been held in the palace after the Queen had left her dinner table and that "male models" had been sneaked into the palace for gay sexual romps. The best-kept secret in this regard is that the young men enjoying all that fun in Buckingham Palace also took photographs of their antics and it is only a matter of time before somebody makes a lot of money by selling them to a foreign newspaper.

Also in 1986, Ralph G. Martin, in his bitingly frank 533-page book *Charles and Diana* (Grafton, 1986), disclosed that the royal palace staffs were "filled with gays" and that there were about sixty on the Queen's staff, about thirty with the Queen Mother, and about six with Prince Charles.

In June 1989 Alan Hancock, one of the Queen's senior aides, was fined £100 after being found guilty of importuning men for immoral purposes in a parking lot used by truck drivers at Shepherds Bush, West London. A forty-four-year-old bachelor, Mr. Hancock started working at Buckingham Palace in 1979 and at the time of his shock arrest he was the chief clerk to the Master of the Queen's Household. He was in regular touch with the Queen and arranged receptions for her as well as controlling hundreds of her staff and advising on discipline. He earned £18,000 a year and lived in a rent-free apartment in the grounds of Kensington Palace until being ordered to resign.

The most notorious gay in royal service was Sir Anthony Blunt. He was the Surveyor of the Royal Pictures from 1945 until 1972, when he officially retired—although he continued to work for the Queen until 1978. Those dates are vitally important because, as far back as 1964, British Intelligence had discovered (from the FBI) that Sir Anthony was actually a deep-cover KGB agent. Yet he was never charged and, incredibly, although the Queen was immediately told, in 1964, that he had confessed to having been a double agent for the KGB, he was still allowed to continue advising the Queen on her art investments and looking after her royal paintings in Buckingham Palace and Windsor Castle.

Fifteen years later, in 1979, when the British government was finally forced to admit that this great lover of the arts had been a traitor to his Queen and country, the public was spun the yarn that he had been "spared" exposure in return for spilling the beans about KGB spying activities in Britian. But the ex-British master spy Peter Wright—who went public because he was not paid the pension he was promised—makes it clear in his book *Spycatcher* (Viking Penguin, New York: 1987) that Sir Anthony spilled hardly any important beans about the KGB.

So why was Sir Anthony spared? The respected British author and journalist Philip Knightley claimed during a 1987 radio program that he had some kind of a hold over the British royals. Mr. Knightley said that while working for British MI5 at the end of World War II, Sir Anthony had carried out a top secret mission for King George the Sixth, the father of Queen Elizabeth. Sir Anthony had gone behind the German lines to gain access to a castle near Frankfurt and take possession of some highly important documents that allegedly exposed just how close certain royals had been with Hitler's Nazi regime. Which royals? Ah, the answer to that question had been given much earlier in an exclusive story Philip Knightley had helped to compile for the British *Sunday Times*.

That article (November 25, 1979) stated that the castle Sir Anthony Blunt had mysteriously visited was the family home of the princes of Hesse. This is a really hot political potato because those princes were none other than Prince Phillip of Hesse and Prince Christopher of Hesse—who were both top-ranking members of Hitler's SS at the beginning of World War II. Phillip and Christopher were brothers-in-law of Britain's Prince Philip, the Duke of Edinburgh—and to make matters worse, these two princes were said to have retained "certain documents" relating to the Duke of Windsor and his friendship with Adolf Hitler.

Answering this claim, Buckingham Palace admitted that superspy Sir Anthony had, in fact, as it so happened, popped into the castle and that while there he had recovered certain papers. But these had been only a few rather embarrassing love letters Queen Victoria had written to a German prince. Why on earth would British Intelligence send one of its top spies just to get a bundle of very old love letters? Buckingham Palace answered that it was necessary to prevent the letters falling into the hands of "vulgar" Americans who might have been tempted to print them in some sensational scandal magazine.

When the elegant gents at Buckingham Palace start using undiplomatic words like vulgar you can be quite sure they are covering up. In this case it seems to be something far more explosive than a few old love letters.

In *Spycatcher*, Peter Wright makes the surprising disclosure that in 1964, before he started interrogating Sir Anthony Blunt about his KGB work, he was called in by Queen Elizabeth's private secretary, Michael Adeane, who told him: "You might find Blunt referring to an assignment he undertook on behalf of the Palace—a visit to Germany at the end of the war. Please do not pursue this matter. Strictly speaking, it is not relevant to considerations of national security."

Many British newspapers have portrayed Peter Wright as a lying old drunken nobody who is such an idiot that he wears an Australian bush hat with corks hanging from it. This is not quite true. Wright was one of the two most important technical experts in British Intelligence and knew more secrets than any sixty-nine British Intelligence agents cuddled up together.

In 1979, when Prime Minister Maggie Thatcher was forced to admit in Parliament that MI5 agent Sir Anthony Blunt had been a KGB double all the time he had worked for British Intelligence, Queen Elizabeth stripped Sir Anthony of his title and he became common communist Tony Blunt. But, because he had that stranglehold over the British royals, he was allowed to continue living gaily in London until he died in 1983 at the age of seventy-six. In his will he left nearly $2 million and a couple of extremely valuable paintings. Some commie he turned out to be.

From all the above, it is abundantly clear that nobody can accuse the royals (or British Intelligence) of discriminating against gays when it comes to giving them employment. There are three main reasons:

First, gays, having a basically feminine nature, are remarkably loyal and dependable.

Second, because they are far more sensitive than "straights," gays have the ability to sense more speedily those delicate differences in meaning, feeling, and atmosphere, which makes them invaluable to the more highly sophisticated needs of the royals.

Third, male homosexuals do not chase the female servants employed by royals—or get them pregnant. This eliminates many awkward problems for those who oversee the huge royal staffs.

One of the oldest and corniest smears used against gays is that they are serious security risks who are open to blackmail. This is arrant nonsense. Heterosexuals can just as easily be lured into "honeypot" sex traps and blackmailed—even more so when they are married.

Furthermore, it is an undeniable fact that some of the most brilliant spies in history have been homosexual, mainly because, having different sexual preferences, they are forced from puberty to live secret lives. This makes them far more geared to deception and social hypocrisy—both of which are vital ingredients for the making of an excellent spy.

# 4

---

## *The Mad Royals*

*M*ost of the people who are mad about royalty do not know how crazy many of them have been. The simple explanation for this is that not much publicity has been given to the tricky subject.

KING CHARLES THE SIXTH of France was a most delicate monarch. He was so convinced he was made of glass that he hated traveling by coach, believing he would shatter into a thousand pieces if jolted.

Charles came to the throne in 1380 at the age of twelve and was apparently so liked by the public that they called him "Charles the Well-Beloved." He deteriorated mentally from 1392 however, and when he started roaming the corridors of his palace howling like a wolf, his wife, Queen Isabeau, decided she didn't want that kind of animal in her bed. She solved this problem quite cleverly by finding someone to take her place. This was Odette de Champdivers, who bore a strong resemblance to Isabeau. The daughter of a poor horse trader, Odette was tickled pink at the idea of living like a queen, so she was dressed in Isabeau's clothing and placed in the king's bed. He never noticed the difference and everyone was happy.

Before dying totally insane, King Charles married off his daughter, Catherine of Valois, to KING HENRY THE FIFTH of England in 1420. That marriage produced a little boy who not only inherited his grandad's mental problems but also experienced a decidedly oddball life as England's HENRY THE SIXTH.

First of all, he was England's youngest monarch, coming to the throne at the age of nine months in September 1422. His next record was to become the King of France in the following month when his madly fragile grandad died.

A good clue that young Henry was to have a mindless reign came at his coronation banquet in 1429 when he was aged eight and some lunatic in charge of the catering laid on a truly mad menu. The first course was soup of an unusual burgundy color due to the thick blood (perhaps ox) floating on the surface. And, whether for their vitamin or entertainment value, rare white lions were swimming around, trying to stay alive, in the huge copper serving vats. Rounding off this senseless bad taste, the royal chef served a fruit dish accompanied by massive bowls full of custard in which baby leopards had been sunk. It may sound crazy, but it really happened.

Apart from that hard-to-digest banquet, Henry had an unhappy life. In 1445 he married fifteen-year-old Margaret of Anjou. But, as is often the case with the royals, no love was involved. The marriage was a political one aimed at securing peace with France. In 1453 Henry suffered the first bouts of insanity that were to plague him for the rest of his life. During these periods of mental instability he was so depressed that he was partially paralyzed, unable to reason or speak.

Bishop Ayscough (who claimed to be the monarch's best friend) warned King Henry not to sleep with his queen while in such a state. When Henry's sanity returned about ten months later, he was astonished to find his wife had given birth to a son. Knowing, without a shadow of a doubt, that Margaret was a totally and utterly virtuous woman who was devoted to only him and God, the lunatic king commented that "the boy must have been conceived by the Holy Ghost." Via the bishop, perhaps?

As well as being chaste, pious, and generous, King Henry was a very naive and trusting man who was the pawn of his strong-willed wife. She ruled him, and for him, much of the time until he was deposed by EDWARD THE FOURTH, who had him stabbed to death in the Tower of London in May 1471.

THEODORE, the Emperor of Abyssinia, was a crazy bandit leader who started his career as a trainee priest but took to warring in the hills with an armed gang rather than jaw-jawing from the pulpit. He was perhaps not insane to begin with as he had the sense to marry a royal heiress and, with her financial backing, overthrew the prince of Tigre and become emperor of Abyssinia in 1855 at the age of thirty-seven.

In 1862 he wrote a letter to Queen Victoria requesting her help against his Mohammedan neighbors but, probably because he had been a common bandido, Victoria didn't bother to reply. This royal disdain is said to have so maddened Theodore that he jailed the local British consul and several other important Europeans. When Victoria sent envoys to deliver a "We are not amused" complaint, Theodore threw them in jail as well.

As diplomacy had failed, Victoria then sent her gunboats and sixteen thousand British troops who rescued all the prisoners after a battle during which Theodore shot himself rather than be captured. This military expedition cost the British taxpayers more than $500 million in today's currency. All because Queen Victoria didn't answer a letter.

Bavaria had several royal oddballs in the nineteenth century. LUDWIG THE FIRST became king there in 1825 and soon had a reputation of being rather eccentric. (This word is often used to describe rich people who are oddballs. Poor people, when odd, are just plain crazy.)

Ludwig fell madly in love with a theatrical adventuress known as Lola Montez. She was a larger-than-life lady who was born Maria Eliza Gilbert in the Irish county of Limerick. At the age of nineteen she eloped with a Captain James but deserted him five years later and embarked on a career as a Spanish dancer, which took her to leading theaters in Britain, France, Germany, and Russia.

In 1846, at the age of twenty-eight, she performed in Munich and danced away with the heart and mind of sixty-year-old King Ludwig. She became his mistress in return for the title countess of Landsfeld, pocket money of $10,000 a year, and a few bags full of rubies, diamonds, and emeralds. But that wasn't all. Lovely Lola quickly became the virtual ruler of Bavaria because the weak-minded king gave her too much rein. She went too far, though, by exercising enormous influence in favor of liberalism and against the Jesuits, which started the 1848 revolution and forced Ludwig to abdicate. Not that Lola minded very much. After taking all her loot to London, she bigamously married a more virile chap of twenty-one years.

The next ruler of Bavaria was Ludwig's son MAXIMILIAN THE SECOND, a headache-prone halfwit who beat his children and, for some strange reason, kept them so hungry that they begged food from the servants. Although he was not actually certifiable, his sister Princess Alexandra was decidedly strange. She was convinced that she had swallowed a full-size grand piano when she was a child, and nobody could persuade her otherwise.

When Maximilian died in 1864, his son LUDWIG THE SECOND took the throne. Ludwig was an outstandingly handsome eighteen-year-old Prince Charming who set all the girls' hearts aflutter, but he became the world's most misunderstood monarch. Although most historians tag him the "Mad King," he was actually a highly intelligent, cultured, artistic, and sensitive person who was kind, generous, and deeply religious.

His ministers thought he was obviously stark raving mad because:

- He didn't care much for girls.
- He loathed huntin' and shootin'.
- He hated being a king and wished he had been born a peasant.
- He was more at ease with servants than with courtiers.
- He always referred to his mother as "that Colonel of the Third Artillery Regiment," which he sneeringly described as her most ludicrous title because he despised the military and everything it represented—so much so that the only time he willingly accompanied his soldiers was on the piano.

While in his early teens, Ludwig heard Richard Wagner's music and was one of the first to recognize the composer's genius. When he came to the throne, he sent one of his court officials to contact Wagner and was astonished to hear that the composer was so deeply in debt that he had gone into hiding and was considering suicide. Ludwig quickly solved that little problem by giving Wagner a large annual pension and a beautiful house, which left the composer free to write such masterpieces as *Parsifal* and *Ring of the Nibelung*.

Wagner and the king wrote to each other regularly, and more than six hundred of their letters are still in existence. Many of Ludwig's letters are so emotional that some cynics have suggested that the king was as much in love with Wagner the man as he was with his music.

Fifty-one-year-old Wagner was definitely not gay though. When he met Cosima, the attractive daughter of the Hungarian composer Franz Liszt, he seduced her, and she gave birth to his baby—although at the time she was married to, and still living with, Hans von Bulow, King Ludwig's personal pianist. Later, Cosima had two more children by Wagner. After a divorce from Von Bulow in 1870, she married Wagner.

Meanwhile, King Ludwig set about creating his own masterpieces—a set of exquisite "fairy-tale" castles. One was the lemon-yellow castle he ordered to be erected on a secluded island in the middle of Chiemsee Lake. Its Hall of Mirrors is nearly 300 feet long, and it took thirty servants twenty minutes to light the 2,500 wax candles in their ornate crystal chandeliers. And that was just one room.

A further indication of the splendor of that castle can be gained from the fact that two hundred seamstresses worked full time for seven years to make the intricately embroidered curtains and upholstery. Fifty artists and twenty-five sculptors worked on this and the Neuschwanstein Castle, that world-famous edifice most kiddies remember from the film *Chitty-Chitty Bang Bang* (the car flew over it and landed in the courtyard). It was also copied by Walt for his Disney World.

When the cost of these and other spectacular constructions sent King Ludwig bankrupt, he told his finance minister to borrow some more money so that more dream castles could be built. When the minister said he had no way of raising the money, Ludwig told him to think of a way—even if it meant recruiting criminals to break into banks in Paris and Berlin. When they finally realized the king was not joking, his cabinet became frightened that they would lose their jobs if they disobeyed him. On the other hand, they didn't wish to risk going to jail for planning bank robberies so they decided it was time to get rid of the king. How to do it, though? They could not just depose him because he was popular among the working classes—and public criticism had to be avoided at all costs.

As several of his relatives were known to be mentally unbalanced, the ministers decided it would be much safer to have the king certified as insane because the peasants, being stupid themselves, would fall for that. Thus a great conspiracy was mounted. It involved four top psychiatrists who signed a nineteen-page medical report alleging that Ludwig was "incurably insane." Three of those shrinks had never met the king, never mind examined him. The well-bribed villain of the piece was Dr. Bernard von Gudden, the director of a lunatic asylum in Munich.

Just before dawn on June 12, 1886, Dr. Von Gudden and a team of heavies grabbed King Ludwig, placed him in a coach, and rushed him to Berg Castle on Lake Starnberg, south of Munich, where he was told he would be imprisoned, though with due respect and in comfort, while a less extravagant king would reign in his place. But Dr. Von Gudden was no match for the wily king, who gulled him into a false sense of security by behaving impeccably.

On the morning after his arrival at Berg Castle, Ludwig asked to be taken for a short walk. Dr. Von Gudden accompanied him with two brawny guards. During the stroll around the gardens Ludwig flattered the doctor and asked him many questions about his most interesting cases. This relaxed Von Gudden so much that when the king asked to be taken on another little walk at 6 P.M., the doctor told the guards not to bother accompanying the two men.

That is where Von Gudden made his great mistake. When a search party was sent out about three hours later, both men were found drowned in the very shallow water close to the shore of the nearby Lake Starnberg. What really happened has been deliberately confused by a lot of double-talk.

Some historians, who clearly believe it would reflect badly on all royals if anyone suggested that he had deliberately murdered the doctor, have tried to claim that King Ludwig suffered a heart attack in the water and Dr. Von Gudden drowned "trying to save him." But this hardly fits with the fact that earlier, Ludwig had told his valet, Weber, "Drowning is a fine death." After saying this, the king had given the valet all his remaining gold coins and some jewelry, saying: "Take it, I shall not need money any more." It is highly unlikely that Ludwig drowned accidentally. At the time of his death, the forty-one-year-old, six-foot-tall monarch was in excellent physical condition and, quite apart from being immensely strong, was a superb swimmer.

(Exactly one hundred years later, on June 13, 1986, in Munich's National Theatre, the Bavarian State Ballet Company held the world premiere of a ballet based on King Ludwig's life and the whole of Bavaria observed a period of mourning for their now much-adored monarch. Why? Because every year more than one million tourists from all over the world make a point of visiting those fabulous fairy-tale castles built by the "Mad King." And while in Bavaria, each of those tourists spends an average of $800.)

When Ludwig drowned, his younger brother, thirty-eight-year-old OTTO, took the crown. Now, it must be admitted that this one was a total nutcase. When he was twenty-seven he caused an almighty scandal by racing into a crowded church during high mass dressed in a shooting jacket and deerstalker cap. After throwing himself facedown at the altar, he screamed out the most amazing list of sexual sins involving page boys. After he was removed, the embarrassed archbishop (who had just finished telling the congregation how wonderful the royal family had been during the previous week) quickly reassured the shocked worshippers that Otto's sexual confessions were untrue. A pack of lies. A load of rubbish. Absolute nonsense and totally impossible.

King Otto loathed his royal doctors because he knew what they had done to his brother Ludwig. As a result Otto developed a strange kink. He firmly believed that he could keep the doctors away by shooting a peasant a day. No, not a pheasant, a *peasant*. So he leaned out of his bedroom window each morning and blasted the brains out of a couple of common or garden peasants as they were clipping the royal rose bushes. Deciding that this was taking class distinction a little too far, his family politely asked him to desist. When he refused and carried on shooting the peasants, saying it was the only way to keep the doctors away, a clever charade was mounted that kept everyone happy.

Every morning, before the king awoke, a servant crept into his royal bedchamber and quietly loaded his pistol with blank cartridges. At the same time a guard, disguised as a dirty peasant in ragged clothing, positioned himself in the bushes below the king's bedroom window. The stage thus set, a servant would wake the king with his breakfast tray and shout "Yonder peasant, who is he?" (or words to that effect). The monarch would grab his gun, rush to the window, and bang off several shots until the acting peasant fell to the ground with an ear-piercing scream pretending to be dead. Delighted with his brilliant marksmanship and secure in the knowledge that no doctor would visit him, the king's mental tension was completely relaxed and he would behave himself for the rest of the day. This killing farce was carried out every morning until 1913 when King Otto was officially deposed.

WILLEM THE FIFTH, known as "the Senseless," became the ruler of the county of Holland in 1356, and some history books say he ruled for the next thirty-three years. Not true. He went insane just two years after taking the throne and others had to govern for him.

IVAN THE FIFTH is said to have been the co-ruler of Russia from 1682 until 1696. Not true. Poor Ivan was a consumptive who was half blind and so mentally backward that he was tsar in name only. His brother Peter was the actual ruler.

KING AFONSO THE SIXTH of Portugal came to the throne in 1656 when he was thirteen, and history books say he ruled until 1683. Not true. From the age of fifteen he was kept virtual prisoner due to insanity. His wife left him and the country was actually ruled by his mother and others until 1667 when he was "persuaded" to surrender the throne to his brother Pedro.

Over one hundred years later his descendant, QUEEN MARIA, took the Portuguese throne and some history books claim she ruled until her death in 1816. Not true. In 1807 she was quietly shipped off to Brazil, not just because she was nuts but also to stop the Portuguese public discovering that insanity had struck their royals again.

Perhaps the saddest mental case was QUEEN JUANA of Spain, who is officially branded Juana "la Loca" (the Mad). This is unfair as it gives a rather false impression. Juana was the daughter of King Ferdinand V and Queen Isabella of Spain, and in 1496, when she was seventeen, she married PHILIP, the archduke of Austria.

Although it was a political marriage in which all the courting had been done by her parents, Juana loved Philip passionately. She worshipped the ground her husband walked on, but he treated her like a doormat and also neglected her sexually—except once yearly when it was necessary for him to sire sons and heirs. Being the handsomest young prince in the whole of Europe, Philip was in great demand with the girls and could not bear to disappoint them when they fell to their knees and begged him to pleasure them. This made Juana so insanely jealous that she refused to let him out of her sight, which Philip found not only boring but restrictive when it came to his whoring.

In 1506 Philip became the king of Castile. He did not wear the crown long as he caught a fever just two months later and died aged twenty-eight. This devastated Juana and sent her totally insane. Refusing to allow the body to be buried, she had it embalmed and said: "We must remain together for eternity." And wherever she went throughout Spain, Philip's body traveled with the queen—in a beautiful and bejeweled coffin. She sat next to it when eating her meals and it lay on her bed every night. Understandably, Juana's subjects started to wonder what was wrong. To stop them finding out she was mad, Juana's father had her locked away in a fortress at Tordesillas.

Although she was offered every possible comfort, Queen Juana preferred to crouch in a pitch-dark room wearing a black mourning dress and talking incessantly to Philip. She stayed in that room for nearly forty-six years and died at the age of seventy-six. In death Juana achieved her heart's desire by being buried in the royal chapel of Granada Cathedral, in the same tomb as her beloved Philip—the handsome young prince of her dreams who had never loved her.

Another sad royal love saga ending in madness was that of PRINCESS CHARLOTTE, the daughter of King Leopold the First of the Belgians. As a teenager Charlotte fell in love with Max, the younger brother of Austria's emperor Franz Joseph. After their marriage the French government offered the out-of-work Max a well-paid job overseas—looking after Mexico. So, in

1864, the thirty-two-year-old Max became EMPEROR MAXI-
MILIAN of Mexico and his pretty twenty-four-year-old wife became empress. Their happiness was short-lived because the
revolting Mexicans, led by Benito Juarez, forced Napoleon the
Third to withdraw his troops. Poor Max was left with only eight
hundred men to look after him while his wife Charlotte was
enjoying a short stay with relatives in Europe.

As Max was Queen Victoria's cousin-in-law, the public was
assured that he had put up a "valiant fight" during the revolution in mid-May 1867, although he didn't have a scratch to
show for it. Max had always instilled that great motto "Death
Before Dishonor" into his soldiers, but truth to tell, this was
not something he personally believed in. After he and his men
were surrounded, Max was found cowering in a cellar. Wine,
of course. In what other kind would you find a royal?

When a smelly and badly dressed Mexican entered the cellar
brandishing a dirty, bloodstained toothpick, Emperor Max
knew the odds were against him. Dropping his ruby-and-em-
erald-encrusted sword and his pearl-handled pistol, he put his
hands in the air and allowed himself to be captured—confident
that he would be released on payment of a huge ransom. No
chance. On June 19 1867, Max was placed against a brick wall
along with several other common prisoners and shot dead by
a firing squad.

Worse was to come. The Mexicans chopped up Max's body,
and fragments of his skull, skin, and hair were publicly sold
in the local bazaars as mementoes. Queen Victoria, writing in
her private diary, described this as "too disgusting and disgraceful," although she added the snide little comment that
cousin Max had been sent to Mexico without her royal approval
anyway. Max's widow Charlotte? She went totally insane and
remained so until she died in Europe at the age of eighty-
seven in 1927.

Perhaps the saddest king in British history was GEORGE
THE THIRD, whose mind started to malfunction one day in
1787 as he was being driven by carriage through Windsor Great

Park. Ordering his driver to stop, he got out, walked over to an oak tree, shook hands with one of its branches, and talked to it at length, believing it to be the king of Prussia.

At first, George only suffered periodic fits of insanity, but when his condition worsened over the years, a crack team of royal surgeons led by Dr. Francis Willis diagnosed that he was suffering from madness. As a leading expert on the subject of lunacy, Dr. Willis pontificated that it was caused by evil and the best way to cure it was to punish the patient.

Another medical expert named Dr. Warren agreed with this great assessment, and the two of them proceeded to slap hot mustard plasters on the king's legs, stomach and chest—working on the theory that they would not only punish the king with pain but would also "draw out the evil in his body." The plasters caused excruciatingly painful blisters to erupt all over the king's body and when he quite understandably tore off subsequent plasters, Dr. Willis "disciplined" him by placing him in a straitjacket, often leaving him in it for twenty-four hours.

As any prison officer, psychiatric nurse, or maniac will confirm, this was pure torture. The constriction of such a jacket, after only a few hours, causes intense cramps and agonizing pins and needles sensations throughout the body. When King George complained, Dr. Willis treated him like a child, screamed at him and threatened yet another torture. This was a special "lunatic" iron chair with steel clamps, which was physically painful and psychologically demeaning. George ridiculed it by nicknaming it his new "coronation chair."

Not appreciating this jest, Dr. Willis placed the king on a wooden bunk, shackled his arms and legs to the top and bottom, and kept his body held down with a tight strap across the chest. At this point it should be mentioned that Dr. Willis ran a lunatic asylum in Lincoln where members of the public were confined. God knows what diabolical atrocities he inflicted upon those poor wretches when we know how he treated the king of England!

The fact that King George was, by now, incurably insane, was kept secret from the public and he was hidden away in the north side of Windsor Castle where he spent the last ten years of his life, shuffling round in his tatty old dressing gown, blind, deaf and totally deserted by his highly embarrassed family until he died at the age of eighty-two.

The British royals get very uptight on the subject of George the Third's insanity because they fear that some really stupid and ignorant people might get the totally wrong impression that madness might run in the family due to inbreeding. In the mid-fifties, Queen Elizabeth went to see the film *Beau Brummel* in which George the Third was portrayed as being mentally unbalanced. Her Majesty was so annoyed by this that she left the movie house without saying thank you or goodbye to the organizers.

In recent years, strong attempts have been made to persuade the public that His Royal Highness King George the Third was not really mad. We are told that he merely suffered from "periodic attacks of a metabolic illness not then understood." Understandably, no less a personage than PRINCE CHARLES has publicly lent his name to this theory.

As we shall see later, George the Third must have passed some of this "metabolic illness" on to his various oddball sons, particularly George Augustus Frederick, who became KING GEORGE THE FOURTH in January 1820. His ten-year reign was marked by debt caused by his excessive gambling, drinking, and whoring. He was also a little odd in the head when it came to his anecdotage because he genuinely believed he had led the German charge at Salamanca (disguised as a famous general). He also claimed to have won the battle of Waterloo and often embarrassed the duke of Wellington at cocktail parties and dinners by loudly telling other guests how bravely he had fought at that battle.

On one occasion he turned to Wellington (who beat Napoleon at Waterloo) and said: "Did I not do so, Arthur?" and the duke tactfully but dryly replied: "I have often heard Your

Majesty relate the incident." The royal doctors were unable to do anything about King George the Fourth's strange life-style, and he died of alcoholic cirrhosis in 1830.

At this stage, we must confess that writing about some of the mad royals, particularly King Otto's shooting of a peasant a day to keep the doctor away, often caused us to smile. But serious mental illness is no laughing matter. It is a terrible burden for any family, and when it occurs in the royal family it is quite understandable that they try to cover it up. Not that they are personally ashamed. Their biggest problem is that they worry about public opinion, because the masses, much helped by the media, have put them up on pedestals and they simply must be seen to be perfect. Walter Bagehot, the perceptive British social and literary critic, summed it up perfectly in the nineteenth century when he wrote that royalty's mystery is its life and "we must not let daylight in upon magic."

That is probably why John, the sixth and youngest child of QUEEN MARY, was hidden away from public scrutiny. Although he was always a problem child, he became dangerous when he was twelve because he was tremendously strong and started making vicious attacks on his older brothers, David (later the Duke of Windsor) and George (later King George the Sixth). His violence was such that the royal doctors advised that he be kept well away from his family. He was moved to an isolated house named Wood Farm on the Sandringham estate where private servants looked after him. Queen Mary described her son John as "a poor little troubled spirit" and she is said to have been saddened in 1919 when, at the age of thirteen, he died in his sleep after suffering a fit. In those days, the Press barons would never have dreamed of letting daylight in on such royal madness, but things have changed since then.

Widespread shock was felt in April 1987 when it was disclosed that Katherine and Nerissa Bowes-Lyon—daughters of the Queen Mother's brother—had spent more than four decades hidden away in a Surrey mental hospital under a veil of secrecy because they were suffering from "severe mental retardation." Nerissa, a first cousin of Queen Elizabeth, died in 1986 aged sixty-seven and was quietly buried in a pauper's grave marked by a cheap and common plastic cross.

When the British press discovered this astounding fact they rushed to *Burke's Peerage* and were equally flabbergasted to discover that some extremely prominent personage had fed this highly respected stud book of the aristocracy the false information that Nerissa had "died" way back in 1940! Equally astonishing, Nerissa's sixty-one-year-old sister Katherine was listed as having died in 1961, yet she was still alive and hidden away in that Surrey mental hospital—along with two other close female relatives who were also suffering exactly the same kind of mental retardation.

When journalists asked Harold Brooks-Baker, the publisher of *Burke's Peerage*, to comment on these mental problems in the royal family he admitted quite frankly: "It was caused by inbreeding."

Buckingham Palace tried to claim that the faked deaths of Nerissa and Katherine was not a deliberate lie. Someone had just made a mistake, that's all. But most of the British press refused to go along with that kind of waffle and the royal family was severely criticized for hiding these women away so heartlessly. The *Sun* newspaper published a particularly scathing story in which it was suggested that the Queen Mother should be asked to quit her position as patron of MENCAP—the Society for the Mentally Handicapped.

Even the Queen Mother's greatest admirer, Sir John Junor, writing in the *Sunday Express* four days later, accurately put his finger on the public pulse by asking: "Why, when so much family money was clearly available, a ward in a public hospital? Why not the comfort of a private clinic? And why on death, a pauper's grave with only a plastic cross?"

This bitter criticism struck home in the heart of at least one member of the royal circle. This was the multimillionaire and personality-plus royal photographer, Lord Lichfield, who is the Queen's cousin. In August 1987, without any publicity hoo-ha, he arranged and paid for a decent headstone to be erected on the grave of the sadly neglected Nerissa Bowes-Lyon and threw away that unfortunate plastic cross.

# 5

## *Royal Flush*

*T*he English KING ETHELRED, "the Unready," was born in the year 968, and as he was being baptized, he piddled in the holy water of the royal font. Although he was only a baby, the churchmen saw this as a bad omen—and they were right. Ethelred grew up to be an unlucky ruler. He was dethroned, exiled, and even when he regained the throne, he had to contest it with his son and the Danish invader King Cnut (Canute).

In April 1016 Ethelred's son, EDMUND IRONSIDE, became the king of southern England. A good and brave warrior, he lasted only eight months because he had a poor sense of personal security—which was madness in those days when everyone went around stabbing each other in the back. One evening in November, the king went into his house to empty his bowels and sat down on the long wooden lavatory box.

What he did not know was that Edric Streona, one of his dissatisfied knights, had secreted himself in the pit below. As King Ironside sat on the seat, Streona twice lunged a sword deep up his backside. For plumbing the depths of indecent behavior in this way, Streona was beheaded.

KING HENRY THE THIRD, who ruled England from 1216 to 1272, was a great builder, a loyal husband, and a religious man who went to mass three times a day. Although he was clearly a good man, the public disliked the heavy taxes he imposed in order to rebuild such places as Westminster Abbey. When it came to spending pennies, however, they thought old Henry was great, because he gave London its first public lavatory. But there is a price to pay for everything. If you use any of the public toilets in London's central parks these days, a percentage of all the pennies you spend goes to H.R.H. Queen Elizabeth. How's that for a royal commission!

Going to the loo in the "good old days" was quite dangerous as there was always a strong risk of catching a disease, not just from touching the lavatory seat but from touching anything. Typhoid was a real killer. The stench was not very pleasing either, so small bags of sweet-smelling herbs were hung behind the door. Being rather more affluent, the royals disguised the smell of effluent by splashing costly perfume all over the walls and floor.

In 1589, however, the terrible problem of disgustingly stinky loos was solved brilliantly by Queen Elizabeth the First's godson, Sir John "Johnny" Harrington, who invented Britain's first flushing toilet. When Queen Elizabeth visited Sir John's home, he asked her to honor it with her royal opinion. She went one better and, after watching it flush away, Her Majesty pronounced it most worthy of the Royal We. Being so highly honored by royal patronage, orders poured in for the fabulous invention and Sir John's fortune was well and truly made. His name too—because, even today, some people still call it the john.

Most history books state, quite truthfully, that England's KING GEORGE THE SECOND died of a coronary thrombosis, but they usually fail to mention the embarrassing extra detail that His Majesty had been suffering from severe constipation for several days and, on October 25, 1760, was so desperate to relieve himself that, as he sat on his lavatory at the palace of Westminster, he bore down so ferociously that the strain brought on a sudden and fatal heart attack.

When QUEEN VICTORIA traveled on the royal train, her lavatory seat was covered in suede because someone in high position had ruled that the original mahogany seat was far too cold for a royal bottom. Victoria apparently didn't care much about other people's bottoms because, apart from her own, hardly any of the toilets in Buckingham Palace worked properly. In 1873 she lent the palace to NASER od-DIN, the shah of Persia, and he found the toilets there "so disgusting" that he and his 100-strong harem refused to use them.

The urinals at the royal country retreat Sandringham were also unhygienic. Victoria's grandson Prince George nearly died of typhoid fever while holidaying there in 1891. The sewage drains at Windsor Castle were just as bad. Victoria's husband Prince Albert caught typhoid fever there in 1861, and it killed him.

Some of those antique loos still exist at Windsor Castle. Fergie, the Duchess of York, really likes them. While touring America recently, she told a group of open-mouthed youngsters: "They're amazing. They don't have cisterns. You have to pull a chain *up* from the ground and water comes rushing *down*. They are great!"

Not many people consider toilets worth collecting, but PRINCE CHARLES, believe it or not, has a private collection of some 140 antique lavatory seats in various shapes and sizes. If you should happen to have an antique or unusual loo seat in good condition and think it would enhance the royal collection, mail it to: H.R.H. Prince Charles, Kensington Palace, The Broad Walk, LONDON W.8.

You could send it as a Christmas present or, if you wish, for his birthday, which is on November 14. No, we are *not* joking. On the contrary, we are sure that if Charles likes it, he will almost certainly send you a royal thank-you letter on palace notepaper.

Charles has no hang-ups about toilets. In one of the loos at his Kensington Palace home he has original newspaper cartoons of himself hanging on the walls.

In January 1974 an Essex newspaper got itself a great little scoop by discovering that Prince Charles had bought two chastity belts from a firm that made them as novelty items. Charles found an excellent use for them—to hold rolls of toilet paper. With a sense of humor like that, he's going to make a witty king.

Prince Charles often spends hours standing in rivers casting for salmon. When nature calls, he admits that he often unzips and adds to the volume of rushing water by peeing in it. But, as he once confided to an American newsman: "I'm always petrified that some cameraman will catch me at it."

While attending a royal garden party at Buckingham Palace in 1971, we discovered some interesting facts about royal toilet arrangements. In the White Drawing Room there was a tall Oriental screen in the left-hand corner discreetly hiding much of a large mirror. In the frame of the mirror was a secret button that, when pressed, operated a spring and the mirror swung outward silently. This revealed a secret door leading to a private "comfort station." The Queen and other female royals could pop into this unobtrusively when attending lengthy receptions in the rooms nearby.

There was another cleverly hidden private lavatory on the ground floor. To visitors, it appeared to be just another large oil painting fixed to the wall in a huge gilt frame, but at the press of a secret switch, the painting swung open and revealed a tiny recess containing a toilet. The palace servants called this "the James Bond loo."

When the queen invites people to her garden parties, they take tea in her forty-five-acre garden. It boasts a large lake populated by beautiful pink flamingoes which ignore the milling crowd and daintily fish with their long and elegantly curved necks under the water. It's a ravishingly poetic scene, but reality is nearby in the form of two green-and-white striped tents that are actually full of lavatories.

In these regal surroundings, it's incongruous to see a long line of immaculately dressed women (wearing the most astonishing hats) queuing outside the tent bearing the sign "Ladies Cloakroom Entrance." It's even funnier to see gray-toppered men looking frightfully embarrassed, by the exit sign, waiting for their lady partners to evacuate. All the plumbing, we discreetly discovered, is actually a permanent fixture, covered over by special strips of grass when the guests have departed and the tents are pulled down.

Another thing we found was that members of the royal family often laugh themselves silly at the stupid antics some prissy dignitaries get up to. For instance, when the Queen visited Totnes Guildhall in Devon during the sixties, the automatic flushing system in a gents' public toilet was switched off so that the distinctive flushing noise would not offend the royal ears. And because the Queen would have to walk past this terrible eyesore, the civic dignitaries voted that local VIPs (mostly rich farmers and big shopkeepers) should stand in a semicircle to hide the "Gents" sign and its entrance.

Not so long ago, cities all over Britain would always arrange for brand-new, never-before-used toilets to be built whenever a royal was due to visit—the theory being that no royal backside could possibly be expected to grace a seat that had been sat on by other bums. In these economically constipated times, though, it would be political suicide for some city councils to spend public funds on such one-off conveniences, particularly left-wing councils like the one in Yorkshire's steel city, Sheffield, which is so scornful of the multimillionaire royals that it voted *not* to send a present to Prince Charles when he married Di.

The Queen now travels with a special lavatory cover made of white kid (we kid you not), which is slipped over the toilet seat by her lady-in-waiting. And when the Queen or other female royals do go for a tinkle, as they sweetly call it, one of their ladies-in-waiting always stands guard outside to prevent lesser mortals barging in.

Yet some firms still go out of their way to make a fuss when the royals come a calling.

- When PRINCESS ANNE attended a concert in Weymouth, she needed somewhere to change her dress and perhaps freshen up. So the local Rembrandt Hotel spent $15,000 on fitting out a bedroom with a brand-new bathroom boasting new carpets, velvet walls, and gold-plated taps!
- When the QUEEN MOTHER visited the BBC TV Centre in Shepherd's Bush, London, they prepared a special loo just in case the little old lady was taken short.
- When PRINCE CHARLES visited the BBC dubbing section in Glasgow, the nearest lavatory was totally refurbished and locked up so that nobody else could pass the time of day in it before Charles. Even funnier, when Charles had been and gone, the mandarins at the BBC thought it would be in bad taste to let others use the same mahogany seat—so they replaced it with a brand-new plastic one.
- In 1987, when PRINCE ANDREW took his fun-loving wife, FERGIE, to the Indian Ocean island of Mauritius for a much-needed holiday, two portable toilets were set up in the shade of a coconut tree on a vast and deserted stretch of gleaming white sand—just in case. What puzzles us about this is: Why two? Were they expecting guests?

One of the funniest royal lavatory incidents happened in the fifties, when PRINCESS MARGARET was due to visit an army camp in the north of England. The commanding officer was worried that Margaret's eyes might be offended by the latrines (those places used by the lower ranks). So he had them all completely boarded up several days before Maggie's visit.

But when you've gotta go, you gotta go, and having nowhere to go, the hundreds of lower ranks watered the nearby grass, which, not surprisingly, turned a nasty shade of brown. To solve this possible last-minute stain on his character, the commanding officer ordered that every blade of grass be painted green. This annoyed one private so much that he leaked the story to a mass-circulation Fleet Street tabloid, which splashed the grass-painting story over a whole page.

Yet, for reasons of "good taste," the newspaper totally ignored the distasteful subject of the boarded-up loos because in those days, nobody would dream of linking the word latrines with a member of the royal family in any shape or form. A lot of water has been passed under the bridge since then. Today, if such a thing happened, some British tabloids would publish a photograph of the boarded-up latrines—with the soldiers "watering" the grass alongside as well. Backs to camera, of course.

While on the subject of passing water, the most hilarious printing error in royal history came when QUEEN VICTORIA visited the Menai Bridge in Wales. Instead of stating that "the Queen then passed over the bridge" the newspaper wrote the word pissed—which caused the Welsh to wet themselves laughing.

Still on the subject of water, QUEEN ELIZABETH never drinks common tap water. Not even when she's at home in Buckingham Palace. The reason is that London's water supply is recycled so often that it has previously been drunk and passed out again by an average of nine people.

Well-traveled people know it is unwise to drink tap water when visiting other countries as it can often cause the runs. If you are not a seasoned traveler, take a tip from the Queen, who moves around the globe a lot. To avoid having to run during her highly publicized walkabouts, she always takes several crates of Malvern Water with her. She cleans her teeth with it, her tea is made with it, as are the ice cubes for her nightly predinner gin and tonic.

The Queen also likes Vichy water and Perrier, but we shouldn't really be telling you that. For patriotic and dollar-earning export reasons, the palace wants you to believe that Her Majesty only drinks Malvern Water—because it's British, of course.

When in a hot climate, the Queen makes a point of drinking at least three pints of Malvern Water every day, to replace the body fluids lost by sweating, though Her Majesty prefers to describe it as "glowing." Great care is taken of the Queen when she travels abroad. If she should become ill, all kinds of diplomatic and political embarrassments could arise; therefore, the best medical experts travel with her. One of them is the brilliant Norman Blacklock, professor of urology at Manchester University, who is—we can't resist telling you—the author of the unusually titled tract: *Bladder Trauma in the Long Distance Runner.*

We now turn to a subject some readers might consider rather indelicate. But to reassure them, we must emphasize that the royal family will definitely not be offended. On the contrary, it's old news to them, although we suspect that on reading it here, they will probably fall about laughing all over again. The subject concerns the passing of wind. And this brings us to the most fabulous royal joke of all—which Her Majesty actually tells against herself, with great relish.

It happened when the Queen was sitting in an open-topped horse-drawn carriage with the president of an African country. One of the rear horses broke wind so violently that it sounded like a thunderclap. Quite involuntarily the Queen heard herself say "I'm terribly sorry . . ." Looking astonished, the African president shrugged his shoulders and, leaning toward her so that the carriage driver would not hear, whispered: "If you hadn't apologized, I would have thought it was the horse."

The best part of this delectable story is that the Queen rounds it off beautifully with a mock-serious look on her face: "And, do you know, even to this day, I'm still not sure whether he was teasing me—or not."

The first Queen Elizabeth of England also had a favorite story about passing wind. It happened when she granted an audience to Edward de Vere, the seventeenth Earl of Oxford

(1550 to 1604). A flamboyant poet of Italian background, he wore his finest apparel when he proudly appeared before her and performed an elegantly deep bow to the throne. But, as he did so, he broke wind, which caused several courtiers to giggle. The earl was so embarrassed by this public loss of face that he left the country and went traveling for seven long years. When he eventually appeared at court again and bowed before her, Queen Elizabeth couldn't resist commenting on the rather strained look on his face and teasingly said: "My Lord, I had forgotten the fart."

The *Oxford Dictionary* describes a fart as "an emission of wind from the anus," but many British teach their kids to use the more refined word "trump" instead. This is a little prissy because all human beings (even the royals) fart. In fact, the average person expels at least one pint of gas from the backside each day.

Every member of the royal family is well aware of what backsides are for ever since Prince Philip made world headlines by telling British industry (some claim he meant the workers) to take its finger out of its backside. Since then, buttocks have been bared before the royals on several occasions.

It happened to Prince Charles and Di when they toured New Zealand in 1983 and came face to cheek with an old Maori who bared his bum to them. People who do that kind of thing are always branded as lunatics. But this cheeky bum was certainly no mental case. His name was Ringa and when he was brought to court on a charge of offensive behavior, he was fined.

His defense was that he had not meant his bare "ring" to be offensive. He had done it to show his utter contempt—this was the traditional way for a Maori to deliver the "ultimate insult." Being a shrewd old political warrior, Maori Ringa brought an outstanding witness to court who confirmed this.

William Parker, a retired senior lecturer in Maori studies at Victoria University, Wellington, told the court that buttock-baring was an established tradition for Maoris wishing to show utter derision. He added that it was also an old royal custom, as there were several recorded cases of Maori queens baring their backsides to silence members of their court who talked a lot of rubbish.

A different case of exposing private parts came when Frances D'Espinay, a mother of three, bared her breasts in front of the queen outside the Sydney Opera House during a royal tour of Australia. Frances was cleared of offensive behavior when an appeals court judge ruled that a display of ample breasts did not constitute a crime. Quite right too. If Zulu ladies can dance totally topless to delight both male and female British royals, why can't a lady down under go over the top?

Aboriginal protestors have also bared their souls and other private parts before the queen, but she does not hold it against the tribe as a whole because an Aborigine provided Her Majesty with yet another of her favorite stories. This happened when she granted the royal pardon to an Australian Aborigine.

When the pardon was read out in court, as legally it must be, there were several sniggers because the pompously worded document began: "Elizabeth the Second, by the Grace of God of the United Kingdom of Great Britain and Northern Ireland and of Her Other Realms and Territories, Queen, Head of this Commonwealth, Defender of the Faith—to HARRY HAIRY-ARSE, Greetings. . . ."

# 6

## *Religious Royals*

*A*lthough the Church of England and the Roman Catholics have traveled a long way along the ecumenical road to peaceful coexistence, the British royals have long had something of a "Berlin Wall" mentality when it comes to Catholics and the throne. The foundation was laid when England's Catholic king, HENRY THE EIGHTH, defied Pope Clement the Seventh by divorcing Catherine of Aragon and established the Church of England with himself at its head. Paradoxically, King Henry remained a Catholic for the rest of his life.

Henry's daughter was ELIZABETH THE FIRST, who officially styled herself as "God's Chosen Deputy on Earth," and even during her last speech to the masses said: "God hath raised me high." Yet when illness laid her low in 1603 and the time came for her to meet her Maker, the seventy-year-old monarch just didn't want to go. On her deathbed she tried to bargain with Him by saying: "All my possessions for a moment of time."

This was no great deal, as God surely knew, because although Elizabeth left a vastly expensive collection of two thousand gowns, she was deeply in debt as a result of her holy war against Catholic Spain and the cost of keeping the Catholics down in Ireland. Which indicates that the atheists might just have a point when they claim there's no life after debt.

On coming to the throne in 1558, Elizabeth had promised she would remain a virgin all her life because she wished only to be "married" to her devoted subjects. She liked to play this role so much that she often emphasized her alleged virginity by wearing pure white gowns. She also ordered court painters to depict her as "the Virgin Queen." But virgin she wasn't. Apart from having a clutch of lovers, she fell madly in love at the age of fifty-four with Robert Devereux, age twenty. During their twelve-year affair she showered him with land, money, a title, and various high offices—which the basically unhappy young stallion earned the hard way because Liz hated to let him out of her sight in case some young wench seduced him.

Their affair ended tragically (for Robert) in 1601 when, becoming disenchanted, he mounted a hare-brained plot to dethrone the queen. To save face, she regretfully had him beheaded in the Tower. Older men who have sex with young girls are often called dirty old men so, in a desperate attempt to prevent anyone calling Queen Elizabeth a dirty old woman, some royal apologists claim she might have loved young Robert because he might have been her illegitimate son, and understandably, she had to keep this quiet. Maybe this was true. Yet if so, doesn't that still tarnish Elizabeth's virgin image somewhat? They can't have it both ways.

Elizabeth really *was* a dirty old woman. In an attempt to hide her age, she caked her face, neck, and cleavage with a thick paste made up of white lead mixed with egg white and the juice of white lilies aged in horse manure. And rather than go to all the trouble of having to scrape it off every night, she added a new layer every morning until it became half an inch thick. Furthermore, she bathed only once every three months, which must have distressed her lovers somewhat.

Queen Elizabeth also swallowed arsenic and candlewax to make her face become paler, and it became highly fashionable for well-bred ladies to copy her ghostly white complexion. Although the use of arsenic might sound dangerous, it was a regular practice for the ancient royals, who lived in fear of being poisoned. They took a tiny dose daily, which helped their bodies to build up an immunity to the poison.

While Queen Elizabeth was not physically clean, when it came to religion she was as pure as the driven snow—depending how far along the slushy road it had been driven. She was so convinced that Protestantism should be the state religion that she gave her royal assent to the passing of severe laws aimed at keeping the Catholics down.

- No man could hold public office unless he first denied the authority of the pope.
- Anyone who converted an Englishman to Catholicism was declared a traitor.
- And anyone caught attending mass was fined, jailed, or placed in the stocks for public ridicule.

When Elizabeth went to meet the Grim Reaper, that gay intellectual JAMES THE FIRST took the English throne. Earlier, the canny Scot had promised to help the Catholics if he became the king of England. But during the first few months of his reign, a Catholic priest named William Watson involved himself in a plot to kidnap King James and hold him prisoner until he guaranteed to show that promised toleration toward Catholics.

After Watson was caught and hanged, Robert Cecil, the head of the British Secret Service, persuaded the king to protect himself against future Catholic plots by ordering all Catholic priests to leave England. This was the direct cause of that other, far more famous plot—in which Guy Fawkes and several well-born Catholics gathered together thirty-five barrels of gunpowder with the intention of blowing up the king as he sat in Parliament on November 5, 1605. This, in turn, caused the now-fearful King James to give his assent to several laws forbidding Catholics to become lawyers, doctors, or clerks and preventing them from acting as executors or trustees. In addition:

- Catholics were not allowed to appear at court.
- They were not allowed to live within ten miles of London unless they were employed in approved professions.
- They could not travel more than five miles from their homes without obtaining permission from a magistrate.
- Any Roman Catholic who had been educated on the Continent was declared an outlaw.
- Special fines were imposed on Catholics whose servants failed to attend services of the Church of England.
- Married Catholic couples had no right to property due to either of them by marriage—unless the wedding ceremony had been conducted by a Protestant clergyman.
- And if a Protestant entertained a Roman Catholic visitor, or employed a Roman Catholic servant without permission, he could be heavily fined.

Not only the Catholics suffered under King James the First. Shortly after ascending to the throne, he told the Puritans that unless they conformed to the Church of England, he would "harry them out of the land." Believing him, a congregation from Nottinghamshire left England in 1608 and settled at Leiden in Holland. Later, in 1620, a group of them left Plymouth Harbour in a ninety-foot-long square-rigged sailing ship and made their way to another place, which they also named Plymouth. Of these 102 (78 men and 24 women) only 35 were actually Puritans, but, in 1799, they all earned their place in American folklore as "the Pilgrim Fathers."

As we have mentioned in the "Gay Royals" chapter, King James was incredibly coarse and profane in his speech, but he still claimed to be a representative of God and ordered his bishops to tell their flocks that he spoke "with the special assistance of God's spirit"—to which a cynic of the time aptly commented: "The spirit of God must be surprisingly foulmouthed."

Undaunted, King James told his Parliament on March 21, 1609: "The state of Monarchy is the supremest thing upon earth: for Kings are not only God's lieutenants [on earth] and sit upon God's throne, but even by God Himself they are called Gods."

God might have thought this was stretching it a bit but probably forgave His lieutenant James because, two years earlier, he had ordered forty-seven scholars to produce a vernacular translation of the Holy Bible—so that more of the masses could be made aware of its teaching. This Bible is known as the Authorized Version or King James's Bible, and is still in use in England.

When James died in 1625, the English throne was taken by his son, CHARLES THE FIRST. He was an extremely religious and fastidious man, so his horror can be imagined when, in 1631, none other than his own royal printers, Robert Barker and Martin Lucas, of Blackfriars, published a Bible urging people to commit adultery! A really ungodly gremlin in the printing works had left out the key word, Not, in the Seventh Commandment so that it read: "Thou Shalt Commit Adultery."

Today such a mistake would get the printers top billing on a prime-time radio or TV show and be the subject of a little nudge, nudge, wink, wink. But back in 1631 it caused such an uproar that the faulty tome was called "the Wicked Bible" and even "the Adulterer's Bible." The royal printers were fined the then massive sum of $6,000. This sent them into bankruptcy, quite apart from the social disgrace. The furor was such that the archbishop of Canterbury insisted that all one thousand copies of that Bible be destroyed, but, human nature being what it is—acquisitive—the men designated to burn them, secretly kept a few copies. At least six are known to exist and are valuable collector's items.

One of those "Wicked Bibles" is almost certainly stored away in the royal library at Windsor because AUGUSTUS, the son of England's loony King George the Third, was so Bible-mad that he had an incredible private collection of 5,300 leather-bound ones.

In 1685 JAMES THE SECOND came to the English throne. Being a staunch Catholic who had an equally staunch Catholic wife, he started appointing Catholics as officers in the army and navy. He also chose Catholics for positions in Oxford colleges and admitted them into the Privy Council. In 1687 he issued the Declaration of Indulgence to protect the religious rights of all dissenters from the Church of England.

Brooking no opposition and exploiting his royal preroga-tives, the king suspended or dispensed with laws and steam-rolled everyone in his attempts to introduce what he described as "complete religious equality." But his detractors saw all these moves as part of a cunning plot, masterminded by Rome, to overthrow the British constitution and the established church in order to bring about a Catholic takeover.

The crunch really came when it was announced that the king's wife was pregnant and the child, if a boy, would naturally become the next king of England. Not liking the sound of this—as it heralded a permanent Catholic dynasty—the king's enemies put out the story that the child would most probably be stillborn or die shortly after birth as the queen's previous six babies had all died in infancy.

Another rumor claimed that the queen was not pregnant at all and that she and the king secretly intended adopting some-one else's newborn child in a last gamble to keep the English crown in the Catholic grip. To silence the latter accusation, King James invited a varied panel of VIP's to be in the queen's bedchamber when she went into labor on June 10, 1688.

For reasons of modesty the actual birth was hidden by blan-kets. Just before delivery, the queen said she felt cold, as moth-ers often do, and called for a warming pan to be placed in her bed. When a healthy bouncing baby boy (Prince James Francis Edward, who became tagged "the Pretender") was born, the king's enemies put out a story that the queen had not really given birth to the child but that it had been smuggled into her bed in the warming pan.

Some historians insist this was a lie and that the baby was definitely the queen's. Others write that there is reasonable doubt because, many weeks before the birth, King James had rushed around "guaranteeing" that the baby would be a boy and, in any case, the little prince was remarkably healthy considering that he was born one month premature.

Within days of the birth a group of British noblemen, powerful millionaire businessmen and clergy, sent a secret message to Holland telling the Dutch-born William of Orange that if he brought an army over to England he could easily snatch the English throne—with their backing. Jumping at the chance, William came, saw, and conquered without firing a shot. His invasion was warmly welcomed by English Protestants and, throwing away his crown, James the Second fled to France.

This then, was the "Glorious Revolution" which brought a Dutchman to the throne as WILLIAM THE THIRD who co-ruled with his wife, MARY, the elder daughter of King James by his first wife, Anne Hyde.

William quickly showed his English backers that they had chosen the right man by giving his royal assent to an Act of Indulgence permitting Christian nonconformists (but not Roman Catholics) to worship freely subject to certain conditions. He also gave his assent to the 1701 Act of Settlement, which laid down that the sovereign of the realm must belong to the Church of England with the proviso that all Roman Catholics, or persons marrying Roman Catholics, were forever to be excluded as heirs to the throne, as if they "were naturally dead." The Act of Settlement excluded fifty-eight superior claims by descent to the English throne—all of them by Catholics.

The mood of that act is still with us because, as recently as February 1983, the Church of England Synod issued its decision that PRINCE CHARLES's son William would be barred from succeeding to the English throne if he chose to marry a Catholic. The fact that little William was not even nine months old at the time just goes to show that someone felt no chances should be taken.

The most recent case of embarrassment involving the British royal family and the world's (then) 621 million Roman Catholics came in 1985 when Prince Charles visited Italy and wanted to share a little prayer with the pope by attending a private Vatican mass. Someone at top level in London said "definitely not, not under any circumstance," and Prince Charles was left standing outside St. Peter's with egg on his face.

When this became a worldwide scandal, Buckingham Palace "leaked" rumors to its agents in the British press that the British premier, Margaret Thatcher, had banned the mass. But Maggie, also no slouch when it comes to media manipulation, told her mates in the press that she was not the woman at fault—which bounced the ball straight back into the queen's court, where it rightfully belonged. The public was never told who was really responsible, but the shock cancellation of that innocent papal mass offended countless millions—not all of them Catholics.

This holy unnecessary shambles was brilliantly summed up in a couple of paragraphs by that deliciously outspoken old journalist of British Establishment fame, Sir John Junor. Writing in the *Sunday Express*, he blamed the Queen and supported Prince Charles by stating: "Why shouldn't he make up his own mind on religious matters? I do not imagine that he has any serious leanings towards Roman Catholicism. But if he had, and even wanted to become a convert, what would be so wrong with that? Isn't the only important thing the fact that he believes in God . . . ?"

Some rather enthusiastic researchers have allowed themselves to get just a little carried away by suggesting that the House of Windsor side of the royal family is descended from the biblical King David. Other experts only go as far as saying they are descendants of KING ALFRED THE GREAT, which is equally fascinating because Alfred (who reigned from 871 to 899) is firmly on record as saying he was "fiftieth in direct descent from Adam"!

This linking of monarchy with biblical characters is not confined to the English royals. Some Welshmen still believe the (Welsh) legend that in the fourth century, one of their kings (BELI, the son of MANOGAN) was "a brother-in-law of the Virgin Mary." Beating even that, the family of the French king CHARLEMAGNE actually claimed they were "descended from the union of the Virgin Mary."

Some rulers went one better than claiming descent from biblical figures. RANA, the maharajah of Dholpur, who was a close friend of England's King George the Fifth in the 1930s, was loony enough to brainwash his subjects into believing he was "descended from the Moon." Another odd Indian ruler was SIR JEY SINGHJI RISHI SHRI SEWAI, the maharajah of Alwar, who told his subjects that he was "the Holy Sage of the Domain." Let's examine this titled chap's holiness:

Although sophisticated and highly intelligent, he was mentally and sexually bent. He had four wives but was a notorious pederast who liked ten-year-old boys and had them tortured if they displeased him. He was also sadistic and considered it great fun to have babies tied up as tiger bait. All the British diplomats (and Secret Service information-gatherers) based in India knew full well about these and other atrocities, yet this weirdo was a guest of King George the Fifth and his wife, Queen Mary, at Buckingham Palace in 1931.

The British royals blanked him out of their social circle later, however, when they discovered, to their absolute horror, that he was cruel to animals. This was after a game of polo during which the maharajah played badly. Blaming his pony, he poured a can of petrol over the hapless animal and set fire to it—in front of a shocked audience of Indian and British VIPs. That was the end of the "holy sage." He was deposed in 1933 and exiled to Paris, where he lived in fabulous luxury until he died in 1937.

Another religious ruler was EMPEROR YOSHIHITO of Japan who died insane in 1926 at the age of forty-seven. He was succeeded by "SHOWA" HIROHITO, who was undoubtedly the modern world's most astonishingly successful fallen god when it came to surviving. But let's start at the beginning of this divine story.

When Hirohito was born in 1901, the Japanese people were told that, as a descendant of the Sun Goddess Amaterasu, he was the "son of heaven." After coming to the throne, Hirohito observed the essential one full year's mourning for the death of the previous emperor. Then, in early 1928, he performed a ritual ceremony during which he had sexual intercourse with the gods.

It may sound outlandish to most Westerners, but throughout Japanese history, this ceremony has always been necessary for any emperor wishing to be invested with divinity. As part of the ritual, every new emperor sits inside a primitive hut in the grounds of the Kyoto Palace. The hut has screens open to the east ("the Sacred Direction") to await the coming of the gods. During this time, the emperor is magically transformed into a temple virgin, has intercourse with the briefly visiting gods, falls pregnant—and is then "reborn" as a god.

Although the subject was largely ignored in the Western press, Emperor Hirohito quietly performed this ritual and, by so doing, became the "heavenly monarch" who was worshipped as "a living god." In December 1941 Hirohito's planes came down from the heavens and bombed Pearl Harbor, and in August 1945 an American aircraft more than settled the score by dropping that ungodly atomic bomb on Hiroshima. When this was followed by another atomic bomb on Nagasaki three days later, poor Hirohito could hardly save his lost face by disemboweling himself in public with his favorite diamond-, ruby-, and emerald-encrusted ceremonial sword because he was a god. And gods, not being mortal, simply can't be seen to die.

So what did Hirohito do? He officially announced he was not a god anymore. Just like that. A living god one day, and an ordinary guy the next. But even then, on becoming a normal mortal, Hirohito still didn't commit hara-kiri. He surrendered, in total and utter disgrace. Yet (just like Kaiser Wilhelm of Germany in 1918) he somehow managed to escape standing in a common dock and facing trial as a war criminal. Instead, Hirohito led his vanquished people in an economic war against the rest of the globe and became so rehabilitated in the business world that, while enjoying a state visit to Britain in 1971, he stayed in Buckingham Palace as an honored guest of Queen Elizabeth.

The old "Divine Right of Kings" theory stated that as kings were ordained and anointed by God, any resistance to their authority was unlawful. This "divine" right is said to have been demolished in Britain by the so-called Glorious Revolution of 1688, when Parliament got the upper hand over monarchy. But tiny cracks had already started to appear during the reign of KING HENRY THE FIRST (1100 to 1135) when he had to knuckle under to the power of the church—which decided it was rather old-fashioned to believe that anointed kings were God's deputies on earth. The church argued, with canny logic, that its priests were in charge of a man's soul and a king's business lay only with his body.

But the royals have always been brilliant tacticians and, to compensate, they resurrected the mystique of the "God-given" royal healing touch. This was first written about in the tenth century by the historian, William of Malmesbury, who disclosed how EDWARD THE CONFESSOR (1042 to 1066) had washed a disgusting-looking sore on a young woman's badly festering neck and it was "miraculously" cured. What Malmesbury failed to spell out was that the good food the woman ate while she was allowed to live in the palace for a whole week most probably effected the cure.

Remembering that great yarn, the palace publicity experts of the seventeenth century put out the story that if the monarch touched sick people, they would be cured. And faith healing being what it is—mind over matter—the royal touch did, now and then, effect a cure. These successes were given front-page treatment to keep them in the public mind, while the failures were studiously ignored, working on the sound principle that if the public was not reminded, it did not matter.

The royal healing touch quickly became popular, and on certain holy days, thousands of afflicted peasants queued up to be touched by the monarch. As part of this superb Madison Avenue-style publicity scenario the monarch also gave each person touched a gold coin—which understandably further aided the healing process because the peasants were then able to buy some decent food.

As soon as the royal product had been firmly cemented in the public mind by this clever advertising gimmick, the "special introductory offer" of free gold coins was discontinued and the royal treasury saved itself a fortune by churning out cheap and mass-produced "touch pieces" which, having been touched and given by the monarch, still brought about 'miraculous' cures.

In his book *Miscellanies* (London, 1696) John Aubrey tells the amusing story of the Welshman Evans who had the most disgusting fungus growing out of and around his nose. Convinced that the royal healing touch would cure him, Evans patiently lay in ambush just inside St. James's Park where the "Casanova King" Charles the Second often took a walk. On seeing the king, he rushed forward and, on the pretense of kissing his hand, used it to rub all over his clinker-ridden and badly seeping nostrils. We are told that Charles wrinkled his nose at this nauseous experience, but cure Evan's nose it did.

Charles was a great exponent of the healing touch gimmick. During one eleven-month period starting in 1682, he touched 8,577 people, which caused a wit of the day to quip that during the whole of his reign the king must have touched half the nation—and that was not counting all the women he had touched up.

History books claim that QUEEN ANNE (1702 to 1714) was the last royal to perform a God-given miracle when she touched the English writer Dr. Samuel Johnson (then an infant) with her "divine power." Many British newspapers seem unaware of this. To this day, they still religiously publish news stories telling of "miraculous" royal cures.

- In August 1985, several British newspapers told how a thirteen-year-old girl had lain in hospital with her eyes closed after an air crash but had "miraculously" opened them for the very first time when PRINCE CHARLES sat on the edge of her bed.
- In September 1986 the *Daily Mail* told how Fergie's husband, PRINCE ANDREW, had met a girl of sixteen in a school for "problem" children. The girl had been "a snarling creature" who had sat limply with her head on the prince's lap. But the charming prince had lifted up her sagging head and told her: "I'm just flesh and blood." He wasn't though. One year later, when the prince met her again (still in that "problem" school), there was a miraculous change. The snarling creature was now "full of smiles" because, she said, the prince had "given her confidence."
- In October 1987, *The Sun* published an article headlined: "DI-VINE HEALER," which quoted a doctor as saying PRINCESS DI was a "miracle worker" who seemed to possess "extraordinary healing powers."
- In May 1989 the *News of the World* explained how Princess Di had once again performed her wonderful magic by bringing a woman "back from the brink of death" after she had been kicked on the head by a horse. The woman was Chloe Teacher, the wife of the Teachers whiskey heir, James Teacher, who is a friend of the royal family. Hailing Princess Di as "a miracle worker," Mr. Peter Gau-

tier-Smith, of London's National Hospital for Nervous Diseases, added: "You could almost compare it to the laying on of hands."

Although they insist the "divine right" to rule theory was killed off in 1688, it is still alive and kicking in many minds. When a public opinion poll was held in England in 1964, it disclosed that 30 percent of those interviewed believed that QUEEN ELIZABETH had been "specially chosen to rule by God." This may or may not be due to the fact that:

- At their coronations, British monarchs are still anointed with Holy Oil.
- The inscription "D.G.REGINA F.D.," ("By the Grace of God, Queen Defender of the Faith") still appears on British coins.
- British royals are still baptized with water from the River Jordan—as was Christ when he was baptized by St. John the Baptist.
- The Royal Arms of England still bear the motto "Dieu et Mon Droit" (God and My Right), which King Richard the Lion Heart used as his war cry at the Battle of Gisors in 1198.

QUEEN ELIZABETH often mentions God in her speeches, her favorite sayings being: "May God bless you" and "I pray that the blessing of Almighty God may rest upon your counsels." On the other hand, it is no secret that her husband PRINCE PHILIP is rather cynical about religion and once classed himself as an agnostic. He certainly had no respect for the cloth when the Archbishop of Canterbury, Dr. Michael Ramsey, confirmed his sixteen-year-old son Prince Charles in St. George's Chapel, Windsor. Prince Philip caused a rumpus by quite openly reading a book throughout the service, and the outraged archbishop later described his behavior as "bloody rude."

Prince Philip has even used the name of God to raise a laugh. After being delayed by a blizzard, he told an audience in Sheffield: "Despite the Ministry of Technology and all the wonderful things in the world, it does still appear that God has the last word from time to time." To which we say:

Amen.

# 7

## The Casanova King

*J*ust because KING CHARLES THE SECOND made no attempt to hide his passion for chasing skirt, most historians prissily describe him as the man who headed "the most immoral royal court in English history."

Several kings and queens are on record as "despising" him (particularly Queen Victoria), but a close scrutiny of their own lives shows that most of them were guilty of exactly the same kind of sexual athletics.

Charles admitted to having thirty-nine mistresses and was a sexual rogue, but the headline-grabbing tales of his amorous adventures have been allowed to overshadow the fact that he was one of England's greatest and best-loved monarchs. This chapter will present the positive aspects of the man who has been labeled the "Casanova king." But let's get rid of the sexy stuff first.

Charles was born at St. James's Palace, London, on May 29, 1630. As he emerged, the midwife correctly forecast that he would grow up to be most liberal in his attitudes because, instead of clenching his fists as newborn babies usually do, he kept his hands wide open. But, as you travel through the sexy stages of this chapter, you might suspect that his hands were actually open in an attempt to grab the midwife's breasts.

His first sexual encounter was at the age of fifteen when Mrs. Christabella Wyndham, an attractive and super-rich woman then about thirty-five, pulled him into bed and showed him what an older woman wanted. Although it was his first taste of sex, it was not Charles's first taste of Mrs. Wyndham for he had suckled at her breasts as a baby when she was employed as his wet nurse and nanny.

His next recorded sexual encounter was in Jersey, Channel Islands, with Marguerite Carteret, who was twenty and taught Charles, then sixteen, what a younger woman wanted. Later she gave birth to a son, said to be by Charles. This boy, named James de la Cloche, became a man of the cloth in Rome. Although his life is cloaked in mystery, it is known he had a letter, signed by King Charles, stating he was of royal birth.

The king's first full-time mistress was Lucy Walter, who is said to have been a little loose with her body. Some refined historians skate over or totally ignore this side of little Lucy's character. But it is a recorded fact that an aristocrat named Colonel Algernon Sidney (who ended up being beheaded) once gave evidence that, in 1648, he had paid Lucy fifty pieces of gold "for her services."

Does this mean that Lucy was a prostitute? Lady Antonia Fraser, in her splendid book *King Charles II* (Weidenfeld & Nicolson, 1979) states quite categorically that "Lucy was *not* a whore." Lady Antonia is a prolific and dedicated wordsmith who has written and edited many excellent books on royalty and is good at her job.

But so is Tony Palmer, author of some seven books, who produced the excellent *Charles II—Portrait of an Age* (Cassell Ltd., 1979) in which he writes: "Nor was the King's reputation helped by the loud-mouthed Lucy, now a prostitute."

Perhaps we should consult a writer of King Charles's time. Who better than Samuel Pepys, sometimes styled the "greatest diarist in the English language," because he compiled a famous 3,000-page diary that starts in 1660 and ends in 1669.

Pepys was friendly with King Charles and often visited him at Windsor. He was also in regular contact with courtiers and mistresses at court and, being a born journalist, assiduously collected whatever gossip he could lay his ears on. In 1664 he wrote of Lucy Walter: "Alsopp [the king's brewer] says it is well-known that she was a common strumpet [prostitute] before the King was acquainted with her." This is confirmed by yet another diarist of the time, John Evelyn, who describes Lucy in his diary as "a beautiful strumpet."

The modern coyness about Lucy's reputation is mysterious. Can it have anything to do with the fact that Princess Di and her sister-in-law, Fergie, are both descendants of Lucy Walter and that no less than five of the dukes in Britain today—the backbone of the real aristocracy—are descended from the various mistresses of King Charles? We don't think so because those dukes are not ashamed of their background; in fact, they brag about it.

Whether Lucy took those fifty pieces of gold from Colonel Algernon Sidney or not, poor Algy was unable to consummate whatever deal they might have negotiated. Just before they could do whatever it was they were (or were not) going to do, Algy heard a bugle blowing. This was the signal that his regiment was leaving town and he had to dash off.

We gather that Lucy did not return his gold. Perhaps she suggested he take a raincheck. Soon afterward she "fell into the possession of" Algy's brother, Colonel Robert Sidney, who might just have been collecting that raincheck on Algy's behalf.

In the summer of 1648, Lucy captured the heart, or purse, of King Charles and nine months later, in April 1649, in Rotterdam, she produced a baby named James. Accepting the lad as his, Charles gave him the title of duke of Monmouth. In July 1650 when King Charles went off on a business trip, Lucy had it off with Colonel Henry Bennet (later the earl of Arlington). In 1651 Charles finally dropped Lucy. Using the false name Mrs. Barlow, she then "embarked on a life of depravity."

From old records on dusty ledges we find that Lucy allegedly went with many men, was charged with murdering a maid (not proven), got herself arrested on allegations that she was a spy (not charged), and was a little naughty in other ways. Charles, having already decided that Lucy was not the right sort of woman to bring up a king's son, had their bastard child removed from her care. It appears that Charles granted Lucy an annual "pension" of £400 at about this time and warned her to behave. She finally settled in Paris but didn't behave herself and died there in 1658. The personal evidence of King James the Second (brother of Charles) tells us that "her wretched life came to an end caused by a disease incidental to her manner of living." Let's not mince words. She died of syphilis.

A seminude painting of Lucy still exists. It shows her sitting with her infant son, James, duke of Monmouth, on her lap. The title of this valuable painting is "Madonna and Child."

King Charles went on to enjoy, by his own admission, thirty-eight other regular mistresses who produced an estimated twenty bastards. He acknowledged fourteen of them. One of his mistresses was the elegant and stunningly beautiful, French-educated, seventeen-year-old Frances Stewart, who had fabulous legs and continually shocked (annoyed) the other ladies of the court by lifting her skirts at any opportunity to display them. This little cutie cleverly gave Charles hot pants by refusing to go to bed with him at first. Royalist writers rush to protest that this "childlike virgin" never *did* sleep with the king. But others insist that she did, did, did.

For those who might wonder why some historians insist on defending this long-dead lass so strenuously, we should perhaps mention that dear, virginal Frances sat as the model for the world-famous "Britannia" symbol. Yes, that most revered lady (once seen on the old British penny) who wears a helmet, holds a shield in her right hand, a trident in her left, and, overlooks the waves she then ruled. She is the very personification of Great Britain. Rule (Mistress) Britannia indeed!

King Charles showered pretty Frances with jewels and was peeved when he popped into her bedchamber one night and caught her lying in bed with the duke of Richmond sitting beside her. Although the duke was fully dressed, Charles knew he was not there to play Parcheesi and banished them both from court. Frances did the right thing though and later married the duke.

The most elegant mistress King Charles had was Louise de Keroualle, who was born near Brest, France, in 1649. She deliberately caught the king's eye and seduced him in October 1671. The English public was taught to dislike her by a whispering campaign orchestrated by right-wingers in Parliament who emphasized that she was French and a Catholic. King Charles tried to cleanse her public image by persuading her to become a naturalized British subject, but it did not work.

It is almost certain Louise was a secret agent planted by Louis the Fourteenth of France. It is a historical fact that Louis sent her to England in the hope that she could "get close" to Charles. Louis knew that Charles had previously met Louise and had fancied her.

It is also an undisputed fact that Louis the Fourteenth was a past master in the art of espionage and that he had a vast army of spies, agents, informers, and covert propaganda spreaders. Even his ambassadors in London have been proved to have been intelligence experts who collected sexual and political gossip that Louis could use to bribe or blackmail prominent and powerful Englishmen.

It is also a historical fact that Paul Barillon, a French ambassador to London, was just one of several middlemen who arranged for King Charles to receive secret bribes from Louis the Fourteenth. Between the years 1660 and 1684 Charles pocketed more than £3 million in personal cash bribes from Louis, who was eager to get English support against other countries, such as Holland and Spain.

But an English king cannot possibly be seen to have accepted foreign payola, so most historians fall over themselves to assure us that in spite of all the promises Charles made to Louis, he actually "gave very little in return." If we are to believe this, then the French king must have been a total idiot. It stands to reason that no sane man would keep paying regular cash bribes (over twenty-four years!) to someone who didn't play ball.

If Louis the Fourteenth had King Charles in his pocket, why did he plant Louise de Keroualle on him—and tell her to "get as close as you can" to the British monarch? So that she could keep an eye on him, of course. And also pick up other valuable snippets of information while operating in the heart of Charles's royal court.

Pretty Louise certainly got close to Charles. She became his number-one mistress, and in 1672 she had a son by him named Charles Lennox, who was created duke of Richmond. Louise also got titles: countess of Fareham, baroness Petersfield, and duchess of Portsmouth. In addition, King Charles gave Louise properties in various parts of England and even large tracts of land in the Irish counties of Dublin, Donegal, and Fermanagh. She also obtained a pension of £10,000 a year and a torrent of jewelry.

Charles the Second's most famous mistress was Nell Gwynne, the cocky little Cockney of Welsh extraction who spent a considerable time between the king's sheets. Eleanor "Nell" Gwynne, better known as "Pretty, witty Nell," is said to have been born in 1650 and as a young girl served drinks in her mother's private little drinking club. This was actually a brothel in London's Covent Garden area. Her parents were hardly conventional. Her dad died in an Oxford prison and her mum drowned in a Westminister ditch while drunk.

Nell got her big start in life at the age of fourteen when she began selling oranges inside (not outside, as all those Hollywood films depict) London's Drury Lane Theatre during the intermissions. When she was fifteen, auburn-haired Nell was talent-spotted by an actor named Charles Hart who, after giving her a roll on the casting couch, gave her a small role on stage. Nell went on to become one of the most famous comic actresses of her time.

Nell did not fall into the conceit trap of self-importance when King Charles openly displayed her as his mistress. On the contrary, she never put on pompous airs and graces. She knew exactly who and what she was. The best example of this came when Charles was also having that torrid affair with the Catholic Louise de Keroualle, whom the public had been taught to hate.

Nell was traveling in a horse-drawn coach near a meeting of Parliament when a section of the large crowd lining the roadside angrily mobbed the vehicle, thinking it contained Louise. As the crowd rocked her coach, Nell leaned high out of the window and shouted, in a raucous Cockney accent: "Pray good people, be civil. I am the Protestant whore Nell, not the Catholic one." Drawing back, the highly amused mob sent up a great cheer. That little speech made her the most popular woman in Britain.

Nell asked the palace paymaster for £500 a year when she was first taken on as an official mistress to the king. The paymaster refused, saying £500 was far too much, considering all the free publicity she would be getting for her stage appearances. But Nell bent the king's ear and ended up getting £60,000 a year.

Nell's first son was born in May 1670, and a couple of years later, when the king was having tea at her home, she is said to have shouted to her toddler: "Come hither, you little bastard, and say hello to your father." When Charles protested about the use of the word bastard, shrewd and pretty witty Nell retorted: "Your Majesty hath given me no other name by which I may call him." Taking the hint, Charles gave his bastard boy the name Charles Beauclerk and created him Baron Hedington and earl of Burford. This very handsome young man was later made the duke of St. Albans and became a great soldier who married a super-rich, intelligent, and titled woman who was also a famed beauty. Lucky bastard.

King Charles was generous to Nell Gwynne. He gave her jewels, settled Bestwood Park, Nottingham, on her, and also gave her a lovely mansion in Windsor. Nell stayed in good favor with Charles and was maintained at great expense (to the taxpayers) until the king died. One of the last sentences he uttered on his deathbed was: "Let not poor Nelly starve."

She didn't. She was rich, famous, and utterly adored by the

working class. When this former fruit vendor died of a stroke in 1687, she was regally buried in a tomb in the Church of St. Martin's in the Fields, at the corner of Trafalgar Square. Just across the road, in the National Portrait Gallery, you can see the excellent portrait of her by Sir Peter Lely.

Charles's most outrageous mistress was the beautiful nymphomaniac Barbara Villiers, who had five bastards by him. For ten years this astonishing woman was known as the "uncrowned Queen of England." She was born in about 1641 of very good stock. Her father, William Villiers, was Viscount Grandison. King Charles first laid thighs on her in May 1660, which produced her first child, Anne. Barbara's husband, Roger, claimed the child was his, but Barbara insisted it had been sired by Charles, and he, always glad to be Dad, acknowledged little Anne as his product.

In 1662 Barbara gave birth to her first boy (Charles Fitzroy) by the king. This did not stop her enjoying the company of other men, however, as a few months after the birth, two officers on watch duty outside Barbara's home just happened to be peeping through her bedroom window and saw her getting into bed with Sir Charles Berkeley. They added that "purely by accident" they had seen this happen on various other nights.

Conservative historians would normally deny any possibility that such an eminent man could two-time his king this way, but in this case they can't. In his Diary entry of December 15, 1662, Samuel Pepys states that Sir Charles Berkeley's greatness was due only to the fact that he acted as a pimp for King Charles. Now there's a majestic example of a knight having it both ways, some nights.

Barbara had affairs with countless titled men, but she was no sexual snob. One lover was Jacob Hall, a handsome and famous young rope dancer whom she picked up at a fairground. His performance in bed was such that she paid him a regular salary for his "personal services."

Another man who jumped into Barbara's bed was a palace footman, but, as he was a real menial, history does not bother to record his name, age, place of birth, physical attributes, social graces, wit, charm, bravery, artistic talents, or the size of his feet.

In September 1663 Barbara Villiers gave birth to her third child, Henry. When King Charles refused to accept fatherhood, Barbara threatened to carry the baby down to the Whitehall Gallery and, in front of a large audience, bash its brains out against a wall. Not wanting that kind of bad publicity, Charles is said to have dropped to his knees and begged Barbara's pardon for having been "wrongly suspicious" of her. He not only acknowledged the child as his, but made him the duke of Grafton.

In September 1664 Barbara gave birth to her fourth child, Charlotte. In December 1665 a boy named George Fitzroy was born. The name Fitzroy, meaning "king's son," was chosen by Charles to indicate illegitimate royal descent. During her reign as royal mistress she had three sons, all of whom were made dukes by King Charles.

Barbara's most famous lover on the side was a man called John Churchill, a rather lower middle-class country boy. She gave this poor but handsome young man £5,000 for one night of love. Few people know Churchill's name, even though his direct descendant was Sir Winston Churchill, the British prime minister of World War II fame.

John is better known in the history books as the duke of Marlborough, the English military genius who never lost a battle. He was relatively impoverished in his early youth while a student in Dublin but, upon returning to England, landed a plum job as a page boy to James, Duke of York (later King James the Second). That is how, after he was given a commission in the British army, John came to meet Barbara Villiers.

She lured the athletic twenty-one-year-old John into her boudoir. He must have performed well, as she gave him the cash gift the next morning. There can be no argument about this payment. It has been so well documented that all historians —whatever their religious or political bias—simply have no alternative but to accept it.

Mind you, the sum was peanuts to Barbara. When one doddering old aristocrat (Sir Edward Hungerford) told her he would very much like to lie between the lovely legs "where the king had been," Barbara told him he could do so if he paid her £10,000. And, as Sir Edward lay on his back while Barbara earned her money, she whispered that if he did not give her a very expensive present in addition, she would tell all the ladies at court that he was totally impotent. Not wishing to lose face around town, the old knight cleverly counterbargained that to prove publicly he was not impotent he would give her a further £10,000 for another night of sex. She agreed.

When King Charles tired of Barbara as a bedmate, he suggested she take herself off to Paris, saying: "Make the least noise you can, and I care not who you love." That immortal line is from the four-volumed *Memoirs of the Court of England During the Reign of the Stuarts* by John Heneage Jesse, published in England in 1855.

In 1709 Barbara died of dropsy, a disease that causes watery fluids to collect in the cavities. Two dukes and two earls were pallbearers at her funeral but no monument was erected—the only nonerection of her career perhaps. History bears no grudge against this woman and her incredibly rampant lifestyle. Some thirty paintings of her are to be found hanging in Hampton Court, the National Portrait Gallery, and the British Museum. It might sound like a joke but several of these paintings depict her as a saint.

The only really saintly woman in the life of King Charles was his long-suffering wife, the Portuguese CATHERINE OF BRAGANZA. Poor Catherine. Charles did not love her one little bit when he married her. This is understandable when you know that their marriage had been fixed way back when Charles was aged twelve and Catherine was just four. As most royal marriages were (and still are), it was carefully arranged. The Portuguese had signed a commercial treaty with the English in 1642 and wished to cement it. In addition, they wished to secure English aid against other not-so-friendly countries, such as Spain.

Charles certainly did not wish to marry Catherine. Apart from being rather plump, she was not pretty and, at twenty-three, she was hardly young—and Charles liked them pretty young. Furthermore, Catherine had a long nose, a swarthy complexion, and protruding top teeth which slightly distorted her upper lip. She waddled like a duck, had terrible halitosis, and was a devout Catholic who frowned on any kind of immorality. Even worse from a king's point of view, Charles had been told by his spies that Catherine was incapable of having children.

Although Charles strongly resisted when the Portuguese kept offering Catherine to him, he weakened slightly when they promised that all English businessmen operating in Portugal would be given total commercial freedom, tax advantages, and import and export facilities. This was rather like telling the cat it could lick off the cream and leave the milk.

Another incentive they offered Charles was a dowry worth about $15 million in today's purchasing power. When he dithered, they threw in Bombay, on the coast of India, and Tangier, the strategic Moroccan port on the Mediterranean, just opposite Gibraltar. Charles immediately said "I do" and the marriage treaty was signed on June 23, 1661.

The wily Portuguese conned Charles with Tangier and Bombay. Both were very hot political potatoes. Bombay cost him far more than it provided, and when he offered to sell it back to Portugal, they politely declined. In desperation, he sold it to the East India Company for a nominal rent of £10 a year.

Tangier was even worse. It was under regular attack by Sultan Moulay Ismail's Muslim followers, and Charles had to send twenty-seven ships carrying three thousand British troops to keep the heathens down. Led by Lord Peterborough, the troops arrived at Tangier in January 1662 and quickly tidied up the town by destroying most of the buildings of religion not agreeing with Whitehall's.

Three months later the Moors wiped out 500 British troops in a brilliant ambush just two miles from the center of town. When another 500 troops set out on the same route later, they were also ambushed—in exactly the same place. Only nine soldiers survived. This was terribly sad for the other 491 and their relatives, but most suspiciously convenient for the near-bankrupt King Charles and his treasury because when they died, all those soldiers were owed two years back pay.

It was a great saving for the British Treasury, but Tangier was still costing 13 percent of England's total annual income —and that was not counting the cost (£2 million) of the beautifully curved harbor sea wall the British had built there. So, in 1684, Charles ordered his troops to evacuate the dreadful place. Before so doing, these dogs in the manger destroyed all their lovely forts—and that excellent sea wall.

Only one thing about Tangier gave King Charles a belly laugh. This was the astonishing fact that in the short space of one month, a pretty local girl named Joyce had sold her favours to no less than 400 of the British forces based in the Kasbah. And all 400 had caught the dreaded pox. Joyful Joyce really was a hard-working busybody, but you will find no mention of her amazing tour de force in the Guinness Book of Records.

When Catherine of Braganza landed at Portsmouth from the royal yacht on May 13, 1662, Charles was not there to meet her. When he finally arrived six days later, he found his unlovely intended lying in bed with a fever, a raging cold, and a streaming big red nose. His first words on seeing her, which he whispered to his aide, Colonel George Legge, were: "They have brought me a bat!"

Catherine quickly showed she had a will of her own. As a staunch Catholic she wanted, nay absolutely insisted upon, a Catholic wedding service according to the rites of Rome. Charles was not really bothered by this as some of his best friends were Catholics. But his Whitehall bureaucrats were appalled. When Catherine said she would take the next boat back to Lisbon—and they could forget about Bombay, Tangier, and that lovely big dowry if she didn't get what she wanted— Charles's noble advisors went into a huddle and emerged to say a Catholic wedding would be all right, Old Boy. No problem—as long as it was held in the utmost secrecy.

Catherine didn't worry too much about this hypocrisy, and

the secret ceremony was held in her bedchamber the next day. To make things look right for the sake of the uneducated English masses (who did not know that two rites could be wrong), a verbally modified public ceremony was performed later in the governor of Portsmouth's house.

When Catherine arrived at the London court, Charles presented her with a list of women who would act as her ladies of the bedchamber. Queen Catherine's spies had obviously done their homework as the only name she struck off the list was that of Barbara Villiers. Not to be outdone, dear Charles punished Catherine by sacking most of her hundred personal retainers and packing them off back to Lisbon. When Catherine protested that she felt lonely and alienated in a strange court without these loyal and trusted aides, Charles threatened to sack even more. Catherine got the message.

Charles then brought Barbara to a well-attended, full-dress, official audience with Queen Catherine and told her, in front of the massed group, that he was bestowing upon her the great honor of having Barbara Villiers as one of her ladies of the royal bedchamber. Being an elegant lady of impeccable upbringing, Catherine could hardly cause a social scandal by openly refusing, so she did the next best thing. Her face went red, then purple. Tears flowed down her cheeks, blood gushed from her mouth, and she fainted flat out on the floor. From this Charles gathered that Barbara had got the job.

Catherine finally decided to close her eyes to the king's affair with Barbara, and she also put up with his long line of one-night stands. So diplomatic was she that, before entering her own (private) dressing room, she knocked on the door—just in case Charles was rehearsing some of his sexual acts with one of her maids of honor, which he often was.

As King Charles came to know Catherine better, he found he respected her. She was well educated, had highbrow tastes, a pleasant speaking voice, and was totally loyal to him in every way. As a result he started treating her quite kindly and sometimes with genuine affection when she was ill or under attack for being a Catholic. The only pressure she put on Charles was to better conditions for Catholics and their religion. Her chapel became a popular meeting place for English Catholics, so much so that in 1667, an order of Council forbade their "flocking there."

In February 1673, as a result of widespread, highly organized anti-Catholic feeling, a Committee of the Lords was appointed to draw up a bill "That no Romish priest do attend Her Majesty but such as are subjects of the King of Portugal" (Catherine's father). The anti-Catholic campaign became so serious that King Charles was forced to assure Parliament of his "readiness to maintain the Protestant religion." Yet Catherine had her way in the end for, as Charles lay on his deathbed in 1685, she persuaded him to become a Catholic.

Catherine made another mark on history. When she first arrived in Britain and an English courtier offered her a tankard of ale to quench her thirst, she wrinkled her nose and said she would prefer a cup of tea. This raised eyebrows as tea drinking was rare in Britain at the time. The national beverage was beer. But a queen is a queen, and when Catherine subsequently served tea to guests at the palace, tea parties became fashionable throughout Britain and later (1773) even in such distant places as Boston.

That's enough about the sexploits of King Charles. Now we must give you details of his lesser-known achievements—as promised earlier. Sorry it took so long, but you will surely agree that Charles really *was* a sexually active fellow.

One historian has described Charles as "an extremely shrewd politician as well as a ready liar." We guess this means he was a shrewd politician *because* he was a ready liar. Some historians have branded him as lazy, but this was often a pose he affected to hide his high intelligence, as he was totally without pretension. Lazy he was not. Most days he was awake at 5 A.M., and worked on letters and papers relating to affairs of state for three hours before being seen by others at court. He spoke fluent French and had a good command of Italian and Spanish. He had an excellent memory, brilliant intuition, and was a superb judge of men. He prevented or softened hostility with his casual humor, which is still one of the most powerful weapons used by present-day royals.

Charles did not gamble, smoke, or drink to excess. He also dined wisely, though he ate rather too much jelly, which he said "refreshed his mouth after sex." He also had a weakness for ice cream, and it is a little-known fact that he was responsible for it becoming popular in England and, later, in America. Charles first tasted ice cream in Paris and, liking it so much, asked his cooks in London to make it for him. He is also credited with knighting a loin of beef at a banquet because the meat was so tasty. Hence Sirloin?

Charles made racing the "sport of kings" by often attending Newmarket racecourse where he quaffed champagne with the jockeys, who were always keen to ask him about some of the recent winners he had ridden. There is no double meaning there. King Charles was a good jockey who actually entered races and won several of them.

Charles liked animals and kept a monkey and a parrot as pets, although he is best known for his famous King Charles spaniels, which slept and pupped in his bed, causing what his servants (and ladies) described as "an awful stink."

He was a brave man in battle and resourceful. After losing the battle of Worcester in 1651, to avoid being captured by his enemies during Oliver Cromwell's Commonwealth (1649 to 1660), he disguised himself as a woodsman named Will Jones. For forty-four days and nights, with a reward of £1,000 on his head, he lived in woods and barns, eating mainly biscuits and cheese. In October of that year he managed to escape by sea to France where he remained in exile until Cromwell died.

Alexander Goldsmith, who worked as a secret agent for British Intelligence in 1715, described King Charles as not having a grain of ill nature in him. Goldsmith's real name was Daniel Defoe, the author of *Robinson Crusoe*, that castaway who had a bosom friend named Man Friday. (In real life, Daniel was gay. The idea of being marooned on a desert island with a Girl Friday made him puke.)

Although Defoe said King Charles was a most kindly man, he could be tough when necessary. After returning to England as king in 1660, Charles allowed a macabre revenge to be taken against Cromwell, who was responsible for having his father, Charles the First, beheaded in 1649. Cromwell's embalmed but stinking body was pulled out of its hallowed tomb in Westminster Abbey and publicly hung on Tyburn Gallows for several hours, after which the head was chopped off and the body buried in the common criminals' pit nearby. Cromwell's head was carried to Westminster Hall where it was placed on a spike and mounted above a doorway. It was left there for many months until it rotted and fell to pieces.

This treatment of the cadaver, though diabolical, was a brilliant public relations exercise as it signaled that Cromwell's dour "Puritan revolution" was well and truly dead. The message was clearly received; the fashionable ladies of King Charles's time exposed their breasts, while their menfolk wore foppish and exaggerated clothing.

Another astonishing manifestation of this relaxation of morals was the way richer ladies attended London theaters not just to watch the action on stage but to find young stallions who would give them sexual satisfaction while their husbands worked late at the office. If the lady was famous, she wore an elegant mask to hide her identity, which excited the stallions even more as the mask made it abundantly clear what she wanted and saved a lot of silly small talk.

Thus England entered into a fabulously exuberant and flamboyant era during which investment soared and trade prospered, largely due to the fact that the English men of commerce gained inspiration and courage from a relaxed and down-to-earth king—who also amused and delighted them with his many sexual exploits. They also liked Charles because he was good-natured, easy to approach, and kind to those suffering serious personal problems.

Having said all those charming and truthful things, it must be admitted that King Charles was a cynic who believed every man and woman could be bought—the only difference being, he once quipped, that some women haggled "more or better" about the price. Yet, whether they were paid or not, the ladies usually got a fair bargain in bed from Charles. He was a good lover, which was most unusual. Kings do not "make love." They are made love to. Nobody with the slightest knowledge of royalty can expect a king to do press-ups while a lower-born mistress lies idle. That really would be ridiculous. No, royal mistresses have always understood that they are there to be of service, not to be serviced. They do the work and the king just lies on his back having his grapes peeled for him.

There is written evidence that King Charles was not selfish in bed: "He was a good lover who kissed his women all over their bodies to please them," wrote Samuel Pepys in his *Diary*. And for good measure, Pepys added that King Charles was "very well endowed." Interestingly, Charles sent special couriers to Egypt to obtain the powdered remains of Egyptian mummies because he was convinced that the dust of these, when rubbed on himself, gave him "enhanced greatness." You can read into that whatever you like.

A good footnote, if you will pardon the pun, is that Charles was the first monarch to use the twelve-inch rule as a measure of length. He was presented with a one-foot rule by his printer, Joseph Moxon, who, perhaps without ambiguity, ventured to declare that it was "the most perfect length." The king agreed enthusiastically, and his use of the twelve-inch rule (when dealing with his tailors, architects and mathematicians, of course) made it popular.

# 8

## *Royal Quacks*

*M*ost of us have suffered at the hands of doctors. But, just to make you feel better, so have many royals.

Sexy old KING CHARLES THE SECOND was as fit as a fiddler on the first day of February 1685 and enjoyed a couple of glasses of wine at a little musical party that night. But next morning, as his long hair was being combed by his royal barber, he suddenly fainted flat out. No less than twelve of England's top physicians were hastily called in, and they decided it was necessary to "purge all the poisons from his body."

They tried to do this by draining off sixteen ounces of blood from a vein in his arm. Then they shaved off all his hair and singed his bald skull and bare feet with red-hot irons.

They pushed sneezing powder up his nose until both nostrils were full. Then they used dried Spanish fly as a "blistering agent."

They stuck hot plasters all over his body and, after they cooled, ripped them off again.

When the king did not improve, they made him swallow

pearls dissolved in ammonia and powdered horse's skull. This was followed by the skin of frogs and some rook's feathers soaked in asses' milk—a *pièce de résistance* of a menu that the combined skills of Mrs. Beeton, Betty Crocker, and Barbara Kafka could never, in their wildest dreams, have cooked up.

The doctors then drew another eight ounces of blood from their victim and generously left him to sleep for a while. Then they slapped hot plasters all over his body and injected gaseous substances into his rectum. They also gave him emetics of white wine to make him vomit after they had forced him to swallow a gallstone from the bladder of a white goat washed down with spirits made from a human skull.

During this treatment Charles had several convulsions during which the doctors forced apart his teeth to prevent him biting his tongue. When he was able to speak, the poor fellow complained that his throat, gums, and tongue were very painful. Ah yes, the doctors explained, this was most probably caused by the steaming-hot medicines they had forced down his throat during the convulsions.

King Charles asked for a chamberpot and, as he used it, screamed out that his urine was scalding hot. Ah yes, the physicians explained, this was most likely caused by the dried Spanish fly. It does affect some people in that way. In spite of all this, Charles managed to keep his sense of humor. To the seventy-odd people who were in his bedchamber watching the drama, he said he was "very sorry" to trouble them by "taking so long a-dying" and hoped they would excuse him. On the other hand, perhaps King Charles was being sarcastic? We shall never know.

We do know that Charles had the constitution of an ox because at 6 o'clock on Friday morning, February 6, 1685, he was speaking coherently. Not satisfied with this unexpected turn of events, the doctors gathered around his bed and decided to bleed him of another twelve ounces of blood. It had worked before, so why not again?

That did it. At 10 A.M. the king lapsed into a coma and died just before noon. During the five days of "treatment," some fifty-eight drugs had been administered to His Royal Highness. The cause of death was said to have been apoplexy, which sounds right. But, being what they are—good at insuring themselves against being sued—the doctors added the cautious rider that the king might have been suffering from kidney disease, which might have been caused by mercurial poisoning, which might have been because the king had been conducting some private experiments into the production of mercury a few weeks before his death. There you are. It was *his* fault.

Nobody bothered to ask for a second (or thirteenth) opinion because when a royal dies the relatives are usually too busy fighting over the spoils and sucking up to the successor. One man did speak out later though. Lord Thomas Babington Macauley, in his renowned five volumed *History of England* (London 1856), described the treatment King Charles received at the hands of those top twelve doctors as "similar to being tortured like an Indian at the stake."

Another king of England who suffered was the king of Spain, PHILIP THE SECOND. No, that's not a mistake. King Philip the Second of Spain, that horrible man who sent the terrible Armada against England in 1588, was also the king of England for several years. British school history books don't bother to mention this very minor fact, probably because they find it too embarrassing to explain that King Philip of Spain became the king of England when he married the English queen "BLOODY MARY" in 1554. And when Mary died in 1558, Queen Elizabeth the First took the crown. She didn't hit it off with King Philip of Spain so, eventually, in an attempt to dethrone her, he sent that massive Armada, which was pulverized by the unbeatable British (and Irish) weather.

Whatever they say about him—and it's usually nasty—King Philip was not such a bad sort. Opera and drama tell us that his deformed and schizophrenic son, Don Carlos, was a liberal who was murdered, yet neither is strictly true. History tells us that Philip was a bad dad. But he was a tender husband and very affectionate to his daughters. He wasn't so cute when it came to politics, but he was a hard-working monarch who refused to delegate and wore himself out doing all the work himself.

He was certainly negligent when it came to looking after his health. During his fourteen-month stay in damp and drafty England, he had caught cold after cold and was never the same man again. His eyesight became bad, he suffered from gout, he developed agonizing arthritis and, worst of all, a serious blood infection.

On July 22, 1598, he became feverish and a large tumor appeared on his right thigh. When the royal surgeons lanced it, something went wrong and boils appeared on both sides of the wound. When the boils spread all over his body, the king screamed with pain every time he was touched so, rather than risk being shouted at, the doctors decided, most unwisely, not to change his bandages. Then the king lost control of his bowels and, because he could not bear to be touched, would not allow anyone to place a bedpan under him. Although attempts were made to remove some of the excreta from the bed, the poor monarch ended up lying in much of it.

The stench became so atrocious that courtiers had to hold hankies to their faces as they gasped out their daily reports to the king, as did the maids who spooned food into his mouth. The physicians, still refusing to allow the servants to move the patient in any way, told the chambermaids not to change the bed sheets either.

Inevitably, one or two flies managed to settle on the king's body, and maggots soon appeared in the gaping and yellow-green sores. When the doctors tried to scrape the maggots out, the king bellowed with pain and said leave them alone. The doctors timidly did as they were told. They had little choice as, in spite of all his pain, the king remained completely rational and was in constant touch with his ministers, who kept popping into the royal bedchamber to receive instructions concerning affairs of state.

When the king's body started to rot away and he was too weak to argue, the doctors became quite daring and tried to cure his sores by placing dozens of live leeches on them. Equally tenaciously, King Philip held on to life, but nothing could stop the ravaging of his body. Eyewitnesses described the rotting process as so horrific that "all that could be seen of His Majesty were his eyes and his tongue." Finally, after fifty-three days of lying physically and mentally tortured on that dunghill of a bed, seventy-one-year-old King Philip died in the early hours of September 13, 1598.

Another king who had a problem with doctors was England's mad KING GEORGE THE THIRD. Quite apart from the horrific treatment he received from them himself, as we have seen in the "Mad Royals" chapter, he had a low opinion of doctors. This dated back to the time when his sister Caroline Matilda married KING CHRISTIAN THE SEVENTH of Denmark.

Christian was born gay, but in an effort to explain this away, the Danish royals put out the story that he had turned gay only after some naughty page boys at court had secretly abused him sexually when he was a child. They also had to hide the fact that Christian had been born mentally defective, so they said his poor little mind had been seriously unbalanced by the brutality of his viciously strict tutor and governor.

King George's fifteen-year-old sister, Caroline, married Christian when he was seventeen and had just been crowned king. Caroline quickly became pregnant and presented him with a son. Their life was going quite nicely, and it looked as if Caroline was weaning Christian away from his homosexual inclinations. But then a rogue doctor came into their lives.

This was Johan Friedrich Struensee who, having hypocritically sworn the Hippocratic oath to be a good doctor, was villain enough to spot King Christian's sexual and mental problems and take advantage of both. Struensee, age forty, accompanied King Christian on a lengthy European tour, and during that time gained complete mental and sexual control over him.

On returning from the tour the king became "completely gay" and, appointing Struensee as the royal physician, gave him the title of count. He later appointed him as a privy cabinet minister. Armed with all this power, Struensee decided he wanted more. So he turned his attentions to the king's wife, Caroline who—now sexually neglected by her husband— jumped into bed with the good doctor.

With the help of his pretty little mistress queen, Dr. Struensee monopolized all power in Denmark until 1772. But although King Christian was mentally unbalanced, he was not quite as mad as he was painted. He smelled something rotten in the state of Denmark and had Queen Caroline quizzed on the subject. After she admitted that Dr. Struensee had "tempted" her into having sex, Struensee was tortured—with his own scalpel, it is said—until he confessed to having committed "treason" with the queen. A rather sweet way of describing (to the public) his adultery with her. When Struensee said the young queen's beauty had caused him to "lose his head," King Christian punished him poetically by having it chopped off and Queen Caroline was banished from Denmark forever, which did not overplease her brother, King George the Third.

Mad King George experienced another traumatic medical problem after his twenty-year-old granddaughter, Princess Charlotte, agreed to marry the German prince Leopold of Saxe-Coburg in 1816. Oh, they were such a lovely couple. He was small, dark, and handsome, and she was a loving, kindly, shy, nice-natured, caring, and well-dressed pretty blonde Princess of Wales. Although it was a marriage of royal convenience, the public lapped up all the usual "fairy-tale romance" and wedding handouts.

Then, in November of 1817, the renowned royal doctor Sir Richard Croft was called in to deliver their first baby, a beautifully formed boy who was alive and well until the delivery. That's when something went wrong. The child emerged dead and the mother died of a postpartum hemorrhage. This was when the great cover-up started.

The public was told that Princess Charlotte had "unwisely" taken no exercise during her pregnancy. A total lie. It was also said that the princess had starved herself for some fifty hours prior to the birth. Another outrageous lie. The diabolical truth was that Dr. Sir Richard Croft had used his hands instead of forceps while experimenting with a "mistaken new system" of delivery.

The other royal doctors knew this and so did everyone at Buckingham Palace. But the royal family could not be seen to have chosen a doctor who was incompetent, so the public was told a mass of lies and Dr. Croft quietly committed suicide three months later. His ghastly mistake changed the whole course of British royal history. As the only child of George the Fourth, Princess Charlotte was expected to take the throne, and if that had happened, Queen Victoria would never have enjoyed her famous sixty-four-year reign.

VICTORIA also had a terrible problem with a pregnancy. This awful saga began in early 1839 when she had been on the throne for only two years and was just a little inexperienced in the ways of the world. She noticed that a certain lady-in-waiting named Lady Flora Hastings appeared to be not just waiting but decidedly expectant because her stomach was bulging most suspiciously.

Getting into a heavy gossip session with her ladies of the royal bedchamber, the queen worked out that Lady Flora must have had a scene with Sir John Conroy, because the two of them had traveled together overnight in a horse-drawn carriage from Scotland to London. Victoria knew for sure that Sir John was a dirty old man because she had heard he had been rather "familiar" with various women—one of them her own mother.

When Victoria called in her royal doctor Sir James Clark and asked him what he thought about Lady Flora's protruding belly, he replied: "It looks pretty bad morally, but let's wait and see." Dr. Clark had said exactly the same to Lord Melbourne, the British prime minister, so the queen was now convinced that Lady Flora was "with child" and wrote those words in her personal diary on February 2, 1839.

Her Majesty decided that somebody must make it clear to Lady Flora that the whole court knew about her pregnancy. But how could this be done tactfully? The ticklish problem was solved with what Victoria thought was great delicacy. On February 16, she told Dr. Clark to go to Lady Flora and whisper into her ear, "Are you privately married?"

Flora was outraged and vehemently denied being pregnant. She denied having it off with Sir John Conroy in a horse-drawn carriage, or anywhere else. In fact, she denied having it off at all. Not anywhere. And not with any man. And she could not be pregnant because, to be quite frank, she was still a virgin. The only explanation for the swelling of her belly, she said, must be wind, or bile, or something, because she often felt rather sick first thing in the morning.

On hearing of this telltale symptom, Dr. Clark brusquely asked Lady Flora to let him see for himself whether she was a virgin or not. She reacted by telling him to go jump in the lake across the road in St. James's Park. This convinced Dr. Clark that Lady Flora was "with child," and he rushed back to tell Queen Victoria that she had been right.

Victoria immediately had Lady Flora banned from appearing at court until such time as she agreed to submit herself to a medical examination. Faced with this terrible social punishment, Lady Flora was forced to prove her innocence by allowing Dr. Clark and another royal doctor to examine her. This was done on February 17, and the two doctors ascertained that she was, indeed, a virgin. Lady Flora then insisted that they sign a medical certificate stating this, so that she could prove quite conclusively that Queen Victoria was a dirty-minded, gossiping liar.

Furious at the suggestion that she was economical with the truth, Victoria rushed to get a second opinion from her beloved prime minister, Lord Melbourne. He called in Dr. Clark and asked him what on earth was going on. Why had he led everyone to believe that Lady Flora was pregnant? At this point, Dr. Clark gave the astonishing answer that he still thought the lady in question could be with child. Why then, asked Lord Melbourne, had he and the other doctor signed a medical certificate stating that Lady Flora was still a virgin?

Dr. Clark gave a fascinating answer. He said he had known

several cases of virgins being pregnant. Although Lady Flora was definitely a virgin, it was still quite possible for her to be pregnant because "there was an enlargement on the womb like a child."

Lord Melbourne then had the most difficult task of explaining this to the inexperienced Queen Victoria. To make it easier, he started off by telling her that "even certified virgins can still be pregnant." When nineteen-year-old Victoria looked totally puzzled, Lord Melbourne repeated in lay terms what Dr. Clark had told him. This is our reconstruction of that conversation:

"Well, you see, your Majesty, some unfortunate men are . . . hum ha . . . well . . . hum ha . . . that is to say . . . not very well, hum ha . . . endowed, if you see what I mean, ma'am. And in any case, actual, hum ha . . . penetration . . . is not always necessary. The er, hum ha . . . male seed hasn't got a brain but, ho hum . . . it knows which way to go, ma'am, and that means, hum, ha . . . now how can I put this? . . . It means that the er . . . hum ha . . . ho hum . . . male member can do its job—without causing any physical damage."

When she finally worked out what the hell Melbourne was talking about, Queen Victoria continued to believe Lady Flora was pregnant and said so privately—all around Buckingham Palace. This infuriated Sir John Conroy, the alleged father of the alleged child in the womb of the nondeflowered Flora, so he retaliated by leaking a few details to Fleet Street. The newspapers had fun printing discreet speculation on the subject but could not go the whole hog, having promised Sir John they would not divulge that he was their secret informant.

Queen Victoria then enlisted the aid of her faithful but half-deaf duke of Wellington who, along with Lord Melbourne, rushed up and down Fleet Street to get the whole matter hushed up. When this was successful, Lady Flora's indignant relatives leaked full details to the newspapers, which really went to town and splashed the scandal. It was all so sensational that confidence in Lord Melbourne's Whig Government was eroded, and it was forced to resign after suffering humiliating defeats in the House of Commons while voting on other matters. Threats were also made to sack most of Victoria's ladies of the bedchamber who, it was said, were "terribly wicked" to have led the poor innocent young queen into believing such a disgraceful rumor.

The general public instinctively knew who was really to blame, though, and showed their displeasure by booing and hissing Queen Victoria whenever she dared to venture out of the palace. One man was rude enough to shout: "A turd on your royal doctors." He turned out to be very wise indeed for, when Lady Flora died in Buckingham Palace on July 5, 1839, a postmortem showed that the poor woman had a huge tumor on her liver. And she was still a virgin.

The press made a big splash about Lady Flora's funeral, and when Queen Victoria tried to recover lost ground by sending one of her royal coaches to accompany the funeral cortege, angry members of the public threw a hail of stones at it. Queen Victoria's doctor Sir James Clark also came out of all this very badly. Other doctors publicly described him as "nothing but a royal quack who had jumped to the conclusion that because Lady Flora's waist was enlarged, her morals must have relaxed."

Arrogance knows no bounds however. Dr. Clark gave the impression that he was not at all perturbed by the fuss when he was interviewed by a rather pushy reporter. "Come now, old chap," he said haughtily. "Anyone can make a mistake or two."

Two mistakes were made by JULIANA, who became the queen of the Netherlands in 1948 at the age of thirty-nine. She was a much-loved monarch whose assessment of people was usually impeccable, but she succumbed to the services of a "psychiatrist" named Greet Hoffman who exerted a strong influence over her in the 1960s—until the shock discovery that Hoffman was a fraud who had no medical qualifications whatsoever!

The public memory is short, though, and what the press described as the "public disquiet" soon quietened down. A few years later the queen heard about a wonderful new psychiatrist: Baron David James Rothschild, who was introduced to Her Majesty by her royal dressmaker. Falling prey to the baron's charm, the queen appointed him as her royal psychiatrist with the result that he became a regular visitor at the Soestdijk Palace in The Hague. Nobody bothered to check the baron's credentials because, after all, he had been chosen by the queen and she wouldn't make the same mistake again, would she now?

Then, in 1978, the thirty-five-year-old baron obtained permission from the sixty-nine-year-old Queen Juliana to hold a World Wildlife party to which he intended to invite the English queen's husband, Prince Philip. However, as the party was to have been held in the grounds of the royal palace, it was necessary for the baron to obtain a permit from the local police. Just a formality, the queen told Baron Rothschild.

Policemen being what they are—people who think everyone else is crooked—they made a routine check and discovered there was no such person as Baron Rothschild. There was, however, a common Dutch laborer named Henry de Vries, who shared a little apartment in town with a woman who made dresses. Yes, you've guessed it. It was that royal dressmaker who had introduced the "baron" to Queen Juliana.

At this stage, please bear with us as we depart from this factual story, just for a moment, so that we can fantasize an imaginary telephone conversation between the Dutch chief of police and someone at very top level at the palace:

"What on earth do we do now, sir? We can't very well arrest this nonmedical rogue, can we, sir? Why not, sir? Well, sir, it's clear that Her Majesty has blundered again, sir. Even worse, sir, this common laborer laid her. . . . No, sir, *Not* a bricklayer. I didn't say that. . . . He's just an ordinary laborer, sir. Now then, where was I? Ah yes, sir, this laborer had Her Majesty on his psychiatrist's couch and . . . Good gracious, sir. No, Sir, definitely not, sir . . . he just talked to her, sir. Well, sir, that's not quite accurate either, he usually just listened, sir. To all her problems and intimate confessions, sir. Can you imagine the ball the tit-and-trivia tabloids will have with that lot, sir, if we bring him to court? No, sir, I meant the criminal court, not your court. . . ."

That conversation never took place, of course. It's a total invention on our part. Not at all factual, so you must not believe one single word of it. The rest of the story *is* fact, though. Baron David James Rothschild, the great psychiatrist, alias the common laborer Henry de Vries, somehow managed to evade the combined resources of the superefficient Dutch police force and never appeared in court to be charged with any offense.

Wearing a brilliant disguise (probably a shovel over his shoulder), he managed to slip through immigration and customs controls and "fled" across the border into France. At the same time, to get away from it all, Queen Juliana and her airplane-loving husband, Prince Bernhard, took themselves off on a long sea cruise after which, in April 1980, Queen Juliana abdicated.

## *Note*

Not all royal doctors have been total idiots, of course. Napoleon's personal surgeon could amputate a leg in fourteen seconds. This made him very popular with the troops as speed was essential in those days when the only anesthetic was a pint of rum—or a large rubber hammer.

# 9

---

## *The Murder of King George the Fifth*

"The death beds of Kings are as inevitably
organised as their lives must be."
—JAMES POPE-HENNESSY, royal
biographer, 1959

*J*ust after 9 o'clock on the evening of Monday, January 20,
1936, Lord Dawson of Penn, the royal surgeon to KING
GEORGE THE FIFTH, picked up a menu card in the household
dining room at Sandringham and scribbled these words on it:
"The King's life is moving peacefully towards its close."

This conjures up visions of the seventy-year-old monarch
slowly fading away peacefully and naturally. But, as he wrote
that rather poetic bulletin for impatiently waiting representatives of the media, Lord Dawson was planning to kill King
George.

It was not a decision he had taken alone. He had discussed
the matter with QUEEN MARY, and she had given her royal
consent. The killing was set to take place well before midnight,
so that the king's death notice would appear in the next morning's newspapers, particularly *The Times*, rather than the more
down-market evening papers.

This might sound preposterous, but Lord Dawson's personal medical notes on the subject are quite specific. He wrote: "The determination of the time of death of the King's body had another object in view, viz: The importance of the death receiving its first announcement in the morning papers, rather than the less appropriate field of the evening journals."

Dawson's notes continued: "The papers knew that the end might come before their going to press and I told my wife on the telephone to advise *The Times* to hold back publication."

A meticulous man, Lord Dawson nearly missed his deadline. He had intended that King George should die just after 11 P.M. But fate played two tricks that slowed down his carefully laid plan and the king did not die at the correct time, which caused last-minute panic in the offices of London newspapers.

First, mainly for reasons of punctuality, King George had always kept the hundreds of antique clocks in the 274-room Sandringham mansion thirty minutes fast. As Lord Dawson was busily attending to the king, he called to someone and asked the time. That person looked at a clock and deducted the thirty minutes of "Sandringham time." Presuming he had been given "Sandringham time," however, Lord Dawson also deducted thirty minutes!

Just before 11 o'clock (real time), Dawson was shocked to discover the mix-up and told King George's son and heir, the Prince of Wales (later the Duke of Windsor). He was furious. Apart from being highly tense, he had always hated the fact that Sandringham time was different from the rest of the world, so he rushed to the phone shouting "I'll fix those bloody clocks" and called Daniel Burlingham, the man in overall charge of them.

On being ordered to Sandringham to turn all the clocks back to the correct time, Mr. Burlingham called a taxi, drove around to collect his assistant, and sped to the royal country retreat—arriving just before midnight. The time of Burlingham's arrival is important because it shows conclusively that he had been telephoned long before King George died.

In later years, when the Duke of Windsor was in exile, many

writers and historians pilloried him by wrongly stating that the first thing he had done after his father had died was to call the clockman and, showing callous contempt for his (still-warm) father, had ordered all the clocks to be changed.

The Duke of Windsor could hardly defend himself against these lies by explaining that he had lost his temper because Lord Dawson had put King George to death at the wrong time, so the legend of his "callousness" remained to haunt him for the rest of his life.

When Lord Dawson realized there had been a time mix-up, he quickly ordered the king's personal nurse, Catherine Black, to administer the life-killing injections. This was when fate played its second little trick. Nurse Black caused another delay by refusing to obey the command. We are not told why. One theory is that she was a religious woman who felt killing was sinful. On the other hand, she might have been worldly enough to realize that if the secret ever leaked out, she could easily be used as the scapegoat who would take the blame.

So Lord Dawson had to administer the injections himself. His medical notes state: "I therefore decided to determine the end and injected myself, gr ¾ morphia and shortly afterwards, cocaine gr 1, into the distended jugular vein."

This was at about 11 P.M. Lord Dawson's notes state that in about one hour, the king's breathing became quieter, his appearance was more placid, and the "physical struggle gone."

At this point, the king's wife, Queen Mary, and the rest of the royal family were called into the room so that they could watch the last moments. Lord Dawson's notes say that the king's life "passed so quietly and gently that it was difficult to determine the exact moment" so we do not know exactly what time it was when the king died, although the world was told it was at five minutes to midnight precisely.

In later years, when talking to his close friends who knew the top drawer secret, the Duke of Windsor tried to distance himself from any involvement in the killing of his father. He told his close friend Kenneth de Courcy (the duke of Grant-mesnil) that the decision was made by his mother, Queen

Mary. He said she had clearly known all about the matter, and he strongly suspected that it was her idea to have King George put down before midnight so that his death notice would appear in the more up-market morning newspapers. Pressing this further, the duke told de Courcy that he had been "truly horrified" when he discovered that Lord Dawson had killed his father.

There is something fishy in the Duke of Windsor's claim of innocence. In his book *A King's Story* (Cassell, 1951), when dealing with the scene at his father's deathbed, he stated: "All was still as we—his wife and his children—stood together by my father's bedside waiting for life to be extinguished." That was a decidely crude word for the duke to use in describing his father's demise.

The dictionary defines "extinguish" as "to put out or quench (light or life)" and when used about a person, means "to destroy, wipe out, or annihilate." One explanation for the Duke of Windsor's use of the word is that he chose it maliciously, to taunt his much-hated relatives in the British royal family with the possibility that he could use his father's murder as a way of embarrassing them.

An equally odd statement was made in the official bulletins issued by Buckingham Palace after King George died. They said he had died of "bronchial catarrh complicated by cardiac weakness." We cannot tell you whether this lie was also falsely entered on the king's death certificate (which has to be completed, by law) because the original of that vitally important and historical document has mysteriously disappeared. At one time it was safely lodged in the highly efficient royal archives at Windsor Castle but, incredibly, they now say it has been "lost."

The killing of King George was kept a closely guarded secret for fifty years. But when Lord Dawson died in 1945, he left behind all the medical notes he had made during his illustrious career as a royal surgeon. They came into the possession of Francis Watson, who published an admirable biography of Dawson in 1950.

Mr. Watson did not mention the killing injection of cocaine in this book because he did not wish to embarrass Lord Dawson's still-living relatives. He did disclose it thirty-six years later, however. Not in a sensational tabloid, which would have paid a fortune for such a shocking exclusive, but in a learned article for the respected and serious magazine *History Today*. This was quickly picked up by leading British newspapers, and, for once, the publicity experts at Buckingham Palace were unable to squelch the story for three main reasons.

They could not deny it because Mr. Watson still had Lord Dawson's medical notes. They could not refute those notes as "forgeries" because they were logged in Lord Dawson's official notebooks, which, as a complete parcel, would have been impossible to forge. And they could not label Lord Dawson as a Walter Mitty–type "mental case" who had suffered "delusions" because his handwritten notes were backed up by notes made by Lord Wigram—another royal doctor who had attended King George.

Faced with these insurmountable facts, Buckingham Palace tried to solve the problem by issuing a bland statement that these "events" had happened a long time ago, the "main participants" were dead—and revealing this matter could hardly give comfort to anyone. This was a sharp little stab at Francis Watson who had dared to expose the secret.

Taking this as their cue, some writers criticized him. One claimed Mr. Watson had "dug up" the scandal in order to sell his biography of Lord Dawson. As an attempted smear, this really was pathetic, and Mr. Watson struck back with devastating logic by pointing out that his biography of Dawson had been published thirty-six years earlier—and had long been out of print. As any author will confirm, there's no money to be made out of that.

Newspapers well disposed toward the royal family (whether for political or sales reasons) tried to take the heat out of the scandal in various other unsubtle ways. The most popular was that King George had not really been killed. Killing was far too strong a word for it. He had just been "put out of his agony." That's all. This was not true. King George had been given an earlier injection of morphia and was completely comatose about ninety minutes later when he was given the lethal injections of morphine and cocaine.

Other newspapers, also balking at the word killed, stated that the king's "demise" was simply a "humanitarian act" that could be better described as a case of euthanasia. This caused more controversy. Doctors and churchmen united to say that although the literal meaning of euthanasia is "die well," it was still an act of killing and, as such, could not be condoned.

Dame Saunders, a doctor who founded the hospice movement for the care of terminally ill patients, said the killing of King George was "Very macabre, undignified and unworthy of the medical profession."

The respected and normally pro-royal journalist Kenneth Rose, who wrote the biography *King George V* (Weidenfeld, 1983), described his death as "murder."

The Royal College of Physicians, of which Lord Dawson had been the president, condemned it as "evil."

In a shrewdly balanced editorial published on November 28, 1986, the conservative British *Daily Telegraph* asked whether Lord Dawson had been "wise" to bequeath his "most private notes" to posterity.

The strange suggestion seemed to be that Lord Dawson should have been sensible enough to destroy his medical notes before he died so that they did not fall into the hands of the press—a rather contradictory stand for an editor to take in view of the fact that the first priority of a newspaper is usually to campaign for and seek out the truth.

Another interesting snippet about King George is that when he died, the public was told that his last words had been the wonderfully patriotic question: "How stands the Empire?" Rather nearer the truth is that Lord Dawson, as he gave the first injection of morphia at about 9:30 P.M., tried to soothe his victim by dishonestly saying: "Cheer up, your Majesty, you will soon be at Bognor again."

Bognor Regis is a seaside resort in West Sussex where the king had spent a long and boring period of recuperation after an illness in 1929. As the hypodermic needle entered his skin, His Royal Highness King George the Fifth acidly retorted: "Bugger Bognor."

# 10

## *Was Queen Mary Also Killed?*

*S*cores of my friends*—and at least a dozen senior journalists in Britain and South Africa—are witnesses to the fact that, during the sixties and seventies, I always wanted to write a news story claiming that Queen Mary had been "put to sleep" by her doctors. I never wrote it because various editors refused to believe that such a thing could happen to a member of the British royal family.

Those editors must have had second thoughts in 1986 when it was disclosed that Queen Mary's husband, King George the Fifth, had been killed by his royal surgeons.

While working as a journalist, I collected little-known facts and unusual snippets about royalty. Although I did this as an amusing hobby, I always hoped to write a book on the subject

*This chapter is written in the first person by Gordon Winter, who discloses how, on March 22, 1953, a senior royal servant accurately predicted that Queen Mary would die between 10 and 11 P.M. two days later.

one day. That day came when the news broke about King George the Fifth being put down.

My wife, Wendy, put it in a nutshell by saying: "I always believed your story about Queen Mary being put to sleep, but I wondered whether anyone else would accept it. That problem has been solved now though. If they could put King George down, it's obvious they could have done the same to his wife. I think it's time you wrote that story."

Here it is:

On the afternoon of Sunday March 22, 1953, a friend took me to Lord Ednam's beautiful house in Regent's Park, which the Duke of Windsor was using as his temporary London base. There I was introduced to a senior manservant who was then working for the duke. I shall refer to this man as "Douglas."

As we sat drinking tea in the kitchen, Douglas explained that while in America, the Duke of Windsor had received news from London that his eighty-five-year-old mother, Queen Mary, was seriously ill and death was being talked of. Yet, instead of flying to Britain in haste, the duke arranged for a berth on the liner *Queen Elizabeth*, which sailed from America on March 6. The liner docked at Southampton and the duke drove up to London on March 10.

Douglas was a likable and animated man who told us many interesting things about the Duke and Duchess of Windsor. The most surprising disclosure came when he stated, quite specifically, that Queen Mary would die two days later on the Tuesday. He not only knew on which day she would die, but also the exact hour. Between 10 and 11 P.M.

He said he had been told this personally by the duke. Douglas also said that the duke had instructed his chauffeur to make himself available for the whole of that particular Tuesday evening. The duke had made it clear he would need to be driven to Marlborough House at some stage that night. When Douglas told us this, he gave us the strong impression that the chauffeur (Lord Ednam's, I think) had not been at all pleased on hearing that he would have to remain on duty all night.

On the subject of Queen Mary's ill health, Douglas told us

that the royal doctors had been faced with a tremendous problem. Queen Mary was suffering from a serious illness. She could not be operated on as her heart would probably not take the strain. She was being given strong drugs without which she would experience great pain.

During previous weeks, said Douglas, the royal doctors had had no option but to slowly increase the strength (or amount) of the pain-killing drugs. During the next few days, they would reach the point where the strength of these drugs might affect her heart and kill her. However, if she was taken off the drugs, the pain might kill her. The doctors were convinced that Queen Mary did not have long to live either way, but if they took her off the drugs, quite apart from suffering great pain, she could linger on for several weeks.

This presented another big problem. The coronation of Queen Elizabeth had been planned for June 2, and if Queen Mary lingered on, her death would force a postponement of the event because, as Douglas explained, the royal family would have to enter into a "decent period of mourning."

This really was a problem. At the start of the century nobody would have considered less than twelve months sufficient mourning for a monarch. But when King George the Fifth died in 1936, his son reduced the period to six months; Queen Elizabeth, on the death of her father, George the Sixth, further cut the mourning time to four months. So what would be the "decent period" of mourning for Queen Mary, considering that coronation day was already only ten weeks away?

The answer, said Douglas, was that she had to die on Tuesday so that a decent "one- or two-month period" of mourning could be observed and the coronation would then go ahead as planned.

The Duke of Windsor had explained to Douglas that any postponement would cause chaos. Hundreds of foreign guests, including other royals and heads of state, had long fit June 2 into their carefully arranged private schedules. Apart from that, vast sums of money were involved. Hotels and boardinghouses were booked almost solid. Holidays had been planned for workers and schools. Church services and street parties had been arranged. Millions of souvenir plates, mugs, and so on, were being manufactured, most of them bearing the date June 2, 1953. Miles of stands were being erected along the coronation route to Westminster Abbey.

The royal family remembered the tremendous confusion caused in July 1902 when the coronation of King Edward the Seventh had had to be postponed because he had been prostrated by acute appendicitis. This had resulted in immense and annoying inconvenience to foreign potentates and a huge loss of tourist dollars. It even led to a riot in Hemel Hempstead, where the villagers were annoyed at being deprived of their promised free coronation meal.

It is important to stress that Douglas was not being disloyal to the British royal family when he told us about the planned death of Queen Mary. On the contrary, he made the strong point that Queen Mary was "so dedicated to the crown" that when the problem of the drugs had been explained to her, she had "particularly asked to be put to sleep"—to avoid the possibility of the coronation being postponed. When he told us this, Douglas said it in an "Isn't she a wonderful old lady?" vein.

It is a well-documented fact that Queen Mary did not wish to endanger the coronation. Several prominent writers and historians have mentioned it, and some of them—who might have been privy to the great secret, but for social or other reasons did not wish to spell it out—nonetheless seem to have slotted certain clues in their writings.

One such is Robert Lacey, the perceptive author of the book *Majesty* (Hutchinson, 1977). He states that Queen Mary was: "Above all, most insistent that her own death, if it robbed her of the pleasure of seeing Lilibet crowned, should not spoil the occasion for the Queen herself or for the nation. She had served the throne in life and she would serve it in death by knowing her position in the order of things precisely, since mourning for an ex-Queen Consort should not impede the crowning of a full Sovereign."

Graham and Heather Fisher are a hard-working married couple who have written many carefully researched royal books. In their book *Monarch* (Robert Hale, 1985) they state: "And it is a fact that, Royal to the last, Queen Mary, as her life ebbed away, insisted that her death must not be permitted to postpone her grand-daughter's Coronation."

Mr. and Mrs. Fisher make it abundantly clear that the royal family knew Queen Mary would not live to see the coronation. Explaining that it was Queen Mary's "dearest wish" to see Elizabeth crowned, they disclose the delightful fact that Queen Elizabeth is said to have taken the royal crown to Marlborough House secretly at night and, "in the bedroom where Queen Mary lay dying, donned it for her benefit."

There is another good clue. From Michael Bloch's book, *The Secret File of the Duke of Windsor* (Bantam, 1988), we know that on February 28, 1953, royal physician Horace Evans wrote a letter to the Duke of Windsor (then in America) telling him that his mother was ill. In that letter Evans stated that Queen Mary was telling everyone she did not wish to go on living as an "old crock."

On the day after meeting the Duke of Windsor's servant, I telephoned the offices of one of London's biggest bookmaking firms and asked what the odds were against anyone knowing when Queen Mary would die. I was put through to a man who was full of beans. He said the odds would be about 20 to 1 against anyone knowing the exact day. When I told him I wanted to bet on the exact hour of her death, the man said the odds for that must be in the region of 2,000 to 1. At this point I said I would pop around to the man's office and place a bet for £5—which would bring me £10,000 if Queen Mary died between 10 and 11 P.M. on March 24.

The man asked me to hang on while he checked with someone higher up in his office. A few minutes later he returned to the telephone and said: "My boss says that even though he would love to take the bet, just for the fun of laying it off, we can't get involved because the bet would be in very bad taste and if the newspapers found out, they would crucify us."

So I never made that bet. Which was a great pity because the Duke of Windsor's manservant Douglas was right on the money. Queen Mary did die between 10 and 11 that Tuesday night. However, something must have gone wrong with the royals' carefully laid plans because Douglas told us later that the duke had not been at been at his mother's bedside when she died. He had arrived there just too late.

This is confirmed in Michael Bloch's book—which contains a letter the duke wrote to his wife, Wallis, on March 27, 1953 (three days after Queen Mary's death). In it he said he had dined with Commander Colin Buist and his wife, Gladys, on the night his mother died. He had telephoned Marlborough House at 10 P.M. and was told he should go there at around 11. But five minutes later he was called and told to hurry over. He did, but his mother had died at 10:15, just five minutes before he arrived.

Even more curious is the duke's statement that when he did get there, only his sister Mary, the princess royal, was present—and that no other member of the royal family showed up that night! This might suggest that the royal family was astonishingly callous. But a more likely possibility is that if the Duke of Windsor's manservant was correct, and the royal family knew exactly how and when Queen Mary was going to die, they would not want to attend as it would have played havoc with their sensitivities.

The next morning the whole royal family gathered at Marlborough House where they were led in prayers by the archbishop of Canterbury to mark the beginning of the official mourning period. The public was told that Queen Mary had "died in her sleep." But, in view of the accurate advance claim made by the Duke of Windsor's servant, it will be fascinating to see if anyone manages to trace and scrutinize the medical notes made by Queen Mary's royal doctors, Webb-Johnson and Evans. (Or will they have gone missing, just like King George the Fifth's death certificate?)

Webb-Johnson was born in 1880. Married to Cecilia Flora, he served in World War I and was mentioned in dispatches three times. He was the royal surgeon to Queen Mary from 1936 until her death. In 1948 he was created first baron of Stoke-on-Trent. He was president of the Royal Society of Medicine from 1952 to 1954 and an honorary member of the American Surgical Association. He toured principal hospitals and medical schools in America and Canada in the 1920s. An expert on cancer, his address was 70 Portland Place, London W1, and he died on May 28, 1958, leaving no heir.

Horace Evans, a Welshman from Merthyr Tydfil, was born in 1903. Married to Helen Davies in 1929, he had one daughter. He was royal physician to Queen Mary from 1946 until her death and to King George the Sixth from 1949 to 1952. On the king's death, he became royal physician to Queen Elizabeth. A past president of the Medical Society, he was an expert on kidney problems. He was created the first baron of Merthyr Tydfil in 1957. His address was 26 Weymouth Street, London W1, and he died on October 26, 1963.

The general public is not always told the whole truth about the lives and deaths of members of the British royal family. When Harold Nicolson was enlisted to write the official biography of King George the Fifth, the top Buckingham Palace aide, Sir Alan Lascelles, specifically warned him that if he discovered "anything discreditable" about King George while rooting through the thousands of documents in the royal archives, such information must "definitely not be written about." Nicolson agreed to this censorship and his book, *King George V, His Life and Reign* (Constable, 1952) was so flattering that it brought him money and fame.

Sir Alan Lascelles also ruled with an iron fist when the social darling James Pope-Hennessy wrote the 685-page officially approved biography *Queen Mary* published by Allen & Unwin in 1959. In that book Pope-Hennessy made a strong point of stating that he was indebted to Sir Alan Lascelles for his "constructive but unsparing criticism."

All authors and journalists who have had their copy slashed or mangled by subeditors will understand exactly what Pope-Hennessy meant by that. He was almost certainly tipping off other wordsmiths that, if they noticed something was missing in his book, it had been chopped out by Sir Alan.

There really was a glaring omission in Mr. Pope-Hennessy's

book: He gave twenty-six lines to the death of Queen Mary's sadly backward and violent thirteen-year-old son, Prince John, giving the place and time of death (5:30 A.M.). He devoted some forty-four lines to the death of Queen Mary's mother, giving the cause of death (heart failure, two hours after an operation), the precise time of death (3 A.M.), the weather outside (thick fog), how she looked after dying ("so beautiful, calm and peaceful with such a happy expression on her dear face"), and how her death affected her husband "Franz." (He became seriously mentally unbalanced and had to be kept in seclusion and looked after by a doctor and male nurses.)

Mr. Pope-Hennessy lavished more than fifty lines on the illness and death of Queen Mary's husband, giving the exact time of death and even the color of the house he died in. Yet, when dealing with the death of QUEEN MARY, the major character in his minutely detailed tome, he told us only this:

"During the evening of the 24th March 1953, Queen Mary died."

That's it. Not one word more. No cause of death. No mention of the time she died or who was standing by the deathbed. No details about the doctors or nurses and no famous last words. Just: "During the evening of the 24th March 1953, Queen Mary died."

We cannot ask James Pope-Hennessy what Sir Alan Lascelles censored from his book because he and Sir Alan are both dead. But it would be fascinating to see a copy of Pope-Hennessy's original manuscript because on page 559 of his book on Queen Mary he did, after all, manage to slip past the eyes of Sir Alan that now very meaningful comment:

"The death-beds of Kings are as inevitably organised as their lives must be."

# 11

---

## *Gone with the Windsors*

*I*n early May 1972, when the Duke of Windsor was dying at his Paris home, he was pleased to hear that his niece, Queen Elizabeth, was due to make a five-day state visit to France and that she would like to pop in and see him on May 18.

Before Her Majesty left England on May 15, however, the British ambassador in Paris called in the Duke's French physician, Jean Thin, and instructed him that it would be quite in order if the duke died before the queen's visit to France—or after she had returned to England—but on no account must the Duke be allowed to die during the five days the Queen was there.

Dr. Thin was told that Her Royal Highness was visiting France to "improve the atmosphere for Great Britain's membership of the European Economic Community," and it would be politically disastrous if the duke expired in the course of her visit.

For that revealing snippet we thank Michael Bloch, the authorized biographer of the Windsors and the official custodian of their personal papers and letters.

We do not know how Dr. Thin was supposed to obey the incredible command (short of putting the duke's body in the bath and covering it with ice if he died during those five vital days). As it happened, the queen's delicate business trip ran smoothly. She returned to England on May 20 and the duke died one week later of cancer of the throat, said to have been caused by his heavy smoking—the only luxury in his life of which his wife disapproved.

Born in 1894, the duke was baptized Edward Albert Christian George Andrew Patrick David, the last four shrewdly chosen names being those of the patron saints of England, Scotland, Ireland, and Wales, which must have made many in the last three areas feel just that little bit closer to the English-born man of mainly German background who was their latest royal highness.

The people of Wales definitely felt closer to this dashingly handsome man when, as King Edward the Eighth of England, he visited their coalfields during the Great Depression in November 1936. After spending two days listening to dozens of desperately unhappy men who had been out of work for years and seeing their children pathetically short of food and clothing, the king was moved near to tears and gave them this promise: "You may be sure that all I can do for you, I will."

He also uttered the more famous words, "Something must be done," which were reported by newspapers worldwide and, not surprisingly, gave the entire British working class the impression that here, at last, was a king who really cared and would "do something" for them.

At the time he made his comments, the wage for a Welsh laborer lucky enough to have a job was about £1 a week. This must have seemed incongruous to the king. Just twenty-two days earlier he had given his American mistress, Mrs. Wallis Simpson, a beautiful emerald and diamond engagement ring that had cost him £10,000.

Not only that. During the previous eleven months he had given Baltimore-born Mrs. Simpson an avalanche of other jewels worth £100,000 as well as £10,000 worth of fur coats to keep her warm in the British cold when his arms were not wrapped around her.

Equally thought-provoking is the fact that two months before his tour of Wales, the king had enjoyed a long holiday sailing around the sunny Mediterranean on a luxury steam yacht, escorted by two British destroyers. He had whacked three thousand brand-new golf balls from the deck of the yacht. This was not only to perfect his swing, but also because he said he "loved the splash" when they plopped into the ocean. The cost of those balls would have fed about nine hundred of the Welsh workers (and their families) for at least one week.

When King Edward insisted on marrying the twice-divorced Mrs. Simpson, it was the British Establishment's turn to decide that something must be done. It was. After being on the throne for less than eleven months, he was forced to abdicate and in December 1936 he went into exile (with eleven servants plus a Scotland Yard inspector as a bodyguard) and became the Duke of Windsor.

From then on the duke pleaded poverty. He haggled with tradesmen, never tipped his golf caddie, very rarely tipped waiters, and sponged free meals from leading restaurants whenever he could because, he said, unlike other royals, he was not a rich man. He claimed he was relatively poor—as he only had about £1 million in savings. Being unable to survive on the measly annual interest from that, the duke was allocated a "pension" of £21,000 a year. This was sluiced through to him via his brother, King George the Sixth, to save the British Government the embarrassment of being seen to pay him obvious taxpayer's money.

As extra perks, he earned about £1 million from the film rights and sales of his book *A King's Story* (Cassell, 1951), and his wife gained a small King's ransom from her opus *The Heart Has Its Reasons* (Michael Joseph, 1956). Knowing of his financial difficulties, the French government later gave him a mansion once occupied by President de Gaulle and charged him a peppercorn rent of only £25 a year for it. The French government also kindly told the "pauvre" duke that he must not worry his poor little head about having to pay income tax, as it would not apply in his case.

The duke repaid this *entente cordiale* by sneakily and illegally changing his annual British £21,000 pocket money on the French black market. He did not break the law himself though. He sent his valet out into the back streets of Paris to obtain the far higher exchange rate. On top of all this, the duke was able to save a few more French francs by buying his whiskey, gin, tobacco, gasoline, and even new automobiles duty free through the British Embassy in Paris.

No wonder the Windsors were able to scratch together enough money to purchase a lovely old mill house on twenty-six acres outside Paris—where they often spent their weekends. The duke also owned a four thousand-acre ranch in Canada, which he had bought for a song in 1919 and sold at a huge profit in 1962, even though he had lost some money by unsuccessfully drilling for oil on that property.

Although the duke often complained about his eighteen indoor servants "eating too much" and paid them relatively low wages, he swamped Wallis with every possible luxury. A good indication of that came in April 1987 when some (not all) of their jewelry was sold at auction in Geneva and fetched just over $50 million.

In 1938 one of Wallis's luxuries was a gold bathtub. Not 14 or 18 carat, but 22 carat. She was quite upset when a burglar broke in and carried away a valuable piece of it. (The plug, no doubt.)

That snippet about the gold bath appeared in *The New York Times* in April 1938, but never before published is what the Duke of Windsor did in his bath or shower. He did very little, in fact. According to information given to us in confidence by a former manservant (a confidence we cannot resist betraying), the duke liked the valet to rub his body down with soap and sponge. And afterward, with his shoulders covered by a large bath towel, the duke stood motionless while the valet rubbed him dry with another towel.

The valet also dressed his master. After putting on the duke's underwear and shirt, he helped him into his trousers. The legs of the trousers were rolled up to the knee so the duke would not lose his balance while stepping into them. Resting one hand on the valet's shoulder, His Royal Highness lifted one leg so the valet could slip it into the trousers. Repeating this for the other leg, the valet then pulled the trousers up to the duke's waist, fastened them, and then carefully rolled down the legs. Some confirmation of this comes from the duke himself. He once admitted: "I'm so ashamed of myself that I am so dependent on a valet. It's terrible to have been brought up that way."

In June 1940 the duke left France to avoid the German invasion and arrived in Spain where, for the first time in his life at the age of forty-five, he found himself without a valet. His attempts to cope were so pathetic that even the duchess had to laugh. The funniest incident was caused by the fact that, unknown to the duke, his valet had always squeezed toothpaste on to his toothbrush to save him having to do it. That is why the duke emerged from his personal bathroom in his boxer shorts complaining that he needed a new toothbrush because his old one was "empty." He looked baffled when it was explained to him that toothbrushes do not have hollow handles from which toothpaste is pumped.

Not having been to the manor born, the Duchess of Windsor could dress herself—and nobody can deny she did it well. Many women were jealous of her fabulous style. When it came to makeup, she was ten years ahead of her time. For over two decades she was voted one of the ten best-dressed women in the world. This is not really surprising as she spent a king's ransom on dresses, gowns, suits, and accessories.

Once, when a newspaper criticized her extravagance, Wallis reacted angrily: "That's ridiculous, I only buy about 100 new dresses a year . . . and most of them only cost me about $250 each." To fully savor that quote it is necessary to mention that $250 then was equivalent to the purchasing power of well over $2,500 these days.

Wallis was lying through her pearly-white capped teeth, of course. The records show that some of her Paris dresses cost $3,000 each, and when she liked a particular Roger Vivier or Christian Dior shoe, the shopaholic duchess had eighteen pairs made in different colors so that she could match them with her varied outfits. For the same reason, she bought four dozen hats at a time. Some costing $100 each.

Wallis also had a vast wardrobe of fabulous fur coats and stoles that were a steal at a mere $8,000 to $12,000. Her crocodile handbags were handmade with platinum or gold rims, and she had six shelves full of them. She also bought fine silk stockings and deliciously laced silk panties by the gross.

Wallis never had to stand at a kitchen sink, iron her husband's shirts, or prepare his breakfast. Her mornings were spent on far more important matters. She would get out of bed at about 10:30 in order to be ready for a personal hairdresser, who was her first visitor every day. As every strand of hair was caressed into place, a manicurist prettied up her finger- and toenails. After that, a masseuse arrived to tone up the duchess's body in preparation for her physically exhausting daily shopping expeditions. When she was expecting guests for dinner, a beautician would pop in to pretty up her face with makeup carefully chosen to match the color of the gown she intended to wear that night.

It would be unfair to suggest Wallis never did any work though. At least three times a week, while her husband played golf or sat in his favorite armchair doing his needlepoint, the duchess spent her afternoons organizing fabulous dinners for her guests. Fabulous is no exaggeration. Her chef and his six kitchen staff had to ensure that all lobsters, prawns, pheasant breasts, quails, slices of meat, pieces of fish—and even lettuce leaves—were exactly the same size. This was not just for stylish uniformity but cleverly indicated that Wallis did not favor any guest above another—whether it was Richard Nixon, Henry Fonda, Marlene Dietrich, or the Aga Khan.

Seeds had to be taken out of all cucumber slices before they were placed in salads or dainty teatime sandwiches. Grapes were stuffed with cream cheese, and another unusual dish was a cold mixture of Camembert cheese and ice cream served in a hot casing of butter-fried bread and cake crumbs.

Each bottle of fine wine they served would have paid a British workman's wage for about twenty weeks, and the six-inch cigar the duke smoked every night after dinner would have taken a workman two weeks to earn.

The Windsors' pet dogs also lived the life of Reilly. They ate out of solid silver dog bowls. But they did not eat leftovers. The chef created special meals of kidneys, fillet steak, and liver, and baked fresh biscuits for them every day. If that sounds fun, it gets better. They had their own menu cards printed each day. In French!

The Windsors' substitute children wore mink collars studded with real diamonds, and their leads were fashioned from gold and silver gilt. And so that their natural doggie stink did not offend the duchess's nostrils, their fur was regularly daubed with Dior perfume.

Talking of poofy stinks, the Windsors never housetrained their pretty pet dogs by rubbing their noses in it and throwing them outside the first time they plopped in the house. Wallis thought that was cruel. Much kinder to train the servants to scoop it up.

One of the duke's dogs was named Slipper, and this hound doggedly refused even to consider defecating when he was led out into the garden by the valet. He preferred to do it in style on the Persian carpets inside. When one of the servants performed a somersault after skidding on Slipper's droppings in the entrance hall, the duke, thinking this hilarious, wittily nicknamed the dog "Slippy Poo."

The dogs accompanied the Windsors when they traveled. So did a forest of wooden sea trunks. After their marriage in

1937, they went on holiday with 183 large trunks and 40-odd suitcases. In Italy they were the guests of the dictator Mussolini and in Germany were royally entertained by Goering, Goebbels, Hess, and Ribbentrop plus spending an hour with Adolf Hitler in his mountain retreat at Berchtesgaden.

Some books, such as Michael Bloch's intriguing *Duke of Windsor's War* (Weidenfeld & Nicolson, 1982) tell how the duke gathered information for British Intelligence in the late 1930s. Every spy story enthusiast will be fascinated to know that the title-conscious duke headed his reports with: "Secret Report By Major-General His Royal Highness The Duke of Windsor, K.G., P.C., K.T., K.P., G.C.B., G.C.S.I., G.C.M.G., G.C.I.E., G.C.V.O., G.B.E., M.C."

Whether the duke was a great spy for the British is not easy to ascertain because other books, such as Charles Higham's *Wallis, The Secret Lives of the Duchess of Windsor* (McGraw Hill, 1988) allege that he was also some kind of agent for the Nazi regime and that he had a secret deal going with Hitler. Even today, this outrageous suggestion sends the British Establishment red white and blue in the face. They say it is absolutely and totally impossible for anyone to believe that a British royal would have even dreamed of such a traitorous act. Yet there are several clues and claims unhappily suggesting otherwise.

- Charles Higham, who has a rare talent for obtaining information from FBI files, says there is no doubt that Hitler hoped to restore the Duke to the English throne, with Wallis as his Queen, after Britain was conquered. This was confirmed to us personally by Sir Oswald Mosley, when we interviewed him in Johannesburg in 1964. (Mosley, a close friend of the Windsors, was the leader of the British Union of Fascists and a German sympathizer who was detained in Britain during World War II).

- Even more specific is the disclosure by Michael Pye in his *King Over the Water—the Windsors in the Bahamas* (Granada, 1986) that the British Prime Minister, Winston Churchill, seriously considered charging the Duke of Windsor with treason in 1940. This was because the Duke was known to have had a secret meeting in Portugal with Colonel Walter Schellenberg, the deputy head of the Sicherheitsdienst, the intelligence arm of Hitler's SS. During that meeting, the colonel had asked the duke whether he would like to be the King of England again after the Nazis had conquered the British. It stands to reason that if the Duke of Windsor had kicked the colonel and his traitorous suggestion out, Churchill could not have considered a charge of treason.
- The British-born duke of Coburg, who became Hitler's emissary in London just before World War II, was the Duke of Windsor's cousin and knew him very well. He described the duke as "an ardent Nazi."
- The duke spent most of the war as governor of the Bahamas, but he didn't have to worry about his home in Paris. During all the time France was occupied by the Germans, Hitler made sure that the duke's mansion was guarded and all its valuable contents were packed away so carefully that nothing was missing when the Windsors returned after the war. Equally surprising, the duke's bank account at the Banque de France was not confiscated by the Germans.
- After the duke's death in 1972, some trusted person (alleged to be Lord Louis Mountbatten, who was banned from the house later) stole some of the duke's private letters—particularly his correspondence with top German, Italian and British fascists. We can only guess why that was necessary.

Whether the duke was a Nazi spy or not, he certainly agreed with some of Hitler's notorious views. In 1931, when he was still the Prince of Wales, he had a big affair with Gloria Vanderbilt's twin sister, Thelma. She was a vivacious beauty, but he dropped her like a hot brick when one of his Buckingham Palace spies alleged she had been to bed "with an Indian" (Prince Aly Khan). Thelma, who had denied doing any such thing, got her revenge by telling all London's social ladies that the so-called Prince Charming was not only "very poorly endowed" but was also totally incapable of satisfying a woman in bed.

Frank Giles, the former editor of the British *Sunday Times* who acted as aide-de-camp to the Duke of Windsor in 1940, states in his memoirs *Sundry Times* (John Murray, 1986) that the duke complained that war could have been avoided if it had not been for "Roosevelt and the Jews."

While he was the governor of the Bahamas, the duke discriminated against black people by making them use the back door of Government House, and he was opposed to them joining local clubs or having any place in government. Other claims of discrimination have been leveled against the duke by Sir Etienne Dupuch, the owner of the *Nassau Tribune*. But Michael Bloch points out, quite reasonably, that the duke had no choice in these matters as such discrimination was imposed by the local white ruling class in the Bahamas. If the duke had tried to buck their system of social apart-hate, they would have made it impossible for him to govern.

On the other hand, Suzy Menkes, in her scintillating book *The Windsor Style* (Grafton, 1987), makes it clear that the Duchess of Windsor was somewhat biased when it came to race. She writes that in the early 1960s the duchess told an American friend: "It was atrocious driving up Park Avenue tonight, where do they get all those Blacks from? And why do they allow them on Park Avenue?"

While the Windsors openly complimented German efficiency and the German way of life, various claims that Wallis was a German spy have to be treated with suspicion. In all the

German documents captured by the Allies, there is no proof she worked for the Nazi regime. It is far more likely she worked as an agent for the Americans because, in her youth, many of her close friends—and her first husband, Winfield Spencer—worked for U.S. naval intelligence.

Many of the major smears against Wallis emanate from a British Intelligence document compiled by M16 in 1934 at the request of King George the Fifth and Queen Mary, who were deeply worried that their son (then the Prince of Wales and heir to the throne) might double-cross everyone by marrying "the completely unsuitable" Wallis after he was crowned king.

Dozens of British agents gathered mainly unsubstantiated tidbits of gossip and rumor, stitching them all together to fabricate what is now known as the China Dossier. It contains the following smears about Wallis:

- She had been the mistress of several Nazi Germans.
- She had aborted a child fathered by an Italian fascist.
- This abortion had made her barren.
- She had been a secret drug peddler.
- She had been "kept" by several rich men.
- She had acted as a "front" for Mafia-style Chinese gamblers.
- She had frequented Chinese brothels in Hong Kong in 1923.
- She had been taught the sophisticated Chinese art of Fang Chung, the practice of arousing the male and preventing premature ejaculation.

The latter claim sounds right. It is a fact that the duke suffered from premature ejaculation and that this had always made him feel extremely insecure. We have personal information that when the duke first made love to Wallis, she totally convinced him she had exactly the same problem. She told him that after only ten seconds of intercourse, she could not prevent herself from having an orgasm. Whether the duchess told the duke the truth or not is irrelevant. On a sexual (and psychological) level, the duke was satisfied. He had found the woman of his dreams. No longer did he feel guilty about his lack of control. Wallis had the same "problem"—therefore it was no problem. No wonder he gave up the English throne for her and stayed with her for the rest of his life.

Whatever the smear merchants and character assassins may say (and they have claimed that the duke was actually a closet gay who married Wallis because she had a boy's figure and was also a "replacement" for his bossy mother), his adoration of Wallis was the Love Story of the Century. Nobody can deny that the duke's love for her was intense and enduring. Why else would he have kept no less than twenty-nine framed photographs of her in his bedroom until the day he died?

His body was flown to England and five days later, on June 2, 1972, the British royal family gave Wallis the full red-carpet treatment for the first time when she flew over for the funeral. Upon arrival at Heathrow Airport, the duchess was met by Lord Mountbatten in a royal limo and, so that she would not be "stared at" while the car stopped at traffic lights, the Queen personally arranged for all traffic to be blocked off at intersections along the route to Buckingham Palace.

(With the greatest respect to your Royal Highness, wouldn't it have been better if you had sent a car fitted with those specially tinted windows that cannot be peered into? In this way, nobody could have "stared at" the duchess—and the thousands of your loyal and taxpaying subjects who were involved in that snarl up of side-road traffic would not have been so inconvenienced.)

Wallis was allowed to occupy a suite at Buckingham Palace, and the media manipulators based there mounted a propaganda campaign aimed at leading the world to believe this signaled the end of the British royal family's thirty-six-year hostility toward the divorced American commoner who had stolen the heart of an English king.

But when Wallis died in 1986 and her body was buried alongside her husband in the royal burial ground at Frogmore, it became abundantly clear that she had never been forgiven. During the twenty-eight-minute funeral service, which was attended by seventeen members of the royal family including the Queen, Prince Philip, and the duchess's greatest enemy, the Queen Mother, the dean of Windsor achieved a minor ecclesiastical miracle by managing to conduct the proceedings without once mentioning the duchess's name!

Commenting on this in the *Sunday Express* of May 4, 1986, Sir John Junor stated: "There was about as much love round that graveside as there are snowmen in the Congo." He added: "Why did they all bother to take part in such a meaningless, hypocritical farce?"

Nobody answered his caustic question, but we suspect that the protocol experts at Buckingham Palace must have advised the royal family that if the duchess's name was mentioned then, technically, it would be necessary to grace her with the title of "Her Royal Highness." This had been the cause of all the friction between the Duke of Windsor and the British royals ever since he had abdicated as King Edward the Eighth.

It angered the duke intensely that Wallis was refused the title of Her Royal Highness, and for years he fought, threatened, and begged for it to be accorded her. Yet we believe that the Duchess of Windsor could quite legally have used that title for the following reasons.

The duke was born His Royal Highness Prince Edward, and immediately after his abdication he spoke to the British public in a special radio program. Just before he went on air he was announced as "His Royal Highness Prince Edward." No mistake was made in this regard because Sir John Reith, then the director-general of the BBC, had quite specifically asked King George the Sixth—and top Buckingham Palace aides—to give a ruling on how he should be named.

If those experts were correct (and when it comes to titles they usually are), the title His Royal Highness was rightfully Prince Edward's from birth and could never be taken away from him—in life or death. Confirmation of this came when the duke was buried. The plaque on his coffin described him as "His Royal Highness Prince Edward, Duke of Windsor."

This means that the Buckingham Palace experts must have chuckled up their sleeves whenever the duke had begged for his wife to be recognized as H.R.H., for they surely knew that Wallis could have used her full title of "Her Royal Highness Princess Edward, Duchess of Windsor"—and nobody could have stopped her! The most ironic aspect of all this is that, although the British royal family rejected Wallis as a "nonroyal" through most of her life, in death she will lie alongside them forever.

The last word on this subject must go to our friend, the Tangier-based millionaire poet Nigel Logan, who, in his waspish 1987 book *Reactionary Rhymes*, summed up the duchess's position perfectly by observing:

> *At Frogmore, where the best find rest,*
> *And Royal Blood alone is blessed,*
> *What honour to recline, supine,*
> *With neighbours all of Royal line.*
> *What, here below, could lend more tone*
> *To one who never graced a throne?*

## Note

The title of this chapter, originally used by Iles Brody for his brilliantly perceptive 1953 book, might give the impression that all the Windsors' money was squandered on totally selfish luxury. Not so. Long before she died, the duchess bequeathed her estate to the Pasteur Institute of Medical Research in Paris.

# 12

## *He Stole the Crown Jewels*

*T*he British crown jewels have always been extremely well guarded, but a fabulous rogue once managed to steal them from the Tower of London.

The son of a prosperous blacksmith, THOMAS BLOOD was born in Ireland in 1618. After inheriting property from his father at the age of about twenty-three, he sailed to London seeking fame and a little more fortune.

Being a handsome and highly intelligent character full of the Blarney, he made good contacts and enlisted as an army officer fighting alongside Oliver Cromwell in the civil war that led to King Charles the First being beheaded in 1649.

At about this time, Blood gave up soldiering and after resigning with the rank of colonel, married the pretty and well-bred Miss Holcroft from Lancashire. He then returned to Ireland where, as a reward for his services against the British crown, the Cromwell family made him a justice of the peace and gave him large chunks of land.

All went well until 1660 when Cromwell's Puritan regime

collapsed and the "Casanova king," Charles the Second, re-captured the English throne. As a former supporter of Cromwell, Colonel Blood was punished by having his land taken away from him.

Not liking this one little bit, Colonel Blood joined up with underground Cromwellians. In March 1663 he took part in a two-pronged plot in which Dublin Castle was to be attacked by eighty soldiers disguised as workmen and the local British gauleiter, the duke of Ormonde, was to be kidnapped.

The plot was betrayed by a traitor, or spy, in their midst and all the plotters including Blood's brother-in-law, James Lackie, but not the colonel, were captured. Blood made an unsuccessful attempt to rescue Lackie before he was executed and for this treasonable act, the British government offered a huge reward for Blood's capture.

No chance. Colonel Blood remained on the run for more than a year by posing as a Roman Catholic priest in various delightful counties such as Kilkenny, Tipperary, and Limerick. We do not know whether he made use of any information he might have obtained during confessionals, but it is definite that he later sailed to Holland where he became friendly with the great Dutch admiral Michael de Ruyter—gathering intelligence for him about English ships and their movements.

In 1665 Blood slipped back into England where he joined up with a group of religious extremists known as the Fifth Monarchy Men. His rise in their ranks was so meteoric that when some of its members were charged with being spy infiltrators he established a court-martial. Even though they were convincingly found guilty, Blood successfully insisted that they should not be executed. Nobody knows for sure what this was all about, but there is strong suspicion that Colonel Blood himself was some kind of freelance agent who had infiltrated the group on behalf of right-wing Puritan elements still remaining in British Intelligence.

If this is true, it certainly explains how Blood managed to escape capture during all those years when there was a huge price on his head. On the other hand, he might have played ball with British Intelligence only when it suited him. The full story will never be known.

Most of the Fifth Monarchy Men ended up in trouble except, of course, dear old Colonel Blood—who took himself off to Scotland where he joined up with an illegal religious group known as the Covenanters and helped them to aggravate the English. He quickly dissociated himself when five hundred of them were killed in a battle on Pentland Hills in November 1666.

Returning to further intrigue in England, he befriended a Captain Mason, who was arrested when it became known that he was associated with the outlawed Colonel Blood. Determined that Captain Mason should not be rescued, the Duke of York (later England's King James the Second) chose eight of his toughest troopers to guard the prisoner as he was taken north for trial. They were not tough enough. With only three men to help him, Colonel Blood attacked the convoy near Doncaster, killed four or five of them and, although he was badly stabbed during the ferocious fight, managed to rescue Captain Mason. A massive reward of £500 was then offered for Blood's capture, but he went into hiding disguised as a doctor named Thomas Allen and advised others how to keep healthy while his own wounds healed.

For his next trick, Colonel Blood captured the duke of Ormonde, his old enemy from the Dublin days. This happened on the night of December 6, 1670, as the duke was traveling by coach near St. James's Palace in London. Blood and five companions disposed of six escorting footmen, dragged the duke out of his coach, and gave him the glad news that he was about to be hanged.

After telling his accomplices to bind and gag the duke, Blood galloped ahead to place a rope on the gallows at nearby Tyburn (now Marble Arch), but just after he left the scene the duke was rescued by his coachman, who had summoned help.

Later, Colonel Blood said he had never intended to hang

the duke but merely wanted to frighten him and keep him prisoner until he agreed to sign a deed restoring Blood's confiscated estates in Ireland.

Six months later, at the age of fifty-two, Colonel Blood embarked on his greatest adventure. Disguised as a parson in full cleric's garb, he went to the Tower of London with a woman accomplice named Jane who posed as his wife. Jane pretended to faint after seeing the crown jewels and Blood asked Talbot Edwards, the keeper of the regalia, to send his wife for some brandy to help revive Jane.

After fetching the brandy, the kindly Mrs. Edwards—being cunningly prompted by Blood—invited the couple into her private quarters where she said Jane could rest on a bed for a while. Ten minutes later Jane said she felt much better and left with Blood after saying thank you at least a dozen times.

Three days later Colonel Blood, still disguised as a parson, returned to the Tower with several pairs of fine white gloves as a present for Mrs. Edwards. While having a friendly glass of beer with Mr. and Mrs. Edwards, he was introduced to their daughter, who was not well blessed in looks or figure and sounded worse when she opened her common little mouth.

Shrewdly assessing that Mr. and Mrs. Edwards had despaired of finding her a husband, Colonel Blood put them deep in promise land by announcing that he had a rich nephew who would surely fall madly in love with their delicious daughter and marry her because she was, quite definitely, the kind of girl his nephew had long been searching for.

Parental love being what it is (blind), Mr. and Mrs. Edwards fell for it and invited this wonderful parson person to join them for dinner. After enjoying a delicious meal, Colonel Blood insisted that the couple and their daughter join him in kneeling to say a long prayer for King Charles and all the other members of the wonderful royal family.

Colonel Blood straightened his clerical collar, donned his long black parson's cloak, and departed, promising that he would bring his rich young nephew to meet their lovely dog of a daughter at 7 o'clock next morning. This was extremely thoughtful of him because it meant that the nephew would have an hour to talk with Mr. Edwards before he opened the Tower of London to its many visitors at eight o'clock.

Next day (May 9, 1671) Colonel Blood, still wearing his clerical garb, arrived right on time with three right villains named Richard Holloway, Tom Hunt, and Bob Parrot. All four men had swords hidden in their walking sticks as well as daggers and pistols under their jackets. Holloway was posted outside the Tower to keep watch, and the three others went into the private quarters of Mr. and Mrs. Edwards where their blushing daughter was all dressed up in her best clothes, dying to meet the (rich) man of her dreams.

Explaining that he wished to wait until his wife arrived, Colonel Blood cleverly created an air of impatience by complaining every ten seconds that his wife was late—as usual. After a few minutes, Blood suggested that Mr. Edwards should show him and his two friends the crown jewels "to pass the time." To reduce the psychological tension Blood had caused by his impatience at his wife's late arrival, Mr. Edwards was only too pleased to go. He pulled out his huge set of keys, unlocked the door leading to the crown jewels, and invited the three men inside.

That's when they bound and gagged him. To make sure he could not shout a warning to Mrs. Edwards, Blood placed a large plug of wood in his mouth. This plug had a small hole drilled in the middle so that Edwards could suck in air to breathe. The plug was tied securely in place by a soft leather belt buckled around his head. And, just in case he tried to raise the alarm by snorting loudly, Blood had thoughtfully brought along a large double-pronged iron hook, which was pressed tight up Mr. Edwards's nostrils and kept in place by yet another soft leather belt.

At this point, Colonel Blood explained that he was not a common thief who intended to steal the crown jewels in order to sell them. He was going to use them as a bargaining lever in order to persuade King Charles to return those confiscated estates in Ireland. Blood also told Mr. Edwards that if he kept quiet he would not be harmed.

Edwards remained still and quiet as Bob Parrot rammed the royal globe down the front of his trousers and Tom Hunt started sawing the scepter in half because it was too long to slide down the leg of his trousers. But the loyal Mr. Edwards went berserk when he saw Colonel Blood irreverently squash the sacred royal crown flat so that it would fit under his parson's cloak.

Although he was securely bound and gagged, Edwards started bouncing around on his back and making a hellish din on the wooden floorboards. When he refused to stop doing this, Parrot bashed him on the head with a wooden hammer. This also failed to stop Edwards from bouncing around so Parrot gave him a stab in the chest with a dagger, but not seriously enough to kill him. Edwards then stopped his nonsense.

Colonel Blood's carefully laid plans were then messed up. The eldest son of Mr. and Mrs. Edwards—who had been away soldiering in France for several months—arrived home unexpectedly for a brief leave. On entering the Tower, he was challenged by Richard Holloway, the man posted outside to keep watch. When young Edwards explained who he was, Holloway allowed him to pass but gave a prearranged whistle to alert Colonel Blood that danger was at hand.

Grabbing their loot, Blood and his men dashed out of the Tower and ran toward the river Thames where they had a boat waiting. But the young Edwards, upon finding his father bound and gagged, sounded the alarm and raced after the culprits with a guard named Captain Beckman, who gathered assistance from members of the public. After a long and tiring chase, Colonel Blood and his men were eventually surrounded and captured.

During several days of intensive questioning, Blood steadfastly refused to confess and repeatedly told all the interrogators that he would only talk to one man in England—King

Charles. Blood was obviously a great student of human nature because the king was so fascinated on hearing this that he actually went to visit Colonel Blood in his prison cell. He was completely bowled over by the astute charmer from the Emerald Isle and within half an hour the two men were bosom buddies.

As they sat swigging wine together, Charles slapped Colonel Blood on the knees whenever he recounted one of his incredible adventures or explained how he had repeatedly avoided being captured by the king's soldiers. He listened in total fascination when Blood disclosed that he had once taken part in a plot to kidnap the monarch himself as he swam in the Thames near Chelsea. With delicious Irish blarney, Blood said he had withdrawn from this plot because he feared his accomplices might have harmed or killed the king. He said his conscience would never have condoned such a dreadful act—"being, as I am, in such awe of your Majesty's sacred person."

As he said this, Colonel Blood let out a sarcastic belly laugh that deliberately contradicted the truth of his words. King Charles could not be sure whether Blood would have let him be killed or not. The king suspected it was double-blarney, but years of being surrounded by simpering "yes men" made the colonel's audacity all the more sweet to the royal ears.

The king pardoned the rogue, took him back to the royal palace and, after a long night of verbal dueling and drinking, also returned to Colonel Blood the value of his forfeited Irish estates in the form of an annual pension worth more than £500.

The two men remained close friends for several years, during which Colonel Blood is said to have carried out a few secret assignments for the king—although he kept getting into trouble of different kinds, wine, women, and political songs included.

In early August 1680, Colonel Blood made an enemy of George Villiers, the second duke of Buckingham, himself a wild and wicked adventurer who was such a rogue that he was incarcerated in the Tower of London on no less than four occasions.

Buckingham claimed that Blood had spread "wickedly vicious lies" about him—one of them being that Buckingham had hired Blood to carry out "dirty tricks" for British Intelligence many years earlier. Buckingham was so incensed that he sued Blood for slander at the King's Bench and demanded damages of £10,000.

When Blood was arrested and committed for trial, the duke of Buckingham tried to stop him getting bail, claiming that the accused was such a slippery eel he would vanish and assume a new identity. Blood charmed the bench, however, and succeeded in obtaining bail. He then went to his beautiful house in Westminster where it is said he fell sick and died of fever just thirteen days later, on August 24, 1680.

But when a funeral service was held at Tothill Fields Cemetery two days later, the duke of Buckingham flashed a rumor around London that insisted that Colonel Blood had conned everybody again. Of course he was not dead. He had planted a dead body in his bed and was living in Ireland under an assumed name, you idiots. Why? Because he did not want to pay that £10,000 in damages, of course.

Knowing that Colonel Blood was quite capable of such deviousness, King Charles ordered that the body buried at Tothill Fields be dug up and identified at an official inquest attended by a couple of trusted, high-ranking men who had known Blood well. This was done and it was officially determined that Blood was well and truly dead.

So ended the life of the remarkable Colonel Thomas Blood. Unless, of course, that inquest was also rigged.


## Historical Note

The most hilarious aspect of this story is that the crown jewels stolen by Captain Blood were virtually worthless. King Charles had already pinched the jewels himself!

On coming to the throne in 1660, he had been so short of money that he secretly sold most of the priceless gems from the Crown, Scepter, and Globe, and had them replaced with paste fakes. It was only in 1910 when King George the Fifth took the throne that the fakes were secretly replaced with genuine gems. (Mrs. Shirley Bury, of the Victoria and Albert Museum, discovered this incredible royal secret in 1988 while helping several other academics to catalog the crown jewels.)

Oh, how King Charles must have giggled up his sleeve when he had all those lovely chats with Colonel Blood. No wonder he pardoned the rogue and granted him a pension!

# 13

---

## *Critics of Royalty*

*I*n a letter to George Washington in 1788, Thomas Jefferson wrote: "There is not a single crowned head in Europe whose talents or merits would entitle him to be elected a vestry man by the people of any parish in America."

Sneering pro-monarchists attacked this criticism as "a ridiculously sweeping generalization," but the American president-to-be was remarkably well informed in those days of slow communications. We now know that at the time:

- Denmark's King CHRISTIAN THE SEVENTH was a lunatic.
- So was MARIA, the Queen of Portugal.
- FREDERICK-WILLIAM THE SECOND of Prussia was a paranoid sexual deviant who curtailed the freedom of the press and religion.
- And England's KING GEORGE THE THIRD was so

mentally unbalanced that he was shaking hands with the branch of an oak tree in Windsor Great Park.

As clinchers, just one year after Thomas Jefferson penned his controversial statement, France collapsed into anarchy and King LOUIS THE SIXTEENTH of Marie Antoinette fame ended up being executed. Three years later the powerless spendthrift GUSTAV THE THIRD of Sweden alienated his noblemen so much that he was assassinated at a masked ball. And three years after that, Prince WILLEM THE FIFTH of Orange was dismissed and had to flee the Netherlands.

Which just goes to show that critics of royalty are not always wrong. But let us take a look at some other critics.

In 1570, when she was thirty-seven, QUEEN ELIZABETH THE FIRST of England rather fancied Henry, the handsome twenty-year-old duke of Anjou, so she wrote to Henry's mother, Catherine de Medici, suggesting that a marriage could perhaps be arranged. Mum wrote back to say this sounded great, but Henry later grossly insulted Queen Elizabeth by saying that nothing wouldpersuade him to marry such an old hag. This was a pity for Elizabeth, as Henry became the king of France four years later.

Having been so cruelly spurned, Queen Elizabeth later turned her attentions to Henry's younger brother François, duke of Alencon. Elizabeth's lust for young men, Frenchmen at that, did not please some of her subjects. One of them, John Stubbes, wrote a pamphlet ("The Discovery of a Gaping Gulf") in which he stated that the love François professed for Queen Elizabeth was most suspicious because, apart from being French, he was very ugly. The queen was too old for this stripling of twenty-six, and, in any case, he added, at forty-six, Liz was rather old to risk childbirth.

Infuriated by this pamphlet, Queen Elizabeth ordered that the right hand of John Stubbes be cut off. As this was done, the loyal Mr. Stubbes raised his bleeding stump, screamed "God Save the queen" and fainted. He was not the only one to suffer. The printer who published the critical pamphlet (his name was ironically Mr. Page) also had his right hand chopped off.

To their great regret, today's royals are not able to punish critics in that offhand way but, with the help of their hatchetmen in the press, they can ensure that such critics get the chop socially, which for some is a fate worse than death.

One man who suffered the slings and arrows of outrageous press verbals was Malcolm Muggeridge, a once-famous British TV pundit. He hit the headlines in 1957 when, in an article he wrote for the *Saturday Evening Post*, he asked whether Britain really needed a monarch. He said the Queen, Prince Philip, their family and doings had come to constitute a "sort of Royal Soap Opera."

He described the Queen as "dowdy, frumpy and banal" and said some people found the ostentation of life at Buckingham Palace little to their taste. He also sniped at the British press because "it minutely reports the doings of the Royal Family and praises them fulsomely up to the point of satiety." He added: "As for the BBC and now the Independent TV network, they are both tireless and unctuous."

As a former British Intelligence wartime agent, Mr. Muggeridge should have known better. When some of his comments were published in Britain, there was a tremendous uproar and he suddenly found himself Public Enemy Number One. He was banned from appearing on the BBC and a weekly column he had just started for a Sunday newspaper was immediately cancelled. He received many poison pen letters, his country home was daubed with nasty slogans, and people in the street spat at his famous face. That's when he stopped criticizing royalty.

Another British Establishment figure who should have known better was Lord Altrincham. In 1957 he wrote in the *National and English Review* that Queen Elizabeth was surrounded by old-fashioned "tweedy" types and the people who wrote her speeches made her sound like "a priggish schoolgirl and captain of the hockey team." As if that was not enough, he wrote: "Like her mother, she appears to be unable to string even a few sentences together without a written text."

The duke of Argyll, a gallant defender of the crown, counterattacked: "I would like to see the man hanged, drawn and quartered." Lord Strathmore agreed by huffing and puffing: "Young Altrincham is a bounder. He should be shot."

That great liberal British newspaper *The Observer*, for which Lord Altrincham had written several articles on progressive Toryism, quickly disowned him. So did the elected representatives of the taxpayers of the ancient town of Altrincham in Cheshire. Lord Altrincham later renounced his title and became ordinary John Grigg, but socially John Doe for quite some time—although a newspaper survey disclosed that a large majority of its readers agreed with him!

The man who holds the record for being the most vocal critic of British royalty in modern times is Willie Hamilton, who is on record as saying:

- "Princess Margaret is a Royal floozy."
- "Queen Victoria was an ill-educated, reactionary busybody."
- "Prince Charles can be the biggest nitwit in the world."
- "Princess Anne and her husband Mark Phillips are bloody parasites."
- "Prince Philip has cultivated the role of a Royal bull in the democratic china shop."

As a Labour Party member of Parliament for over thirty years, Mr. Hamilton says he was unfortunate enough to meet Her Majesty twice. He found each of these events to be: "Tedious and demeaning—lined up to touch the gloved hand as if about to enter the gates of Heaven to meet my Maker."

The royal family will be relieved when this rogue of a loyal subject does go, although they probably disagree about his presumed destination. This is not as wicked as it may sound because Mr. Hamilton never stood to attention and hummed "God Save Our Noble Queen" when it was played at the end of every public movie performance. On the contrary, his favorite refrain is: "If every member of the Royal Family were ditched in the English Channel tomorrow, I would sleep soundly."

Why does Willie Hamilton dislike them so much? The answer is that in the mid-1920s, when he was about ten, one of the female royals visited his home town of Durham, where his father was a poorly paid coal miner. Along with all the other children in the area, little Willie was forced by his school headmaster to stand in the street to watch and wave to the Great Personage as she swept by in a luxurious limousine with a cocktail cabinet in the spacious passenger section.

"I thought, why should she drive in a car like that when no one in our street could even afford a push bike?"

That is why Willie joined the Labour Party and, having his finger on the pulse of the working class, he became a member of Parliament in 1950. He then poured scorn on the fact that Queen Mary had more than sixty personal servants to tend her every wish and received a yearly wage of £70,000 from the British taxpayer—at a time when £5 a week was a good wage for many workers. Most of the British newspapers gave him a hiding, but he received thousands of letters from members of the public who agreed with him. Realizing there was great publicity potential—and votes—to be obtained from abusing the royal family, Willie Hamilton jumped on the gravy train and made his name.

These days he sometimes wishes he hadn't. Not that he regrets lambasting the royals. He feels that by specializing in monarchy-bashing he missed out on the more serious political and social problems.

"Every time a Royal sneezed or fell off a horse, the Press telephoned me for a comment and I became the bloody Court Jester," he says with a tinge of regret.

But, as the famous proverb says: No man can play the fool so well as the wise man. Willie Hamilton was able to slip some mind-bending political propaganda into print now and again. Not easy in the fifties and sixties, when most newspapers owners had a title, or wanted one.

One of his quotes about royalty was: "The process of indoctrination starts early. History teaching in our schools is still often taught by reference to the reigns of Kings and Queens. Royal photographs appear daily in newspapers, in women's magazines and on TV. There are endlessly, parades of brassy toy soldiers on beautiful horses. Horses which live better than old-age pensioners. We have our national slogans 'For King And Country' when soldiers are needed for savage wars, and toasts 'To The Queen' at every business dinner or Tory nosh up . . ."

One of his most withering snipes at the royal family was: "It is a human equivalent of the London Zoo, but giving much less pleasure than the chimpanzees' tea party, and running at much greater cost."

On royal parades, weddings, the opening of Parliament, and so on, Willie Hamilton once asked: "Yet would not a circus do as well? Colour, pageantry, glitter and lots of coaches—clowns in ridiculous clothes and prancing horses? The difference is that the British people must also soak up a lifelong brainwashing about the value of the Monarchy, in schools, in the rapidly emptying churches, and in a Press which is largely and sycophantically pro-Monarchist."

From all this, it might appear that Willie Hamilton is a vainglorious loudmouth. Not so. He is an unassuming, gentle, shy, and courteous fellow, even if he is the author of the most critical book ever published in England about the royal family. This was *My Queen and I* published by Quartet in 1975. Some idea of how vitriolic that book is, in parts, can be judged from the fact that he starts it with a quote made by the American author Thomas Paine (1737 to 1809): "It could have been no difficult thing in the early and solitary ages of the world, while the chief employment of men was that of attending flocks and herds, for a banditti of ruffians to overrun a country and lay it under contributions. Their power being thus established, the chief of the band contrived to lose the name of Robber in that of Monarch; and hence the origin of Monarchy and Kings."

Not surprisingly, the British ruling class made sure that Willie Hamilton was never considered for high office, and certainly not for any title. But he still managed to survive as a long-term royal critic.

Anthony Wedgwood-Benn, better known as Tony, was born the son of Viscount Stansgate in 1925. He studied at Oxford, was an eighteen-year-old RAF pilot in World War II, then entered politics and, after being the British postmaster-general during the Labour government, became the Minister of posts and telecommunications in 1974. He inherited his peerage in 1960 but quickly renounced it, saying he didn't wish to lord it over anyone. If you see him mentioned in the British tabloid press today, we guarantee that he will, more often than not, be dismissed as a member of the "loony Left."

This might be due to the fact that when he became the postmaster-general in 1964, he refused an invitation to enjoy a glass of sherry with Queen Elizabeth. Tony Benn does not like the Queen much. He says she is "the enemy of freedom and the symbol of wealth and archaic privilege."

The funniest story about Tony is that as soon as he was appointed postmaster-general, he tried to have the Queen's head taken off British postage stamps. He was so enthusiastic about this that in 1965 he had special designs for new stamps set up and took them along to Buckingham Palace to show the Queen.

During that official ten-minute interview, Tony got down on his knees and spread the proposed new "headless" stamps all over her carpet. The queen did not join him on the floor but remained seated. When Tony asked her if she approved of being beheaded on the new stamps, she didn't say yes and she didn't say no. She said she would think about it.

Later Tony was told by Premier Harold Wilson that the Queen had decided she would prefer to keep her head. Tony does not give in easily, though, and kept pushing for the headless stamps. He finally got a letter from Number 10 Downing

Street that said that if, as the postmaster-general, he kept pressing the matter officially, "the Queen may be obliged to reject his advice."

Tony Benn says that letter was probably the most important he ever received in his life about the Constitution because: "If the Crown personally can reject advice then, of course, the whole democratic façade turns out to be false."

In September 1987, as the Labour Party member of Parliament for Chesterfield, Tony Benn caused outrage when he called for the Queen to be sacked and replaced by an American-style (elected) president.

Way back in 1917, the world-famous author H. G. Wells had written a letter to *The Times* advising the British nation to copy the Russian people by doing away with the monarchy and its "alien and uninspiring Court." King GEORGE THE FIFTH took the steam out of that by joking: "I may be uninspiring but I'll be damned if I'm an alien."

King George scored another victory in the 1920s when "extremist" Labour Party MPs started agitating against the royals. Knowing that these little jumped-up cloth-cap peasants from deprived backgrounds secretly envied the life-style of the upper classes, the king pandered to their pretensions by inviting them to royal garden parties.

Throwing away the cloth caps that had got them voted into power by their own working-class supporters, those revolutionary Labourites betrayed everything they allegedly stood for by donning spats, boiled shirts, and top hats, and, with their absurdly overdressed wives on their arms, strutted up and down the lawns of Buckingham Palace gobbling rich cakes and sipping Earl Grey tea as they hobnobbed with dukes and duchesses.

Oh, how King George must have laughed at these idiots being suckered into becoming symbols of the very privileged society they had been elected to destroy. It was no laughing matter for British Intelligence though. Realizing that full advantage could be taken of the situation, they devised a cunning operation. Using limousine liberal-type Socialist ladies (who may well have been secret undercover agents), they master-minded the formation of a little set-up named "the Half Circle Club," which gave lessons on etiquette to other Labour Party wives keen to gain acceptance into the highest echelons of society.

The "Club" taught the Labour wives not to call table napkins serviettes, not to cool their hot tea by pouring it from the cup into the saucer, not to say "Pardon" but "What did you say?" not to say "Pleased to meet you" but "How do you do," and not to spit in the fireplace. Far better to do it into a handker-chief while pretending a dainty cough.

The Half Circle Club also hired the ballrooms of London's top hotels where exclusive evening dress parties were held at which minor members of the royal family would make ap-pearances so that club members could later boast about their close proximity to the royals. Some dedicated Labour Party MPs tried to stick to their principles, saying they would not attend such posh dos—but their wives said otherwise. And so British Intelligence's Divide and Rule tactic put a speedy end to most of the tricky problems King George the Fifth was then suffering from the anti-royal Labourites.

Royal garden parties are still held. Every year there is one for 8,000 Scots at Holyrood House, Edinburgh, and three on the lawns of Buckingham Palace where some 27,000 mayors, magistrates, merchant bankers, minor dignitaries, members of the clergy, eagle-eyed village post mistresses, heavily medaled generals and admirals, shopkeepers, football managers, and even pop stars are invited. Ordinary people don't actually sup tea with the Queen at these parties. She has her own roped-off royal tea tent.

John Lennon, who upset many by saying the Beatles were more famous than Jesus, did not consider it an honor to drink tea in the same garden as the Queen. Another honor he did not like was his MBE (Member of the British Empire) decoration—which he returned, saying it was "an embarrass-ment and a humiliation" as he did not believe in royalty and titles.

Another pop singer who is unlikely to attend a royal garden party is Steven Morrissey of The Smiths, who has often attacked the royal family. He upset them in 1987 by callously saying he would not mourn when the Queen Mother died. Instead, he said: "I would be hammering the nails in the coffin to make sure she was in there and stayed there."

More macabre was the plot set up by an underground group in Britain which said it was opposed to members of the royal family "setting a bad example" to the public by taking part in blood sports such as shooting partridges and hunting foxes. Calling itself the Hunt Retribution Squad, the group went to the graveyard at Badminton's Parish Church in the early hours of Saint Stephen's Day 1986 and started digging up the Duke of Beaufort, a leading figure in foxhunting who had died two years earlier at the age of eighty-three.

After digging out most of the earth covering the coffin, they apparently gave up when their shovel broke on the frozen ground just inches from the body. It was alleged that the would-be grave robbers had intended to chop off the duke's head and mail it to Princess Anne because she was also a keen bloodsports fan. But later some of the culprits said they had not really intended to carry out such a horrible desecration. It was just a bluff aimed at attracting publicity for their anti-bloodsports campaign.

When journalists try to get Buckingham Palace to comment on matters that cause the royals great displeasure (because they are true), the stock answer is usually: "Her Majesty has no interest in that subject" or "His Royal Highness does not read that newspaper." This simply is not true.

Prince Charles reads the *Times* every morning. He does not have time to read all the other newspapers, but his personal secretary does. If Charles's name appears in any article, however small the mention, it is carefully cut out and all such clippings are given to the Prince at breakfast time. The same is done for the other royals, so that they are *au fait* with everything that has been written about them and have their answers ready before they walk out of their front door. Fore-warned is forearmed.

In addition to her Press clippings, the Queen is kept up to date by a specially appointed Parliamentary Sketch Writer (usu-ally an MP) who compiles a quick "need to know" summary of everything important said in the House of Commons and the Lords each day. It includes all the political and sexual gossip circulating among the press correspondents based at Parlia-ment.

The royals have an incredible love-hate relationship with the Press, which they regard as a painful necessity. On the one hand, they loathe being pestered by constant attention, on the other, they have to keep in its good books because it is their most valuable image-making machine. It is also their most important organ of power, which they constantly use to shape public opinion. Not only about themselves but also on shrewdly chosen (and sometimes subtly disguised) moral, re-ligious and yes, even political, subjects.

The British journalist Judy Wade put this very succinctly in her 1987 book *Inside a Royal Marriage* (Angus & Robertson) when she wrote that the royals realize only too well that with-out the media they would have trouble staying in business. Miss Wade also put her foot through the thick royal icing by daring to discuss some of the ups and downs in Prince Charles's marriage to Princess Di. For that, Graham Lord of the *Sunday Express* described her book as "vicious, impudent and imper-tinent."

One of the biggest fallacies about royalty is that they can't defend themselves against their press critics—or fight back. This deliberately misleading claim is used regularly, but it is blatantly untrue. The royals not only have a sophisticated pub-licity team working almost around the clock, they also have a select network of friendly journalists (and editors or news-paper owners) who are only too willing—for patriotic or pat-ronage reasons—to write anything which will defend the Queen they love.

It is also a fact that the royals have secret information-gathering agents (call them spies, if you wish) on the staffs of London's major newspapers, particularly on those busy news desks where high-grade information and gossip floods in round the clock. These agents, often unknown to their Editors, give the Buckingham Palace press office advance warning about any potentially damaging story being compiled by the newspaper. Once again, forewarned is forearmed.

British Intelligence also has a special propaganda section which churns out letters for publication in the Letters to the Editor pages of mass-circulation British newspapers. Such letters not only defend the royal family when necessary, but also give support to political themes being pushed by the British government.

One of the favorite devices used by Buckingham Palace to suck sympathy from the public is to complain periodically about "spying" journalists and photographers who "harass" the poor royals by "invading" their private lives.

Several years ago, when a world-famous film star brought an action against a journalist who had written something un-complimentary about her, a High Court judge decided that famous public figures do not actually have a private life as such because they are public property. The judge also pointed out that the film star in question had never complained about all the flattering things written about her private life over many years.

Keeping that in mind, does not the same apply to the royal family? Are they not also public property? Even more so than a film star because the British public actually pays them to perform their real-life roles. That being so, don't all taxpayers have the constitutional right to know about the secret *Dallas* and *Dynasty*-type antics going on backstage?

Not so very long ago, Buckingham Palace could rely on Fleet Street's total deference. Editors who played ball were not only invited to private lunches at the palace, but were also rewarded with titles or other honors. We know a famous tabloid editor who, when he politely declined a title in the sixties, laughingly said: "Give it to my political correspondent instead, he would be tickled pink." They did.

That kind of thing still goes on but these days the royals get criticized more often. The first serious damage to the regal image came in the early seventies when the popular British satirical magazine *Private Eye* regularly entertained its readers by publishing embarrassing or scandalous (but true) little snippets about individual royals. Not directly by name. Each member of the royal family was given a nickname and although the magazine never really disclosed who was supposed to be who, the readers talked among themselves in pubs and clubs and worked out that Brenda was the Queen, Keith was Prince Philip, Yvonne was Princess Margaret and Lord Snowbum, naturally, was Margaret's ex-husband, Lord Snowdon.

Then, in the eighties, along came that ribald but brilliant TV puppet show "Spitting Images" which not only attacked pretentious and lying politicians but also portrayed some of the royals as clowns or pompous twits occupying palatial palaces and sitting on gilt-ridden antique chairs and chaise-longues blissfully unaware that they were living in a totally different world.

Quite apart from its technical excellence, "Spitting Images" was a devastating success because the producers not only managed to place their fingers on the public pulse with unerring accuracy but used the only weapon against which royalty has no defense. Humor.

The British public has learned to laugh at the incredible antics and scandals of the royal family now regularly being exposed by the tabloid press. This has caused the man in the street to become increasingly bored by true blue newspapers that carry daily reports about how "caring" the royals are, what wonderful things they do and how wonderfully they do them. Opinion polls have also shown there is growing disenchantment in the public mind about the high cost to the taxpayer of keeping some of the minor royals in out-dated luxury.

All these things have caused a definite shift in the mood of leading British newspaper columnists during the last twelve months. Things are now being written that would have been inconceivable ten years ago. Even normally pro-royal newspapers have made astonishingly critical comments about the Queen, particularly in relation to her role within the Commonwealth.

Peregrine Worsthorne of the conservative *Sunday Telegraph* wrote: "The Queen's instincts in this matter are by no means as sure as one might wish."

A. N. Wilson of the *London Evening Standard* wrote that the recent row between Margaret Thatcher and the Queen about the Commonwealth made constitutional monarchy seem like "an empty farce" after Mrs. Thatcher had, "in effect lifted two fingers, not just to the Commonwealth, but to the Queen."

Jean Rook, the top columnist of the conservative *Daily Express*, has written that although the Queen is "Upright, moral, stern and dedicated, she stands increasingly alone. At her best like a noble statue, at her worst, like an anachronistically dressed 5-foot 4-inch wax doll."

In October 1989, the *British Sunday Times* quoted the top social diarist Nigel Dempster as having forecast that Prince Charles will never take the throne because he (Dempster) believes the monarchy will end with Queen Elizabeth.

Another top columnist is George Gale of the conservative *Daily Mail*. He wrote: "The way the Royals carry on is enough to make anybody a republican. Certainly, it is making me one."

An equally withering blast came from Julie Burchill who writes a regular column in the conservative *Mail on Sunday*. In November 1989, she wrote: "I'll make my bias clear—I don't approve of monarchies. The conferring of massive privilege based on the randomness of birth is offensive to every good capitalist."

Every year, Her Majesty the Queen broadcasts her famous Christmas message to the British public. On Christmas Day, 1989, she made a strong point of dealing with topical "Green issues." One of her comments was, "Some species of wild plants and animals are, sadly, bound to become extinct." On this subject, Her Majesty also said, "It is not too late to reduce the damage if we change our attitudes and behaviour."

Shortly after the Queen made that speech, her daughter, Princess Anne, went to church wearing a beautiful £10,000 fur coat. For that, the popular *Daily Mirror* columnist, James Whitaker, roundly criticized the royal family for not getting its act together.

One month earlier, the *Sunday Mirror* had delivered a stinging attack on the Queen's daughter-in-law, Fergie, because she had shocked the nation's Greens by ordering sixteen chairs made from endangered rain forest trees. Costing hundreds of pounds each, the chairs were for the dining room at Fergie's £5 million new home.

Five days later, in an obvious effort to recover from these embarrassing blows to the royal Green image, Buckingham Palace casually let the media know that Prince Charles had persuaded his mother to install solar panels on top of one of her holiday homes. And as a further attempt to reduce pollution, Prince Edward had decided to cycle the quarter of mile from Sandringham House to the stables, a journey he usually did in the comfort of his chauffeur-driven car. This just goes to confirm that the royals really do know how to fight back against the media.

Sometimes, they win on a knockout. This happened on November 19, 1989, when Wendy Henry, the editor of Britain's mass-circulation Sunday newspaper, *The People*, published large color photographs of seven-year-old Prince William doing a little piddle (back to camera, of course,) on some grass. The caption underneath one of the photographs stated: "Willie's sly pee in park."

The same edition also carried pictures of Prince William's five-year-old brother Prince Harry looking decidedly unhappy as he was being teased by other kids during playtime at his posh private school. Headlined "His Royal Cry-ness" the story described Prince Harry as "a right royal cry baby" who turned on the tears whenever his schoolmates were rough.

Prince Charles and Princess Di took strong exception to all this and an official statement was quickly issued which said they found these photographs of their sons to be "intrusive and irresponsible." The owner of the newspaper, Mr. Robert Maxwell, agreed and within twenty-four hours of publishing those photographs, editor Wendy Henry was sacked.

Yet there is one section of the press that often gives unfair hidings to the royals, and nobody can do a thing about it. This is the fashion beat. If the Queen wears a dark lipstick, they say it makes her look "old and tired." If she wears a bright new color, who's she trying to look like, Joan Collins? If she wears a pink suit, the pink is described as "retching pink." Turquoise is "shrieking" and lemon yellow is "acidulous."

Princess Di is the best thing that ever happened to the British rag trade and has made it millions of dollars in exports. But the fashion-beat writers are unbeatable. They flatter Di one minute, by saying her figure is fantastic, then the following week they will carp about her getting fat. When they have the knife in, they refer to Di as "the Royal Stick Insect," yet don't be surprised if, in the very next edition, they extol the virtues of a brand-new Sawdust and Custard diet allegedly favored by slim, trim Di.

When Di visited Australia in 1985, she was still smarting from the bad publicity she had received when a newspaper disclosed that she spent over $150,000 on new clothes every time she visited another country. So, when she visited a reception in Canberra, Di wore the same red dress she had chosen for a reception in Melbourne the week before. The fashion writers didn't compliment her on her shrewd economy though. They criticized her with catty jibes of "Second-hand Di."

Yet when it comes to real insults, Prince Andrew's wife, Fergie, holds the record. No female in the British royal family has been so viciously savaged about her figure and taste in clothing. For instance, when Fergie returned from America in November 1989, the British columnist Nina Myskow gave her a pasting during a TV show by spitting: "Fergie arrived back from holiday with fifty-three bags of luggage and the biggest bag of all was the fifty-fourth who carried it." As if that was not enough, Nina added: "Fergie is vulgar, we all know the woman is vulgar. That's why the Queen is spending £5-million on building her the biggest pig sty in Europe."

Men can be equally bitchy. In January 1988, the fashion expert Paul Mathur wrote in the glossy *Blitz Magazine* that Fergie was "the ugliest woman alive." But even that ghastly untruth was eclipsed by Tom Bussmann of *The Guardian* in March 1989. Commenting on the $3,000 leather coat Fergie had bought from Yves St. Laurent he wrote: "The photographic evidence would indicate that it looked better on the original cow."

The royals very rarely agree with their critics. But the Queen once did. This was when she and Prince Philip were being chauffeur-driven down a narrow lane near their holiday home at Sandringham. Prince Philip was busy scribbling some rough notes for a speech and was surprised when he saw his wife quickly turn to look out of the rear window and say loudly: "I quite agree with you, Madam." Looking back, Prince Philip saw an obviously well-to-do woman wearing tweeds yelling with fury and shaking her fist at them because the car had splattered her with mud. Fascinated to know what the woman had shouted, Prince Philip asked his wife: "What did she say?"

"Bastards!" replied the Queen.

# 14

---

## *Sexy Modern Royals*

When Queen Victoria died senile in 1901, her elder son Albert Edward came to the throne as KING EDWARD THE SEVENTH. Although he was a fair old monarch who gave his name to what became famous as the "Edwardian" age, Edward was a sexual cowboy who spent his whole life chasing skirt in order to get as many notches on the butt of his pistol as possible. More than ten thousand notches is a fairly conservative estimate because he sampled at least four women a week from the age of nineteen until he died at sixty-nine. The actual figure could be between fifteen and eighteen thousand, though, because in good weeks he managed six or seven different bed partners.

To regain his strength, Edward usually devoured an eight-course breakfast, and his dinners often ran to twelve courses. When it came to sexual intercourse, however, Edward's eyes were greedier than his famously fat stomach. Proof of this came when he tried to seduce an outrageously sexy blonde wearing a long slinky silk dress at a party—only to discover to his horror that the "blonde" was actually the transvestite Russian prince Felix Yusupov, wearing full drag. (Source: *Prince Felix Yusupov: The Man Who Murdered Rasputin* by Chris Dobson [Harrap, 1989].)

Rather more amusing for the king was the millionaire Indian prince who was so impressed by His Majesty's sexual comings and goings that he sent him an unforgettable birthday present: a golf bag made from an elephant's penis.

Edward's best-known mistress was Lillie Langtry, the most outrageous "Scarlet Woman" of her time. During the height of her affair with Edward (then the Prince of Wales), a gossip columnist cunningly wrote this sentence in a weekly London journal: "There is nothing whatever between the Prince of Wales and Lillie Langtry." Readers were mystified by this dotty denial but in the very next edition, in exactly the same place, appeared the four words: "Not even a sheet."

Although she was a parson's daughter, Lillie Langtry was an uninhibited character who disrupted many a sedate cocktail party with her outrageous antics. But Edward's ardor for her cooled permanently when she jokingly poured a large helping of melting strawberry ice cream down the back of his neck at a boring dinner party.

Having fallen from the royal gravy train, Lillie took advantage of her notoriety as a former Buckingham Palace intimate by becoming an actress. During a whistle-stop tour of America in the early 1880s, she stayed overnight in a newly formed settlement in Texas where she charmed the local judge Roy Bean so much (by her skill at poker) that he named the town Langtry in her honor.

Lillie also had an affair with Prince Louis of Battenberg (father of Lord Mountbatten) and by him is said to have given birth to an illegitimate daughter named Jeanne Marie. Later still, Lillie married a baronet's son and became the rather more sedate Lady de Bathe. She died in 1929 at the age of seventy-six.

Another of Edward's sleeping partners was the even more

famous actress Sarah Bernhardt. She not only had an affair with Edward, but also claimed to have had one with his son, Prince Eddy. She was also the mistress of the Belgian prince Henri de Ligne, and her bastard son Maurice was said to have been sired by him.

Sarah Bernhardt was as dramatic offstage as on. She kept a silk-lined coffin in her bedroom, and the spiciest tidbit of gossip in London at the time was that she once had sex with Edward as he lay supine, but very much alive, in that coffin. Just before she died in 1923, at the age of seventy-nine, Sarah coyly indicated that she had "entertained" other famous lovers, such as the French novelist Victor Hugo and Napoleon III, in the coffin and that its pink silk lining had to be changed quite regularly—for wear-and-tear reasons.

Edward's longest serving mistress was Alice Keppel, the wife of an earl. She spent six weeks of every year making love to His Royal Highness in the then-popular French coastal resort of Biarritz. Alice was a real survivor who held Edward's hand as he lay on his deathbed in May 1910 and sobbed that if he died she no longer wished to live. This was not quite true. She clung to life until 1947, when she died at the age of seventy-eight.

Another long-favored mistress was "Daisy" Warwick, the wife of Lord Brooke. But soon after King Edward died, Daisy tried to blackmail the royal family by producing a collection of his sizzling love letters. Although everybody in London society knew all about His Royal Highness being an adulterer, these letters were political dynamite because their publication in a newspaper would have proved it to the workers—who were not supposed to know.

So Buckingham Palace arranged for an urgent application to be made to the High Court, restraining Daisy from selling the letters to the gutter press. Daisy then threw the royals into a dither by threatening to sell them to one of America's biggest newspapers. At this stage, Arthur du Cros, of the famous Dunlop rubber (tire) company, stepped in and paid off £64,000 worth of Daisy's debts in return for the love letters. Mr. Du Cros was later created a baronet. Daisy, by the way, died in 1938, at seventy-six.

The most revealing story about Edward the Seventh—in terms of social hypocrisy—is that while staying in a friend's house one night, he felt rather randy and had to make do by calling for a maid. This was Rosa Lewis, who was made to measure for Edward as she not only served him adequately but told him about several other pretty little young servant girls who would simply adore to be in royal service.

After accepting many of Rosa's recommendations, the king realized she was far too talented to remain in belowstairs service to the top nobs and should give them pleasure upstairs instead. So he gave her the money to open London's (now respectable) Cavendish Hotel in Jermyn Street, just opposite the back door of Fortnum and Mason's Royal Grocery shop.

There, from 1902 until she died in 1952, Rosa ran Britain's most famous high-class brothel where she provided classy harlots for members of Parliament, high-ranking military officers, and much of the aristocracy. The hotel-brothel became so famous that in the forties and fifties many members of the British nobility took their sixteen-year-old sons there to introduce them to the pleasures of the flesh and, often, to discreetly ascertain whether or not they were gay.

Rosa's guests were not all Brits. Her hotel was used by thousands of visitors from overseas, including many of America's most prominent politicians and millionaires, who were taken to the Cavendish by trusted friends in London for discreet afternoon sessions of tea and crumpet. And tarts. This world-famous cat house somehow managed to escape the attention of Scotland Yard's vice squad. Not once during her fifty-year reign as Britain's Queen of Sex was Rosa Lewis charged with keeping a brothel.

Although King Edward the Seventh was a regular visitor at this house of pleasure that he had bankrolled, he still admired his faithful wife Alexandra, the lovely daughter of Denmark's King Christian the Ninth. Alexandra didn't mind the fact that her husband had sex with thousands of other women. What upset her was that all those other ladies knew what a terrible sex life she had with him as he took less than a minute to complete the sex act. In spite of this, Alexandra managed to produce three daughters and three sons. Two of those sons went on to great fame.

Son number one was PRINCE ALBERT VICTOR, known as Prince Eddy. Born in 1864, he was lazy, a poor reader, an atrocious speller, and such a total dunce that his tutors despaired of him. Yet this did not stop a university awarding him with an honorary doctorate of law.

When the truth leaked out about his backwardness, the royal family tried to cover up by claiming he was "slightly deaf." They said this made it difficult for him to hear what his teachers said. Some people might wonder why this normally spoiled young prince was not supplied with an ear trumpet if he did have a hearing defect. But of course he didn't, because when it came to sex, Eddy was a genius who could hear the rustle of silk knickers two boudoirs away.

The most disgraceful but nonetheless intriguing rumor about Prince Eddy is that he was Jack the Ripper. Several books have linked him with the sensational murders that rocked Britain in 1888. The common denominator in these books is that Prince Eddy contracted syphilis from one of the thousands of prostitutes in London's deprived East End area.

Some say Prince Eddy obtained his revenge by returning to the East End one night and killing the disgustingly diseased tart by disemboweling her. Other books state that her fellow prostitutes were murdered by Queen Victoria's royal physician, Sir William Gull.

When Britain's Thames TV showed its three-part *Jack the Ripper* series, starring the actor Michael Caine in 1988, it categorically named Sir William as the Ripper. Viewers were told: "We have come to our conclusions after careful study and painstaking deduction. Other researchers, criminologists and writers may take a different view. We believe our conclusions to be true."

Possibly to protect itself against hostile reaction from admirers of the royal family, Thames TV did not suggest that Sir William Gull had been "recruited" by Queen Victoria, or Prince Eddy, to kill the prostitutes. The filmmakers explained that problem away by saying the royal physician was just "insane."

But the late Stephen Knight, in his book *Jack the Ripper: The Final Solution*, took the subject further. He said Prince Eddy had fallen in love with a Catholic shopgirl named Anne Crook, had secretly married her in a *Catholic* ceremony, and that she had given birth to his child, a girl named Alice. To prevent a religious scandal erupting, which could easily have toppled the then unpopular Queen Victoria, Sir William Gull was commissioned to kidnap Anne. He did, and rendered her insane by operating on her brain—after which he had placed her in a mental institution.

According to Mr. Knight, this disgraceful plot backfired because Anne Crook had left her baby in the care of Mary Kelly, an amateur prostitute living in London's East End who, in collusion with three full-time whores, tried to blackmail the royal family.

The result, stated Mr. Knight, was that the British prime minister, Lord Salisbury, sent Sir William to "eliminate" all those dangerous guttersnipes in a desperate last-ditch attempt to protect the British monarchy. To give the impression that a total madman was responsible, Sir William Gull had cut out the prostitute's wombs and ovaries or committed other atrocities, such as chopping off their breasts or ears.

Sir William is said to have died in 1890, but there is doubt about this because, contrary to usual medical ethics, his death was certified by Dr. Theo Ackland, who just happened to be his son-in-law.

Stephen Knight's findings were so well researched and convincing that somebody thought him dangerous. Perhaps that is why he was smeared by several newspapers, which tried to claim he had got his facts wrong. He hadn't. His book, which was originally published by Harrap in 1976, has been reprinted twelve times since by Grafton Books of London.

The whole Ripper saga has been confused, perhaps deliberately, by various conflicting claims—the most ridiculous being
that Moscow had sent a Russian spy over to kill those prostitutes, just to embarrass the British government. No, that is not
one of those anti-Kremlin jokes. The claim appeared in *Things
I Know* by William Le Quex in 1923.

Three years after the Ripper killings, Queen Victoria decided
that Prince Eddy, then second in line to the English throne,
needed a strong-willed wife to keep him in line. The woman
chosen was the Princess of Teck, and she agreed to take on
the job. Their marriage was planned for February 27, 1892,
but Prince Eddy died suddenly six weeks before that. The
Buckingham Palace version is that he died of influenza, though
other sources insist it was caused by a softening of the brain
due to syphilis.

His intended bride plunged herself into one year of mourning for her lost beloved. After emerging from that mourning,
Queen Victoria called her in and told her there had been a
change of plan and she must marry Prince Eddy's brother,
Prince George.

We are told she was "affronted and embarrassed" by the
idea. But the truth is, she was most eager to be a possible
queen and willingly obeyed. The story was then put out that
the Princess of Teck had never really loved Prince Eddy but
had always secretly loved his brother George, and the couple
were speedily married two months later in July 1893. They
enjoyed their honeymoon at Sandringham—where poor
Prince Eddy had died just eighteen months earlier!

When King Edward the Seventh went to heaven in 1910,
Prince George and his wife came to the throne as KING
GEORGE THE FIFTH and QUEEN MARY. The diaries of various
royals unnecessarily confirm that their marriage was one of
total convenience and that no love was involved on either side.
But the public was later told that their marriage developed
into "a deep and lasting love."

Although she was a very German lady with not a drop of
English blood in her veins, Queen Mary's ramrod-back de-

portment was seen to epitomize British royalty for over forty years. Her regal appearance hardly changed. Jeweled toques topped her tightly packed curls, and there was always the same style of coat and silver-topped cane. Her loyalty to the Crown was beyond any possible criticism—even to the point, as we have seen, of being willing to die for it rather than endanger the coronation of her grandchild, Elizabeth, in 1953.

There has never been one breath of sexual scandal about her. It is not unkind to emphasize that she had not the slightest interest in sex. Some historians have made this abundantly clear by recording her own comment that when her husband did visit her royal bedchamber to provide heirs, she "closed her eyes and thought of England."

This does not mean Queen Mary's character had no blemishes. The big skeleton in her cupboard is that she was "unfortunately afflicted with kleptomania." This is a disease affecting only the rich. When poor people steal, they are thieves. If Queen Mary liked a Georgian snuff box or a similarly valuable silver trinket when visiting the home of a friend, she swiped it.

So many aristocrats complained to Buckingham Palace about her theft of their *objets d'art* that Queen Mary's lady-in-waiting was told to watch her like a hawk when she went visiting. If she slipped something into her handbag, the lady-in-waiting would later retrieve it and mail it back to the owner with a covering letter stating that it had been taken "by mistake." Some psychiatrists say this kind of unnecessary stealing, particularly shoplifting by rich women, is a subconscious substitute for sex.

Queen Mary was a disinterested mother who gave little love or cuddles to her children. When she died in 1953 her son, then the Duke of Windsor, told his wife, Wallis: "I'm afraid the fluids in her veins have always been as icy cold as they now are in death."

Queen Mary's husband, George the Fifth, had sowed plenty of wild oats in his youth. At one time he shared a girl with his sexy and alleged "Ripper" brother, Prince Eddy. They kept her in a luxury apartment in London's St. John's Wood area. But, after marrying, George is said to have settled down, and we are told he was a "paragon of virtue."

There is, however, one strange story about George. This surfaced in a French newspaper named *The Liberator* when he became king. Copies of the article were sent to all members of Parliament—obviously to ensure that the royals did not get the news smothered. It was terribly embarrassing because the story claimed that while in Malta, when he was still Prince George, the king had legally married a British admiral's daughter, Mary Culme-Seymour, and had sired several children by her.

This was political dynamite because, if true, those children were claimants to the English throne. Furthermore, it was alleged that Prince George had decided to abandon Miss Culme-Seymour only when his brother Eddy died and the royal family delicately pointed out to him that, as second in line to the throne, he should quickly discard this little commoner.

The journalist who wrote this story was an E. F. Mylius and not surprisingly, he was charged with writing lies. If he had been allowed to get away with it, some nasty-minded people might have thought that King George's marriage to Queen Mary was not legal, which would have meant that her children were illegitimate.

During the court hearing evidence was given that, quite apart from never having married Prince George, Mary Culme-Seymour had not even met him during the years in question (1879 to 1898). Journalist Mylius was found guilty in 1911 and sentenced to one year in jail. After serving his sentence, he had a pamphlet published in New York in which he produced evidence, in the form of British newspaper clippings, that witnesses had lied at his trial.

This showed that Prince George had, in fact, met Mary Culme-Seymour in August 1891 when she opened the dancing with him at a large ball in Portsmouth. Ah yes, said Mary Culme-Seymour, "I had forgotten about that." Mr. Mylius, who was still unable to get the justice to which he said he was entitled, commented that he found it rather difficult to believe a pretty young lady could forget the great honor of opening the dancing at a ball with a handsome prince.

In 1917, toward the end of World War I, the British public developed such a hatred of anything German that they kicked innocent little dachshund dogs in the streets. Some people even suspected the German-blooded British royal family of having secret sympathy for the hated "Kaiser Bill"—Wilhelm the Second—who was, of course, Queen Victoria's grandson.

The publicity experts at Buckingham Palace urged King George to change the German name of his royal British house from Saxe-Coburg-Gotha. So the magic royal wand was waved and overnight the royal family became known by the much more English-sounding name, Windsor.

Another patriotic little story about King George is that he did not want to give Britain's Victoria Cross medal to America's "Unknown Soldier" when that revered serviceman was to be buried in Arlington National Cemetery in 1921. Quite definitely not, said the king. Even when his advisors explained that America had given its Congressional Medal of Honor to the British Unknown Warrior one year earlier, George was not impressed.

He said it was ridiculous to compare the illustrious British VC with the Medal of Honor, which, he sneered, having been instituted in only 1862, "has no history behind it." The British VC, by the way, was instituted by Queen Victoria in 1856. So six years was obviously a long time in the mind of old George Five. In the end, however, he was forced to grant the VC to the anonymous American when the Whitehall diplomats pointed out that America was a valuable ally and could not be insulted with a lesser medal.

Fate sometimes plays cruel tricks, King George the Fifth insisted that his royal physician, Bernard Dawson, be sworn of the Privy Council—an extremely unusual honor for a doctor. As we have seen, Lord Dawson of Penn went on to thank King George by murdering him in 1936.

When that happened, George's son came to the throne as KING EDWARD THE EIGHTH. Although his marriage to Wallis

Simpson was described by Winston Churchill as "one of the greatest love stories of history," King Edward had sown a lot of wild oats in his youth. But he was double smart. To prevent the gossip columnists writing scandal stories about his affairs, he only bedded married women. Their husbands did not complain as it usually raised their social standing and even helped them make better contacts in the City, which brought them juicy contracts.

One of his mistresses was Giulia Barucci. She was so open about it that she went around London bragging "I'm the greatest whore in the world." He also had a fling with Gloria Vanderbilt's twin sister, Thelma, Lady Furness. She was not his first titled lady. At the age of twenty-one he had quenched his sexual thirst with the much older Lady Coke. But it wasn't the real thing so he moved on to Freda Dudley Ward, wife of a Liberal member of Parliament.

Later, in September 1934 (when Wallis Simpson was away on vacation), it is said he dallied with Freda's sister Vera, who gave birth to a boy in mid-1935. After being educated at Eton, that boy become an actor and played the part of Ned opposite Marlon Brando in the 1962 film *Mutiny on the Bounty*. His name is Tim Seely, and in March 1988 the British Daily Express ran a front page story naming him the Duke of Windsor's "secret son."

In this article, fifty-three-year-old Mr. Seely admitted that he bore an extraordinary resemblance to the duke. "It is something I have had to live with most of my life," he said. But it has not hurt him socially. He still rides to hounds with the upper set—sometimes in the company of Prince Charles.

When King Edward the Eighth abdicated for the love of Wallis Simpson and went into exile as what the royal family described as the "Puke of Windsor," his brother took the throne as GEORGE THE SIXTH—although all his family called him Bertie.

As a child he was knock-kneed so they put his legs in painful iron braces to make him walk properly and appear perfect. It didn't work. To make matters worse, his father, King George the Fifth, was a bad-tempered old bully when it came to disciplining kids and would threaten to punish the left-handed little weakling if he didn't stop whining. That is probably why the highly nervous Bertie became terribly shy, developed an appalling stammer, nervous facial twitches, and a chronic stomach complaint.

When Kingship was unexpectedly thrust upon him in 1936, he told his wife he was terrified he would be unable to cope. Without that wife, he never would have managed. In truth, Elizabeth was the real ruler behind the throne but, just like any loving wife, she gave the outside world the impression that he wore the trousers. Even more shrewdly, she pressed the point that her husband was a shy and sensitive man who, in spite of his terrible stammer and ill health, was absolutely determined to be a good king for them. Pure unadulterated brilliance. No wonder the British public came to love and admire him.

Nobody in the history of the British royal family has ever manipulated the media as brilliantly as Elizabeth Bowes-Lyon—who was later to become world famous as the "Queen Mum."

In 1940 when Buckingham Palace was slightly damaged by a German bomb, she took full public relations advantage by telling journalists: "I'm glad we have been bombed. It makes me feel I can look the [badly bombed] East End in the face." No wonder Adolf Hitler had earlier told his Nazi propaganda expert, Joseph Goebbels, to describe her as "the most dangerous woman in Europe."

The Queen Mum scored another victory during World War II. With the help of her husband, she gave the royal family the appearance of being typically "English" once more. She helped to condition the British public into forgetting about the German blood in the royal veins and the incredible background of names such as Schleswig-Holstein-Sonderburg-Glucksburg, Saxe-Coburg-Gotha, Wurttemburg, Teck, Hanover, and Wettin. Yet even today, the real top-drawer aristocrats smile patronizingly at the Royal House of Windsor, saying "They are still Krauts after all, old chap."

Although she was born in England, the Queen Mother usually described herself as a Scot. Great mystery surrounds her birth. It is definite that her mother, Lady Glamis, gave birth to her in August 1900. But incredibly, nobody seems willing to say where. Her father, Lord Glamis, illegally forgot to register the birth, and for that he had to pay a fine of seven shillings and sixpence. And when he did register the birth he deliberately, or accidentally, gave the wrong place of birth—for which he could have been fined under the Forgery Act.

So where was the Queen Mum born? In her wickedly irreverent book *Queen Elizabeth, a Life of the Queen Mother* (Viking, 1986), the brilliant writer Penelope Mortimer tells us that the odds are strong that she was born in the backseat of a horse-drawn vehicle going through central London (or parked under a lamppost). When asked to confirm or deny this, the Queen Mum answered, through a spokesman, that she "had no interest in the subject."

Way back in 1923, when Elizabeth Bowes-Lyon married her husband in Westminster Abbey, she showed that she understood all about the mystique of monarchy—by agreeing with the archbishop of Canterbury that the BBC should not broadcast the ceremony over the radio. Why not? Because "Some disrespectful people might hear it while sitting in public houses with their hats on!" She was obviously referring to her disgustingly vulgar working-class subjects, because the more refined English do not wear hats when they sit in up-market hotels and cocktail bars.

The Queen Mother also understood pictures. Skim through any of the thousands of photographs showing the Queen Mum standing outside Clarence House celebrating one of her many birthdays and you will see that she usually tilted her head slightly to one side. Some Hollywood film stars can learn from that clever trick as it puts "movement" into what could otherwise look like a stiff or posed picture. Whenever the Queen

Mum did it, she gave the impression that she was nodding to each and every one of us. Pure genius!

Just like Queen Mary, there has never been one breath of sexual scandal associated with the Queen Mother although several gossip columnists forecast she would marry her long-time friend, Sir Arthur Penn, after her shy, sensitive, and re-tiring husband died. But obviously, Sir Arthur was not one of the marrying kind.

The only commoner we know to have kissed the Queen Mum full on the lips was the American president Jimmy Carter. He clearly did not turn her on, as the comment she leaked to the press was: "He will *never* be forgiven for that!"

When King George the Sixth died of lung cancer in 1952, his daughter came to the throne as QUEEN ELIZABETH THE SECOND. Just like her mother, she has a perfect genius for the right kind of publicity. Perhaps the best example of this came when a TV film unit was allowed to photograph her enjoying a family picnic in the grounds of her holiday home at Balmoral.

The Queen shrewdly made a point of allowing the camera-men to film her helping to wash and dry the plates and cutlery at the end of the meal. And, exactly as intended, this down-to-earth ploy gave tremendous psychological reassurance to mil-lions of suburban housewives who turned to their husbands snoring on the sofa and cooed: "There you are, you see. She's just like us really, isn't she?"

Without a shadow of doubt Elizabeth the Second is the best queen the English have ever had. The only scandalous thing we have read about her was written by Nigel Dempster, who has long been famous as the high society and royal gossip columnist of the *Daily Mail*. On the very first page of his super-spicy book *H.R.H. The Princess Margaret. A Life Unfulfilled*, (Quartet, 1981) he wrote that when Queen Elizabeth married her first love Prince Philip, she was: "as virginal as her epon-ymous ancestor."

WOW! That raises a most fascinating question: Did Nigel not know that the queen's ancestor, Elizabeth the "Virgin Queen" who ruled from 1558 to 1603 was certainly no virgin? That she had several young lovers *and*, at the late age of fifty-four, even started a twelve-year affair with a handsome young fellow of twenty? Really, Nigel, you should never have associated *our* Queen Elizabeth with a shady lady like that.

To be fair though, it must have been a genuine mistake because the Queen's name had never been tarnished by British press speculation about her love life.

In fact, only one English person has ever dared to mention the subject of sex in relation to Her Majesty the Queen. This was her son Prince Andrew, who once said: "You know, the one thing I can never possibly imagine is my mother and father making love." Randy Andy's comment is said to have made his father "furious" and "outraged" his mother. (Source: *Charles and Diana* by that entertaining American writer, Ralph G. Martin [Grafton Books, 1986.])

In 1941 an American named Henry "Chips" Channon made the most astonishing prediction. Writing in his diary, he stated that the handsome Philip of Greece "is to be our Prince Consort, and that is why he is serving in our Navy."

This really was an incredibly accurate prophecy because Prince Philip did not propose marriage to Princess Elizabeth until six years later in 1947—and even then, it took the world by surprise.

How on earth could Henry Channon have been privy to such a secret? The answer is that he received it from an impeccable source—none other than Princess Nicholas of Greece, who told him, on January 21, 1941, that a marriage was "being arranged" between Philip and Elizabeth!

This rather contradicts the fairy-tale love-at-first-sight stories churned out by Buckingham Palace. Could this be the reason why Sir Henry "Chips" Channon has been denigrated by many historians as an "unreliable diarist" and "an American snob who was obsessed by titles and money?"

Overseas newspapers and magazines have nibbled at the subject of the Queen's marriage to Prince Philip by claiming (about seventy times) that it was "on the rocks," that he had a long-term woman friend who had an interest in a top-society nightspot, and that there was a gigantic cover-up about his alleged involvement in the infamous Profumo "sex and secrets" scandal—which, in truth, should have been tagged the Stephen Ward scandal.

The son of a vicar, Ward was born in 1912 and traveled to America when he was twenty. After studying at the College of Osteopathy in Missouri, he returned to London as a doctor and achieved success by giving relief to top-drawer people suffering backache and other muscular problems—such people as Winston Churchill, Mahatma Gandhi, Paul Getty, Nancy Astor, and Ava Gardner.

A sophisticated and elegant man, Stephen Ward also sketched portraits in pencil and crayon of such famous people as Princess Margaret, the Duke of Kent, the Duchess of Gloucester, and Prince Philip. Ward was not your tradesman's entrance type of artist who was summoned to the palace to do his sketches. He was friendly enough with Prince Philip to have lunched with him in central London. Philip also visited Ward's home several times.

In the early sixties, Ward turned from giving the nobility relief for their back pains and focused on other parts of their anatomy. He introduced them to pretty young working-class "models," such as Christine Keeler and Mandy Rice-Davies— who were only too delighted to oblige the noblesse by having sex with them, and even dressing up as nannies and spanking their bare bottoms for them.

In 1961 a British Intelligence officer named Keith Wagstaffe recruited Stephen Ward as an undercover agent for MI5's Counter Intelligence Section. Ward's assignment was to persuade a London-based Russian naval attaché, Captain Eugene Ivanov, to defect. The son-in-law of Alexander Gorkin, the chairman of the Soviet Supreme Court, Captain Ivanov was known to be an undercover agent for Russian Military Intelligence (GRU).

Ward introduced Christine Keeler to Ivanov, but the plot

went seriously wrong because Ward had also introduced Christine to John Profumo, who was then Her Majesty's war minister. Profumo had several sex sessions with Christine, the most famous of which took place in the bed of Profumo's actress wife, Valerie Hobson. When Fleet Street became aware of this adulterous relationship, Profumo tried to silence them by lying to Parliament that he had never had sex with Miss Keeler and that he would sue the pants off anyone who dared to say he had.

When he was proven to be a liar, Profumo was forced to resign in total disgrace. This made world headlines and brought horrendous embarrassment to the Tory government. To deflect the massive media heat from government, the British Establishment had to find a scapegoat. The man chosen was Stephen Ward, who was framed on a charge of living on the immoral earnings of Christine Keeler and Mandy Rice-Davies —although both women later admitted telling lies against Ward after being subjected to police pressure.

Stephen Ward denied all the charges. He said he had first been introduced to Captain Ivanov by Sir Colin Coote, then the managing editor of the British newspaper the *Daily Telegraph*. (Sir Colin, who died in 1979, is now known to have been a long-term propaganda agent for Britain's MI6.) Ward said he had later been recruited by British Intelligence to persuade Captain Ivanov to defect, but that the intelligence boys had disowned him in order to avoid becoming embroiled in the Profumo scandal. Ward was not believed at the time but, years later, several MI5 officers admitted to various journalists that Ward had been telling the truth about being a secret agent for the British.

Anyone wishing to know the full details can read two excellent books on the subject. *An Affair of State: The Profumo Case and the Framing of Stephen Ward* by Phillip Knightley and Caroline Kennedy (Cape, 1987) and *Honeytrap* by Anthony Summers and Stephen Dorril (Weidenfeld, 1987). Both books convincingly demonstrate how Stephen Ward was framed by evidence produced in a manipulated trial, during which some of the main prosecution witnesses were later shown to have lied under oath.

Stephen Ward cheated the court that found him guilty of living on immoral earnings. He committed suicide by swallowing a large number of Nembutal capsules. At the time, his sketches were on show in a Bloomsbury art gallery and something very odd took place there. A tall, elegant, and well-spoken man walked into the gallery, selected every drawing of the royal family, including those of Prince Philip, paid £5,000, and carried them away without giving his name. The man was never identified although some journalists insist he was Sir Anthony Blunt, the British Intelligence agent (later exposed as a double agent for the KGB) who then worked at Buckingham Palace as Keeper of the Queen's Pictures.

So ended Britain's favorite high society bedtime story. Until 1987, that is. This was when Anthony Summers (co-author of *Honeypot*) made the shocking allegation that photographs removed from the home of Stephen Ward showed a likeness of Prince Philip alongside various naked girls. Buckingham Palace did not react publicly to this distressing claim, although they let it be known that they considered it "outrageous."

Today Christine Keeler lives quietly in a modest, low-rent apartment about two miles from Buckingham Palace in an area of London aptly named World's End.

Millionaire John Profumo is still a member of high society. After cleansing himself morally and publicly by working for a charity in London's East End, Buckingham Palace arranged for him to be photographed shaking hands with Queen Elizabeth in 1971. In effect, this gave the royal seal of approval to the man who once laid a dubious lady on his wife's bed and then lied to Parliament. Four years later, just to prove that Her Majesty's highly bred, elegant, honorable, repentant and totally reformed former Minister of War really had been completely forgiven, the Queen agreed to the now sweet-smelling Profumo being accorded the high honor of the CBE—Commander of the British Empire.

Another naughty fellow who was given the cleansing royal handshake in public was Major Ron Ferguson, the father of Prince Andrew's wife, Fergie. His sexy saga exploded in May 1988 when the British Sunday newspaper *The People* front-paged a fantastic scoop disclosing that Fergie's dad had been a regular punter at a high-class London brothel.

Covering its back against the predictable cries of "Lies, all damned lies," the newspaper published a photograph of the galloping major licking his lips salaciously as he emerged from the brothel, which, for reasons of "respectability," called itself the Wigmore Massage and Sauna Club. *The People* not only told how Fergie's father had paid blonde, brunette, and redhead pro-stitutes, but also published photographs of three of the girls he had paid for sex and other excitements! One of the girls described what the major looked like without his clothing—including his freckles and "patchy scabs like eczema."

Even more revealing was that during one session with a girl, Fergie's father had asked her: "What does it feel like to be dealing with royalty?" We can't help wondering whether the girl was quick-witted enough to ask him what it felt like to be felt by a nonroyal.

The sexploits of Fergie's disgraced dad presented the Queen with a major problem. Although she was privately "fuming with anger" about his immorality (or stupidity in being caught), it was more important to put on a great display of royal family unity. Ron Ferguson could not be fired from his job as polo manager to Prince Charles, and he could hardly be dropped socially as this would have been demeaning for his daughter, Fergie, the Duchess of York—as well as reflecting badly on Fergie's husband, Prince "Randy" Andy.

That is why, on June 5, 1988, the Queen gave Major Ron Ferguson that now-famous "royal pardon" handshake at a polo match. Not by coincidence, several press cameramen were there to record the royal "cleansing"operation, and next day, most British newspapers carried photographs of the Queen clasping the hand that had caressed those blondes, brunettes, and redheads. That handshake was a clear royal message to the terrible tabloids, which had been enjoying themselves immensely. It was: "Now shut up."

But five days later, *Sun* columnist Fiona Macdonald Hull, who is as delectable to behold as she is to read, accurately placed her finger on the public pulse by writing: "The Queen has muddled me. She obviously thinks that perverts who consort with prostitutes are acceptable, while tax-fiddlers are not." (Fiona mentioned tax-fiddlers because earlier, the Queen had withdrawn the Order of the British Empire decoration from Britain's most-loved jockey, Lester Piggot, who had been jailed for failing to disclose all his earnings to Her Majesty's tax inspectors.)

Fiona criticized the Queen for removing jockey Piggot's OBE with one hand "while she extended the other to warmly greet Major Ronald Ferguson." Pointing out that it was the Queen's duty "to set us all a moral example," Fiona said that if any ordinary person had done what Major Ferguson had done, he or she would not be allowed within "spitting distance" of the Queen.

"But when it's one of their own, the Royal Family will forgive ANYTHING. And you or I can either like it or lump it." Fiery Fiona ended her article by stating: "If this is what Monarchy is all about, we are better off without it."

Another married member of the royal family who caused great embarrassment to the Queen was Princess Michael. In 1985 a British paper secretly photographed her entering a London house for an alleged overnight rendezvous with Texas billionaire John Ward Hunt. But this whole affair was solved when Mr. Hunt, being a perfect gentleman, refused to say one word to the British press and flew back to America on the next possible flight.

The Queen then ordered Princess Michael to repair some of the damage caused to the family name by being photographed in public cuddling up to her long-suffering husband, Prince Michael, and gazing into his face with absolutely sincere love and total adoration in her eyes. Although she did it brilliantly, most people were not really fooled.

Despite all the sexual scandals and problems the Queen has had to tolerate within her family, her marriage to Prince Philip is perfect—as far as the British public is concerned. They know that their Queen, as Defender of the Faith, is a good woman. She must be, because she is the keeper of the nation's conscience and the guardian of Britain's (fast-sliding) morality.

And publicly, Elizabeth and Philip really do try to set a good example. They are proud when their children score a success, they adore their grandchildren, and Philip is always loyal and protective toward his Queen to the point that we are told her face still "lights up with pleasure" when she sees him walk through the door.

Throughout the 1980s, the royal with the biggest marriage problem was PRINCESS ANNE—though Buckingham Palace tried to convince the public otherwise. When it comes to Anne and her husband, Captain MARK PHILLIPS, we have personal knowledge that the palace is not always totally honest. In April 1973 (when it was no secret in Fleet Street that Mark was in love with Anne), we applied to the palace for guidance in connection with interviewing the handsome twenty-four-year-old Queen's Dragoon Guards officer.

After telling us how to contact Mark, the assistant press secretary at the palace, Anne Hawkins, warned us: "For goodness sake, don't bore him with questions about Princess Anne. You pressmen seem determined to marry him off to the princess, but they are both on record as having said there is no romance as such."

One hour later Mark Phillips gave us an exclusive interview, which was published. Mark has been unkindly described as "Foggy" by some members of the royal family who seem to think he is "thick and wet," but we found him to be totally straight, honest, and intelligent. Obeying the palace request, we conducted that interview without once mentioning Princess Anne's name. How stupidly trusting we were! Six weeks later Anne and Mark announced their engagement.

Yet even then we did not expose Buckingham Palace's double-talk. Instead, to keep in their good books (so that they would continue to feed us other stories), we wrote a shoe-licking story telling how wonderfully Mark had proposed to Princess Anne. In our published article, to our everlasting shame, we repeated how "even the Royal corgis had seemed to approve" and how they had wagged their tails when the engagement was officially announced. Now there's a perfect example of how a Buckingham Palace tale wagged the dog.

Princess Anne married Mark in November 1973 but the couple, although they continued to share their home in Gloucestershire, agreed to go their separate ways in other ways in 1980, at about the time Princess Anne was pregnant with her second child, Zara (Arabic for "Morning Star"). They led virtually separate lives but, to keep the public happy, they pretended to be man and wife for the sake of appearances. Yet even when they made official overseas trips together, they stayed in separate hotels.

This did not go unnoticed by the gossip columnists, who repeatedly told their readers that Princess Anne's marriage was on the rocks, although the Buckingham Palace press presti-digitators, with hands on heart, solemnly denied any such thing. There was no doubt about it though, because Mark was regularly photographed in the company of various women—including the controversial good-time naughty girl Pamella Bordes, who made world headlines when it was discovered that she had increased her bank balance by spending romantic £500 evenings with various politicians and millionaires she had met while working as a researcher in Parliament.

Princess Anne also made some friends of her own. One of them was her handsome personal bodyguard, Sergeant Peter Cross of the Royal Protection Squad. This affair reached a climax when a Buckingham Palace spy discovered Anne was kissing and cuddling Peter privately, and he was quietly removed by Scotland Yard for being "overfamiliar" with the princess.

At that stage, Peter Cross presumed he had been ditched by Princess Anne because she had tired of him. But later, just before Christmas 1980, when Princess Anne was four months pregnant with Zara, he met her secretly at her Gatcombe Park home and discovered she had been informed that he had left the Royal Protection Squad for domestic reasons.

Realizing that he had been "framed," Peter decided to get his revenge by offering a kiss-and-tell story to Fleet Street newspapers. He is said to have asked for $700,000 on the basis that he had enjoyed a "special relationship" with the princess. He did not get anywhere near that amount, but a carefully worded part of his story was later published by *The News of the World* in September 1985.

It was a fantastic scoop. Peter Cross said he had met Princess Anne secretly on several occasions whenever she telephoned him and asked him if he would like to spend "a day in the country" with her. Sometimes they met at a cottage in the grounds of Princess Anne's country estate but also two or three times at a friend's modest little house in Surrey where they spent several hours together, completely alone.

Their friendship was such that the princess telephoned her former bodyguard to say she was going into hospital to have baby Zara. Next day, on May 15, 1981, Anne telephoned Peter Cross at his home to say: "I've had my baby—it's a girl. We're both fine." One month later Peter was invited to Princess Anne's home for lunch, and after the meal she took him to the nursery to see the baby. Peter said he had given the little girl a teddy bear he had bought for her and, one year later, he gave Zara a jumpsuit for her first birthday.

Buckingham Palace did not appreciate Peter's disclosures one little bit, and, in an attempt to trash his credibility, they let it be known that he was "a vain man who had indulged in several extramarital affairs." Tut-tut. *The News of the World* was proved correct though. In September 1989 it was officially disclosed that Princess Anne and Mark Phillips were to be separated.

This "shocked" those members of the British public who had believed all those denials of a marital rift issued by Buckingham Palace. But some of the damage was quickly repaired by gushing newspaper stories that Anne and Mark still "admire each other" and, although separated, will remain "the best of friends."

It is also reassuring to know that Princess Anne's two children "understand," and that the problem of "sharing" them has mostly been solved by the fact that their son, Peter Phillips (born in November 1977) likes going out with his dad, whereas daughter Zara, who has a much stronger bond with her mother, mostly accompanies her.

The big gossip around London town these days is that Princess Anne will definitely apply for a divorce after paying Mark off with a big cash settlement in the region of $2 million. Not that Princess Anne has any intention of remarrying at the moment. Her friendship with former bodyguard Peter Cross ended in November 1983 when she telephoned him and asked him if he would like to enjoy "a day in the country." He took a raincheck by saying he had a new girlfriend. Peter Cross is now married to Angie, a dental nurse.

The latest man to be linked closely with Princess Anne is the dashingly tall dark and handsome "Tiger" Tim Laurence. Their friendship came to light in April 1989 when a Buckingham Palace servant of humble background who was earning $10,000 a year (live in), became so annoyed by the opulent life-style of the royals that she took possesion of four intimate letters from Princess Anne's unlocked writing desk. The letters had been written to Princess Anne by the Queen's equerry Tim Laurence, and, in them, he made it abundantly clear, that he was madly in love with Anne.

Cleverly using a front man to protect her identity, the royal servant sent the letters to Rupert Murdoch's newspaper *The Sun*, the only newspaper in Britain that has consistently proved that it is not at all overawed or frightened of the royal family.

In this instance, however, realizing that they did not possess the copyright to Princess Anne's letters, *The Sun* behaved impeccably and returned them to the palace unpublished. But word leaked out and the super spicy story was chased by every newspaper. That's when Princess Anne's love life once again hit the fan.

The tragedy here is that Anne is the most honest and down-to-earth member of the royal family. When she married Mark Phillips, it was considered unthinkable that he could remain middle-class Mark without a title to his name. But Princess Anne felt otherwise. She refused pointblank when the Queen offered to give him an earldom, as had been done for the commoner Tony Armstrong-Jones when he married Princess Margaret. Anne said it seemed rather pompous to her that Mark should be given a high falutin' title just because he was marrying a woman who was a princess by an accident of birth.

The same applied to Anne's children, Peter and Zara, who—at the time of writing—are the only members of The Family not to have titles. The Queen was insistent that they should be known as Prince Peter and Princess Zara, but Anne said no way. Her actual comment on this subject was: "They are not royal. The Queen just happens to be their grandmother."

Princess Anne is an original who likes to do it her way. She has no intention of copying Princess Diana's engaging but shrewd way of saying "Cheese" for press cameramen and refuses to behave like a performing seal for them. She prefers to wear trousers, jumpers, and check shirts rather than flashy dresses, saying she would like to be judged by what she does, not by what she wears. Unlike Princess Di, Princess Anne does not have vast walk-in closets containing thousands of garments, and she does not have a private hairdresser who visits her every day. Neither does she have a manicurist in daily attendance, as can be seen from her often chipped and unpolished fingernails.

The hardest working member of the royal family, Anne hates trotting out much of the tripe written for her by Buckingham Palace. Tripe, because she has told friendly journalists that it's often "ridiculously pompous and even patronizing." She loathes pretentious people and also those who show off or crawl to her. She refuses to have the usual army of royal kitchen maids at her country home and keeps a small staff who help her by "mucking in" with the housework, with everybody wearing blue jeans. When competing at horse trials, she likes to drop her Princess title and asks to be known as plain Anne Phillips. In other words, we admit to having a sneaking regard for her.

Compare all that with the Queen's cousin, LORD LOUIS MOUNTBATTEN, he who was Mountbatten of Burma, Viceroy of India, Chief of the Defence Staff, and a truly brilliant but sneaky man who handled himself and manipulated everybody else so well that he was known as the shop steward of the British royal family. That is until 1979, when the Irish Republican Army blew his body to pieces while he was fishing on a small boat near his magnificent Classiebawn Castle in the Irish county of Sligo.

Mountbatten was not only the most crashing snob in royal history but also one of the naughtiest sex-wise. Yet he always managed to get away with it. Most senior British journalists knew that Mountbatten and his vastly rich wife, Edwina, spent most of their married life jumping in and out of other people's beds. It was also no secret that Mountbatten was a bisexual, which might explain why his wife searched for affection in the arms of well-known public figures such as Indian Prime Minister, Pandit Nehru.

Anyone wanting further details about Lord Louis can read *The Mountbattens* (Constable, 1989), written by Lord Lambton who is no amateur when it comes to sex scandals. He was a Cabinet Minister serving as Parliamentary Under-Secretary at the Ministry of Defence and was in charge of the Royal Air Force. In 1973 he was forced to resign after being secretly filmed in bed naked (and smoking pot) with London's then-famous prostitute, Norma Levy.

Millionaire Tony, who now lives in happy exile in a sixteenth-century villa near Siena, Italy, discloses in his meticulously researched book that Mountbatten was not only a charlatan and a snob but also a pathological liar who disguised his ancestry ("pastry cooks, tailors, and pastors") in order to enhance his claims to royal status.

Not mentioned in Lambton's book are the latest and most astounding claims against Lord Mountbatten. Someone in British Intelligence is leaking rumors to authors and journalists that Mountbatten was a Soviet sympathizer who secretly helped the Russians during the Cold War. Equally incredible is the claim that Mountbatten was murdered on the orders of the KGB, as they feared he might have been intending to disclose his role as a Russian agent.

This rumor was ridiculed by some but in August 1989, top British journalist Richard Ingrams opened a new can of worms. In his weekly *Observer* column he stated that Mr. Alan Clark (now Britain's Minister of State for Defence) had told him the same story about Lord Lambton.

It's a strange world. Apart from Her Majesty the Queen, nobody in the royal family is safe from naughty disclosures these days. Except perhaps the Queen's gentle and sensitive bachelor son, PRINCE EDWARD, who was called a wimp by his angry father when he deserted the famously tough Royal Marines in 1987 because he found their assault coarse.

Being a great lover of the performing arts, Edward decided to learn his desired trade from the bottom up by taking a job as a tea boy working backstage at a London theater. But you can safely bet that in years to come he will end up laying them in the aisles as a famous impresario mounting some great stars in a spectacular musical.

At the moment however, central stage is being occupied by the astonishing antics of three of the prettiest young female royals. This unusual soap opera started in October 1989, when newspapers in Italy, France and Germany disclosed that Princess Margaret's unmarried daughter, twenty-six-year-old LADY SARAH ARMSTRONG, was living with her actor boyfriend Daniel Chatto who was described as "the illegitimate half-brother of the two famous movie stars, James and Edward Fox."

Major London newspapers disclosed this to the British public rather tactfully by saying Lady Sarah was "quietly and discreetly" living with Daniel. Sarah's father, Lord Snowdon, reacted by acidly telling a journalist: "Sarah is a student and Daniel is a 'resting' actor. How can they get married yet?"

Another shock for Buckingham Palace came when it was disclosed that twenty-six-year-old LADY HELEN WINDSOR, the unmarried daughter of the Duke and Duchess of Kent, was also "quietly and discreetly" living with her art gallery boss, Tim Taylor.

As both girls are in line to the throne, these revelations caused severe embarrassment to the Queen because she likes to perpetuate Victorian values and cannot possibly be seen to condone any suggestion that her young relatives are "living in sin." She was horrified when she heard that foreign "paparazzi" cameramen were responsible for uncovering such naughty goings on. They had shadowed the two pretty young ladies night and day and had discovered they were keeping their bedroom slippers at the homes of their boyfriends.

But the biggest shock for the Queen came a few days later when her twenty-three-year-old unmarried cousin, MARINA OGILVY, created the most diabolical royal scandal by telling her parents (Princess Alexandra and businessman Sir Angus Ogilvy) that she was several months pregnant by her commercial photographer boyfriend, Paul Mowatt, aged twenty-four. Mum and Dad quite naturally suggested that a marriage should be speedily arranged so that the royal baby would not be born a royal bastard.

Being a fiercely independent girl, Marina said she didn't want a shotgun wedding and that she was determined to live with boyfriend Paul for a while to make sure they were right for each other. But as Paul did not have any money, Marina asked her millionaire father to buy her a house.

Both parents were appalled at the idea of a young lady royal living in sin while carrying a "love child" (only common people have bastards). So much so that they not only refused to buy her a house, they also threatened to cut her off from the family completely. And, as a little taster—to show they meant business—they stopped Marina's monthly pocket money of $420 and also instructed their lawyers to block her from touching any of the substantial funds being held in trust until her twenty-fifth birthday. To round all this off, Marina's boyfriend Paul was told that if he ever darkened a royal doorstep again, the police would be called and he would be arrested.

Marina was so incensed by all this that she went public and gave her story to a British tabloid newspaper. The very first royal in British history to do that! Suspecting that Buckingham Palace might arrange some kind of kidnap in an effort to suppress the story, the newspaper (*Today*) spirited Marina and her boyfriend off to a secret hideaway in Ireland. When the story hit Page One, Buckingham Palace leaked some viciously wounding stories to friendly newspapers. One was that Marina and her boyfriend Paul hit the bottle just a little too much because at least $750 worth of empty liquor bottles had been seen in the trash bins outside the love nest they were sharing.

That shaft was presumably aimed at Paul, to indicate he was a bad influence on sweet naive little Marina. But Marina did not escape the vitriol either. Another story leaked to the newspapers alleged that she was not quite right in the head, poor dear. She had earlier gone through a "personality change" you see. And this had worried her distraught family so much that they had thoughtfully placed her in a posh private clinic in Surrey, where she had spent some time having "psychiatric counselling."

Being mightily displeased by the suggestion that she was off her rocker, Marina made an astounding counter attack by going on television and telling millions of viewers all her problems. The very first British royal to do that! During the program she cried her heart out and begged her parents to telephone her, saying: "I want you to stand by me and love me. I am your child. I want you to understand that this is what I want."

British newspapers had a field day. Some of them lashed out at Buckingham Palace for being "old-fashioned," whereas others said the Palace must not knuckle under to permissive attitudes. The papers were equally divided about Marina. Some described her as "a bewildered and rather naive young mother-to-be," while others portrayed her as "a vindictive and manipulative, Royal brat" who had betrayed her class.

When Marina's parents refused to weaken in the face of all this scandal, she played her trump card and caused another avalanche of bad publicity by writing a six-page letter to the Queen. Starting it with "Dear Cousin Lilibet" (Queen Elizabeth's family nickname) shrewd little Marina begged Her Majesty: "Please help me to save my unborn child." She rounded this off nicely by alleging that her parents had tried to trick her into having a secret abortion during "a routine check" with a top Harley Street doctor.

That did it. Her Majesty the Queen simply could not risk becoming embroiled in a highly religious controversy involving the royals in an alleged abortion attempt. So Princess Alexandra took some of the heat out of the explosive issue by denying she had wanted her daughter to have the unborn baby's life terminated. She said poor little Marina must be confused. In royal terms, that meant: "She's either mad, or a liar."

For some strange reason, Marina suddenly stopped shooting her pretty little mouth off in public. Cynics claim she was paid to shut it. But even then, she still put two fingers up many upper-class noses by moving into the modest terraced home of her boyfriend's parents who live in the relatively social backwater of suburban Kingston. This was a most unusual act for Marina when you know she is twenty-fifth in line to the English throne! Goodness gracious, whatever next?

# 15

---

## *"Some Day My Prince Will Come . . ."*

*T*he only man PRINCESS MARGARET truly loved was Peter Townsend, a slim, handsome man on the brink of thirty, who arrived at Buckingham Palace in March 1944 to start work as a temporary equerry to her father, King George the Sixth.

The appointment was a superb publicity gimmick aimed at boosting the morale of the war-weary British, and it gave the royal family's image a much-needed update because Group Captain Townsend was a brave battle of Britain fighter pilot. His main claim to fame was that in February 1940, he was the first pilot to bring down a German bomber over British soil. It crash-landed near the Yorkshire seaside resort of Whitby.

Today Princess Margaret admits that when Peter first appeared at the palace, she had a terrific crush on him. "But there was no question of romance until much later—as he was a married man," she says. That is quite incorrect. The reason there could be no question of romance was simply that Margaret was only six months past her thirteenth birthday and no man, not even a heroic fighter pilot, could legally have a romance with a girl under the age of sixteen.

The fact that Peter was a married man didn't seem to matter in 1948 when the eighteen-year-old princess was seen dancing, with her head blissfully resting on his chest, in a ballroom in Amsterdam.

Peter Townsend was not divorced from his wife until four years later, in December 1952.

We are told that then, and only then, did Peter fully give his heart to the princess. They were not allowed to marry, though. The evil snake in the woodpile, according to Princess Margaret, was Sir Alan Lascelles, one of the top brass at Buckingham Palace whom she despised because she thought he was a narrow-minded, supercilious old fogey. Although the whole royal family had long known of his love for Margaret, Peter made the big mistake of trying to make it official by telling the all-powerful Sir Alan.

Looking as if his face had been slapped with a dirty old sock, Sir Alan told Peter: "You must be either mad or bad." And from that moment on the British Establishment was united against this jumped-up and divorced palace employee who had the audacity to presume he was good enough to marry an exalted royal.

Everyone in the palace knew about the affair. All the politicians knew. Top society knew, and so did all the leading newspaper editors. But it was kept an open secret. Open to the privileged few, but a closed book to the public because the British newspapers remained loyally mute.

All that changed when Princess Margaret attended her sister's coronation on June 2, 1953. As she stood talking to Peter Townsend in Westminster Abbey, Margaret made the biggest mistake of her life—the kind any woman deeply in love could easily make. Seeing a piece of fluff on Peter's uniform, she carefully picked it off—the universal act of women proclaiming ownership. This possessive gesture was spotted by a female reporter who turned in astonishment to other journalists and said: "Did you see that, did you see that? She picked a piece of fluff off his shoulder!" Hearing this, a male reporter quipped: "Now there's a good story, she must be his bit of fluff."

The British press did not mention this fluff, but the European and American newspapers gave it headlines. It took eleven days before a British newspaper dared to broach the highly delicate subject. The *Sunday People* stated: "It is high time for the British public to be made aware of the fact that newspapers in Europe and America are openly asserting that the Princess is in love with a divorced man and that she wishes to marry him." Then, boxing clever, the newspaper balanced its shocking disclosure by adding: "The story is, of course, utterly untrue. It is quite unthinkable that a Royal Princess, third in line of succession to the Throne, should even contemplate a marriage with a man who has been through the divorce courts."

That was the end of Peter Townsend. He was quickly shunted out of the country as air attaché at the British Embassy in Brussels. The general public was solemnly told that the two lovers did not see each other again for two whole years. Not so. The truth is that Peter Townsend often skipped over to London and secretly met Her Royal Highness several times, and they snatched a few moments of bliss by enjoying "discreet weekends" at the homes of Margaret's trusted friends.

In 1955, when she was twenty-five and, in theory, free to marry Peter if she so wished, the public was told that Margaret had decided against it. "I have reached the decision entirely alone," she said. This was also not true. Peter Townsend was the one who made that decision. But, as it would have been unthinkable for the British public to know that a commoner had refused to marry a royal personage, we were told that Princess Margaret had turned Peter down because she was: "mindful of the Church's teaching that a Christian marriage is indissoluble. . . ."

In his book *Time and Chance* (Collins, 1978), Peter Townsend stated that he had decided not to marry Princess Margaret because he felt he could not have compensated her for the loss of her royal prestige and pay (then $10,000, but today $238,000 a year).

Peter Townsend was wrong. Princess Margaret might have lost her prestige in the eyes of many in the British Establishment, but not in the minds of the public. An opinion poll showed that the British masses were overwhelmingly in favor of the couple getting married. The public mind was eventually proved right, because Princess Margaret was hardly "mindful of the Church's teaching that a Christian marriage is indissoluble" when she later divorced her husband, Lord Snowdon, after many years of married blitz.

As for worrying about not being able to support Princess Margaret, Peter Townsend clearly had not done his arithmetic. It is inconceivable that the British royal family would have thrown her on skid row. To keep up the all-important royal image, they would have been forced to give her an allowance enabling her to live in stylish comfort, just as they did for the Duke of Windsor when he opted out of the royal nest in 1936.

Being worth £6.9 billion (Source: *Fortune magazine*, September 1989), the Queen is the world's richest woman. On the other hand, accepting that she can't really sell such things as her priceless art treasures, jewels, and her crown estates (280,000 acres), her personal fortune might more realistically be estimated at a mere £3 billion.

So, if she had given her sister Margaret the relatively piddling sum of only £5 million, and told her to try to make ends meet on the yearly interest from that, the Queen would hardly have been left short.

Even if Margaret had been given nothing from the royal coffers, she and Peter Townsend would not have starved. Many multinational companies would have gladly paid Peter handsomely, just to have his name on their letterheads—as a board director for prestige reasons.

But it was not to be. By a strange quirk of fate, another woman had thrown herself at Peter Townsend's feet. This had happened two years earlier in 1953 when Peter had attended a horse show in Brussels and pretty little Marie-Luce Jamagne, age fourteen, fell from her horse just in front of him. Ever gallant, he jumped from his seat and went to her aid as she lay dazed on the ground. Romance, of course, did not come until later.

Having lost Peter Townsend, Princess Margaret shut out the pain by becoming a keen jazz, jive, and jitterbugger at London's top nightclubs. She was escorted by a long line of rich and titled boyfriends, but even when she thought her prince had finally come, he always rushed to the altar with some other woman after finding Margaret rather volatile for marriage.

One would-be prince who did measure up to Margaret's expectations was the wealthy playboy socialite Billy Wallace, to whom she became engaged. But he tarnished his gleaming silver armor by having an affair with a lithe and sun-tanned young woman while in the Bahamas, and Margaret dropped him like a hot brick.

Much later, another suitor was Robin Douglas-Home, a society columnist who fell madly in love with Princess Margaret. Eventually he fell foul of her, and it was said that he offered some of Margaret's personal letters for auction in New York. When this act of alleged treachery became known, he was disgraced socially and later committed suicide.

In October 1959 Princess Margaret received a letter from forty-four-year-old Peter Townsend in which he said he intended to marry Marie-Luce Jamagne, then twenty. That very same night the princess decided she would also get married. Her choice was the handsome and talented society photographer Antony "Tony" Armstrong-Jones. Although not a prince, as a distant relative of King Edward the Second, he could claim noble birth.

It was planned that Jeremy Fry, son of the famous chocolate company family, would be Tony's best man, but Buckingham Palace disagreed. Special Branch files disclosed that Mr. Fry had a homosexual conviction dating back to 1952.

Tony had also wanted a man named Jeremy Thorpe to be his second best man, but Special Branch files alleged that he too had homosexual tendencies, so his name was also dropped from the list. This turned out to be a wise decision because although Jeremy Thorpe later became the leader of the British

Liberal Party, he made world headlines in 1976 when Norman Scott, a young male model, told the world that he had been Thorpe's lover. In 1979 Thorpe appeared in court charged with conspiring to kill Norman.

During that infamous trial, the judge had the last word by refusing to allow any mention to be made in court of a male member of the British royal family who had allegedly once been friendly with Norman Scott. Although Mr. Thorpe was found not guilty, two of his three co-accused later admitted, in affidavits to journalists, that they had, in fact, discussed ways of getting rid of Norman Scott. Jeremy Thorpe's political career was ruined.

For his best man, Tony Armstrong-Jones finally chose Roger Gilliatt, the son of the queen's gynecologist. After the lavish fairy-tale wedding took place in Westminster Abbey in May 1960, Tony was made an earl and became known as Lord Snowdon.

As Princess Margaret was barely five feet tall in her stockinged feet and her husband stood at only five feet three inches, the British satirical magazine *Private Eye* told its readers that the couple were "the two highest-paid performing dwarves in Europe." This was a cruel joke, as Tony is touchy about his lack of height. While a student at England's poshest school, Eton, he contracted polio, which left him with a withered leg one inch shorter than the other.

Princess Margaret gave birth to Lord David Linley in 1961 but before her next child Lady Sarah was born in 1964, the marriage had started to crumble and Margaret and Tony were occupying separate bedrooms. Some gossip columnists have openly criticized Princess Margaret for being "unfaithful" to her husband, but their use of that word was rather unworldly. Margaret did have affairs during the later years of her marriage, but she was not unfaithful to him in the usual sense of the word.

When members of the upper classes find that their marriage has lost its sex appeal, they often solve the problem in a highly civilized manner by "doing a deal." For the sake of their children, but also to keep up social appearances, they agree to continue living together but not sleeping together. Each can take a lover on the side as long as it is kept discreet. There is no great secret about this kind of promiscuity. It's just another of those open secrets known to all in high society but concealed from the masses, who must always be set a good example by their "betters." Otherwise they too would join in the fun and games—thus endangering the all-important moral fabric of the nation.

Nobody knows this better than the royals, and that is why, when Princess Margaret finally took a full-time lover, she went to great lengths to keep it a secret—and succeeded for more than two years. She met this young man in the most peculiar way. It was early September 1973—when she was feeling rather depressed and lonely and desperately needed someone to make her laugh. A married couple who were her closest friends decided it would be rather nice to find a witty young man to act as the princess's escort when she spent a few days at a country estate in Scotland.

Not knowing any suitable young bachelors, the couple phoned an elderly society lady in London who knew lots of young men because she enjoyed entertaining them at her home. After rummaging through her three-volume address book, she recommended Roddy Llewellyn, a well-bred but impoverished young man who was working as a $25-a-week researcher in London.

Roddy was contacted and told that his presence was requested at a luncheon party being held for Princess Margaret and several friends in the Café Royal in Edinburgh. On being assured he would not have to pay for the airfare to Scotland, Roddy threw his dinner jacket into a suitcase and took the next bus to London Airport. When he arrived at the restaurant, twenty-five-year-old Roddy could not fail to notice that there was an empty chair waiting for him next to forty-three-year-old Princess Margaret.

It was a meeting of hearts. They adored each other on sight, and later that afternoon the diners drove to the 9,000-acre country estate of Lord Glenconner where several other guests arrived, including Drue Heinz, the vivacious wife of H. J. "Jack" Heinz II, of the American "57 Varieties" canned food family.

That night Princess Margaret and Roddy held hands at the dinner table and then entertained the other guests further by playing the piano together as they sang various popular melodies. Then, when it was time to retire, Princess Margaret said good night to everyone and, as she walked out of the room, Roddy followed her.

There now, isn't that a lovely, heart-warming story? Yes, it really is, and grateful thanks must be given to our source. It appears in chapter 8 of the rollicking book *H.R.H. the Princess Margaret—A Life Unfulfilled* by Nigel Dempster (Quartet, 1981). Nigel, who is married to Camilla, the daughter of the eleventh duke of Leeds, is the extremely well-connected society columnist on Britain's *Daily Mail* newspaper.

In his cleverly worded book, Nigel states that after one year of knowing Princess Margaret, Roddy found that "the physical side of the relationship was proving difficult to sustain." Doubting that he could keep it up, Roddy fled to Turkey for a holiday alone—which upset Princess Margaret tremendously. Nigel Dempster's disclosures infuriated Princess Margaret so much that she gave her royal assent for a book to be written giving her side of the story—which completely ridicules that much-repeated old claim that it is terribly unfair to criticize the poor "defenseless" royals because they are unable to answer back.

The sympathetic wordsmith the princess assisted was Christopher Warwick, the consultant editor of *Majesty*—the best-informed magazine on British royalty. For those interested, it is published monthly from 80 Highgate Road, London NW5.

A gently spoken and sensitive person who adores the arts and interior decorating, Christopher Warwick enjoyed twenty lengthy interviews with Princess Margaret at her apartment in Kensington Palace and then banged out the 191-page *Princess Margaret* (Weidenfeld & Nicolson, 1983). While it was professionally written and entertaining in parts, the book was so friendly that the learned writer on royalty, Tom Nairn, slated it as "a strained cover-up job."

On the first page, Mr. Warwick described the princess as "one of the most fascinating women I have ever known." Referring to Margaret's relationship with Roddy Llewellyn, Mr. Warwick skated over it somewhat by saying it was just "a loving friendship" in which the princess had "found some happiness."

After recuperating during his holiday in Turkey, Roddy was reunited with Princess Margaret, and she flew him off for a restful stay with her at her luxury villa on Mustique in the Caribbean. It was there, during yet another holiday in early March 1976, that Roddy became world famous as Her Royal Highness's secret boyfriend. This scoop was obtained by the New Zealand journalist Ross Waby, who managed to avoid the princess's Scotland Yard bodyguard and sneaked a photograph of Margaret sitting with Roddy at a table outside a beachfront bar. The snapshot was an unusually intimate one for a member of the British royal family as both were sporting casual beach clothing.

When this photograph was published by Britain's biggest Sunday newspaper, *The News of the World*, there was such a scandal that the professional royal critic Willie Hamilton stood up in Parliament and suggested that the luxury-loving Princess Margaret was "a wayward woman" who should be sacked. Princess Margaret's advisors tried to cloud the issue by complaining that Roddy and Her Royal Highness had not been alone when the photograph was taken. A couple of other people had been with them, but the *News of the World* had cut them out of the picture to give the wrong impression that it was a more "intimate" occasion.

This feeble excuse did not wash. The newspaper had done its homework and knew full well that Princess Margaret had not taken Roddy to Mustique several times just to plant cucumber seeds in the large garden she has there.

Lord Snowdon jumped on the bandwagon by saying the photograph of his wife with Roddy had caused him "humiliation" and made his position "quite intolerable." Princess Margaret retorted that his "injured husband" act was ironic because, she alleged, for the previous fourteen months Lord Snowdon had been enjoying a romance with the attractive young Irish-educated divorcée, Lucy Lindsay-Hogg.

Yet no matter what was said, within days of that photograph being published, it was announced that Princess Margaret and her husband had agreed to live apart. As it would have been dreadfully demeaning for a royal to be divorced by a commoner, Princess Margaret applied for the divorce (after settling a reported six-figure sum on her husband) and the decree was granted in 1978 during a speedy 113-second High Court hearing.

Taking full publicity advantage of his now-notorious friendship with Her Royal Highness Princess Margaret, Roddy Llewellyn launched himself into a career as a pop singer. Naturally, he obtained some good publicity in England, but in early 1979 he made the mistake of flying to the United States and appearing on Ned Sherrin's TV show, *We Interrupt the Year*.

After hearing Roddy sing "There's Something About You," one of the panelists on the show quipped: "It should shoot up the charts—to about number 160." An even wittier panelist dryly drawled: "You could dance to that if one leg was shot off." This just goes to prove that some Americans simply do not know how to behave when in the presence of someone who has actually performed, at a piano, with a princess of the royal blood.

Princess Margaret also failed to shoot up the popularity charts when she visited the United States in October of that year to hustle money for London's Royal Opera House. Funds failed to flow in when the Chicago newspaper columnist Irv Kupcinet had the dashed audacity to disclose that Her Royal Highness had called the Irish "pigs" during a private dinner party in Chicago.

During that meal, somebody had mentioned the assassination of the royal family's beloved "Uncle Dickie" (Lord Louis

Mountbatten), who had been blown to smithereens by the IRA two months earlier.

Princess Margaret denied calling the Irish "pigs." It was absolute balderdash and pure bunkum. She had not said anything like that. Not at all, at all. This denial became suspect when Chicago's mayor, Jane Byrne, tried to take the heat out of the highly political subject by saying Her Royal Highness had been talking of "Irish jigs," not pigs. This brilliant rhyming failed to placate the people of Irish background in San Francisco later. They shouted "You are the pig" at the princess and threatened to release a large grunt of piglets in her path.

After her disastrous fund-raising tour, Princess Margaret shot off to spend another rejuvenating holiday with Roddy Llewellyn on Mustique. There she claimed that the "Irish are pigs" incident had just been a cunning IRA plot "aimed at discrediting the British monarchy." This was weird in more ways than one because we are constantly told that the British royals never make comments that could possibly be seen to be of a political nature.

The "Irish are pigs" was not the only mishap to befall Princess Margaret during her American gig. In Los Angeles Hollywood producer Ray Stark had staged a fancy cocktail party where top-flight film stars lined up expectantly for the princess at 6:30 P.M. But she arrived seventy-five minutes late, by which time some of the important celebrities had left, after deciding they had more interesting things to do.

The overworked royal publicity advisors tried to explain this rudeness away by saying Her Royal Highness was unused to Californian punctuality. This excuse was not only pathetic but laughable because it does not take much brainpower to work out that punctuality in Los Angeles is no different from punctuality in London, Lisbon, or Lisdoonvarna.

In 1980 Princess Margaret became friendly with a man named Ned Ryan. Although he was born in Ireland, the princess did not think he was a pig. In this she was correct because Ned is a delightful character. The talented son of a Tipperary farmer, he is a former conductor. No, not one of those woolly-haired virtuosos waving a baton before a melange of musicians at the Metropolitan Opera House. A conductor who collected fares from passengers on London's number 21 bus route.

After working at a big department store in Dublin, Ned moved to London where, in 1964, he worked at Liberty's store during the day and served drinks in a pub at night to earn the rent for his small, $5-a-week bed-sitting room. Later he sold silver and antiques from a wooden stall on the sidewalk of the famous Portobello Road secondhand market where the money-conscious Princess Margaret, wearing large sunglasses and a faded scarf around her head, likes to hunt for bargains incognito.

Ned Ryan quickly became Princess Margaret's favorite companion because he's a no-nonsense type of chap who makes no attempt to hide what his detractors call his "bog background" and exaggerates his thick Irish accent when it suits him. But no ways is he thick. He's highly intelligent and a brilliant raconteur who never needed to kiss the Blarney Stone.

Being Irish, Ned Ryan has a great sense of morality. Once, when he escorted Her Royal Highness to an open-air rock concert, a male streaker ran past. Ned whipped off his dinner jacket and held it in front of Margaret's face so that her royal eyes would not be offended by the man's disgracefully naked navel. That was when the British media worked it out that Ned had a special friendship with the princess. But not all the newspapers reported it as a romance. Instead, they merely reported that "he makes her laugh." This is a coy phrase used by some newspapers to describe a close royal relationship.

Taking the mickey out of this new in-phrase, the British *Daily Mail* wittily described Ned Ryan as "the Court Jester"—this being at about the time when Roddy Llewellyn had apparently stopped making Princess Margaret laugh. But you can't keep a good Irishman down. When Ned was asked whether he and Margaret were enjoying a romance, he quipped: "I'm waiting for Her Royal Highness to become a Catholic before I would even consider marrying her."

Princess Margaret is a great sport. She laughed heartily when this remark was relayed to her, but the Queen put on what Buckingham Palace staff call her "Miss Piggy" look. She doesn't like religious jokes—particularly not when made by an Irish commoner. Although he is not Buckingham Palace's idea of a prince, fifty-six-year-old Ned is now a very successful property developer who remains one of Margaret's close friends.

Roddy Llewellyn, who today writes a gardening column for a British newspaper, married freelance travel writer Tania Soskin in 1981, but he and his wife are welcome guests at Princess Margaret's home.

In 1979 Lord Snowdon married Lucy Lindsay-Hogg, and today they live happily at his $1 million house, which is close to Kensington Palace.

Margaret has only one big love in her heart these days— her two children, who are her only real success in love because she was always a good mother to them. If Princess Margaret was ever neglectful in her public duties, as some critics have alleged, it was usually to be with her kids. She wisely insisted on protecting them from ill health by breast-feeding both from birth, even getting up in the middle of the night to do so— which is rare for a royal. Another thing in Margaret's favor is that she was always totally honest with her children and never hid her highly personal boyfriend problems from them, which probably explains why both are remarkably well balanced and able to cope with life.

Princess Margaret is still waiting for her prince to come, but our palace mole says it is unlikely that she would marry him even if he did arrive. She is far too set in her ways. Once the most social of the royal family, she is now a rather solitary lady who no longer goes out nightclubbing until dawn.

She's still a night owl, though, staying up until the early hours in her twenty-one-room apartment at Kensington Palace. There she sits, in her favorite armchair, often eating her supper from a tray on her lap and smoking cigarettes in that famous long holder, as she wallows in nostalgia watching familiar and favorite golden-oldie Hollywood films on her video cassette recorder.

# 16

---

## *The Rebel Princess*

*T*here is always a "black sheep" in the British royal family and if there isn't, the popular press will quickly create one. Princess Margaret held the title for many years until Princess Anne won it from her by telling press cameramen to "naff off"—which is a royal euphemism for "go forth and multiply."

Today's black sheep is PRINCESS MICHAEL OF KENT who was born Marie-Christine von Reibnitz in Czechoslovakia in 1945. This vivacious blonde Roman Catholic was raised in a working-class suburb of Sydney, Australia, and became a member of the royal family in 1978 when she married PRINCE MICHAEL, the grandson of King George the Fifth.

Usually tagged "Princess Pushy," she is the most maligned and misreported female royal in modern history. If a British newspaper mentions her, the odds are that the story will contain a snide sneer or cheap crack.

In 1985, the William Hickey gossip column of the British *Daily Express* rubbished Princess Michael by describing her as "the divorced Roman Catholic cuckoo in the Royal nest" and in December 1986, Britain's biggest-selling Sunday newspaper, *The News of The World*, gleefully disclosed in a front page story that the princess was a descendant of Count Dracula!

Princess Michael could easily have got her own back by asking the newspaper why, if it was keen on playing the "Sins of the Father" game, it did not mention the fact that Prince Charles was also descended from Dracula (via Vlad Dracul of Rumania) or even that Princess Di is related to Lord Lucan, the high-gambling peer who murdered his children's nanny in 1974 and remains the world's most famous uncaptured killer.

Princess Michael is hardly the most popular member of the royal family. Princess Margaret says she has "that certain nothing." Prince Charles once nicknamed her the "Rent-a-Princess," and Prince Andrew stopped talking to her after she said his wife, Fergie, was "common" and "a frump" who devalued the royal currency.

It is no secret that the Queen also dislikes Princess Michael. In fact, the two royal ladies have been insulting each other for years. Not face to face, of course. That would be far too unladylike. Instead, they do it in the time-honored way by "leaking" little snippets to friends or journalists. Bitchy little tidbits which can always be denied later, if necessary.

The war of words started in the late 1970s when Prince Michael announced that he intended to marry the sophisticated and highly intelligent Baroness Marie-Christine, who proudly told people she was of truly royal stock dating back to Queen Philippa of Portugal.

Queen Elizabeth's reaction was: "She sounds much too grand for us." This light-hearted jibe was made to appear rather bitchier when it was reported in the media and the would-be bride hit back later by issuing the counter-insult: "I may be many things, but at least I'm not boring."

The rift between the two royal ladies widened when Marie-Christine married Prince Michael. Instead of attending the ceremony, the Queen sent Princess Anne and the blushing bride took this as a personal slap in the face.

Marie-Christine was a Catholic and in terms of the 1701 Act of Settlement, any member of the royal family who marries a Catholic must be excluded as an heir to the throne. In spite of great pressure, she had refused to give up her religion, so Prince Michael had to renounce his right as sixteenth in line. Princess Michael, as she then became, took the attitude that the Queen should have honored the marriage ceremony with her presence because Prince Michael, as the grandson of King George the Fifth, was of "truly royal blood."

Indirectly referring to this later, the princess infuriated the Queen by making it clear she felt that Prince Michael was "more royal" than the monarch herself. Queen Elizabeth saw this as a barb aimed at her mum, Elizabeth the Queen Mother who, although by birth a Lady (Elizabeth Bowes-Lyon) was not born a royal.

In 1980 Princess Michael further angered the Queen by writing to the Duchess of Windsor. Addressing the envelope to "Her Royal Highness" (the title always denied to Wallis by the rest of the British royals) the princess stated in the letter that she had "deeply admired" the duke and duchess all her life. Reacting to this, the publicity experts in Buckingham Palace leaked a sneer smear to friendly journalists that Princess Michael was just currying favor in the hope that the senile old Wallis would leave her some jewelry in her will. A few months later Wallis gave Princess Michael a pair of her valuable earrings. Hearing of this, Queen Elizabeth angrily told her: "You must never wear that woman's jewelry in my presence."

Princess Michael put her foot in it again when she asked what kind of clothing she should wear at a state funeral and was told to wear black. The day after the funeral she received a memo from Buckingham Palace which stated: "When I say black, I mean black. Not a black handbag with gold clasps."

The Queen was further nettled when Princess Michael was the guest speaker at a luncheon party and she said: "You may wonder why I always speak of myself and the Prince. This is mainly to avoid saying my husband and I."

On another occasion, the princess arrived nearly one hour

late for dinner being hosted by the Queen and infuriated Her Majesty by saying teasingly to all the seated guests: "Oh, please don't bother to get up anyone."

When she is being interviewed by newspapers whose editors are known to be fiercely pro-Buckingham Palace, Princess Michael cunningly disguises her deliberate verbal arrows against the Queen. A good example of this came when she told a reporter of her great love for cats. This seemingly innocent remark was a sly stab at the Queen—who detests cats and keeps a pack of corgis.

Later, she twisted the knife in the wound by stating on a chat show that she sometimes felt like shooting the Queen's corgis. Queen Elizabeth lost her cool when she heard this and cattily sniped back with: "They are better behaved than she is."

Princess Michael was absolutely right, though. The unruly royal corgis have savaged so many ankles that in late 1988 the Queen called in the now-fashionable British doggie psychiatrist, Roger Mugford. He was assigned to discover whether the corgis were mentally maladjusted due to being the pets of the most important person in Britain. (By the way, if your chihuahua has been savaging sheep lately and you need Dr. Mugford's expertise, his address is: The Animal Behaviour Clinic, Hardwick Court Farm, Chertsey, Surrey.)

The Queen wittily calls her corgis "my dorgies" and in her eyes they can do no wrong. A palace policeman once had his ankle savaged by one of the dogs after he had kicked it. The Queen was not amused and fired him when he wittily explained that he had kicked the dog in self-defense because it had tried to kick him first—with a raised back leg.

The corgis do not eat dog food from a can. Their favorite nosh (apart from ankles) is the best quality liver, fresh rabbit, pork and chicken. Every day at 5 P.M., a footman goes to the Queen's sitting room carrying a tray of dishes containing their meat, gravy, and dog biscuits and Her Majesty dishes out the food to the dogs with a silver spoon and fork.

We do not know what Dr. Mugford discovered when he got

the royal corgis on his couch because, just like any other psychiatrist, he refuses to disclose any details about his patients and their mental problems. But one thing is sure. The Queen's corgis have snapped at Princess Michael's ankles on at least two occasions. There could be two reasons. Either the corgis sense that their mistress dislikes Princess Michael, or they do not recognize her as one of The Family—which boils down to the same thing.

As we wrote this chapter, the news broke that five or six of the royal corgis had savaged the Queen's favorite dog, Chipper, to death. This horrific incident happened at Windsor Castle, and the news was so earth-shattering that *The Sun* (May 6, 1989) covered its front page with the story. One of the tongue-in-cheek headlines above the article was "Grief Over Savaged Chipper." But we doubt whether Princess Michael went into deep mourning. Dear old Chipper was one of the hounds that found her ankles irresistible.

In Buckingham Palace they refer to Princess Michael by the cruel nickname "B.T.L." This stands for "Billiard Table Legs" because, being a six-footer, the princess has very strong legs and even stronger thighs. This is why she usually wears long dresses. During an "off the record" interview with a newspaper reporter, a senior aide at Buckingham Palace bitchily commented: "You will never see Princess Michael in a bikini." This crack spread like wildfire through Fleet Street and, inevitably, a reporter telephoned the princess to ask her what she thought of it. She retaliated by saying: "When you see Her Majesty Queen Elizabeth in a bikini, I too, will pose in one for you."

In 1984 Princess Michael was photographed riding sidesaddle on her horse, which has the regal name State Occasion. It may well be that she rode sidesaddle because a riding skirt was more flattering for her broad thighs than tightly fitting jodhpurs, but Buckingham Palace took it as another slight because, at that time, the Queen was the only royal to ride sidesaddle in public—during the Trooping the Colour ceremony.

When Marie-Christine became engaged to Prince Michael, he was known as the "invisible prince," because of his natural shyness and dislike of publicity. A bowler-hatted soldier, he earned less than $20,000 a year although he worked for intelligence in a section of the Ministry of Defence. Born in 1942, he was christened Michael George Charles Franklin, the last name given because Franklin D. Roosevelt was chosen as his godfather.

Marie-Christine loves Americans. But she once upset Buckingham Palace mightily by telling a journalist: "I feel content in the United States because anyone can make it with normal intelligence and tons of hard work. But in England, you have to fight prejudice."

Yet when it comes to race prejudice, Marie-Christine seems to have photographic-type light meters in her large blue eyes. In the eighties, she upset race relations organizations in Britain by saying: "Wogs begin at Calais." Another gaffe she made was to say: "I suppose your nickname is Chalky?" when introduced to a famous black actor.

After marrying Michael, Her Royal Highness Princess Michael of Kent plunged into work and took on a large number of public engagements. Being a good businesswoman, she made sure she was paid fees of up to $4,000 for some of the commercially linked functions she attended. This was when Prince Charles wittily nicknamed her "Rent-a-Kent," and "Rent-a-Princess."

The British royal family never stop acting as sales reps for British-made products and constantly publicize them on their highly sophisticated business gigs overseas, particularly in the United States. They draw the line at flogging hot dogs and hamburgers however. Not quite understanding the regality of being a royal, Princess Michael agreed to open an American-style fast-food joint in England. The Queen thought this was going just a little too far and curtailed the princess's public appearances by sending around a curt memo indicating that members of the royal family did not lend themselves to "commercial activities." This is most strange because Princess Anne has done that on several famous occasions. So has Prince Charles.

After the Queen penned that "stop making money out of being a royal" memo, Buckingham Palace aides leaked stories to the media stating that the royal family was "appalled and embarrassed" that Princess Michael had accepted money and lavish gifts "from men" (they meant businessmen). Princess Michael must have been mightily puzzled by this, as it is no secret that every member of the royal family has received many expensive presents. Some of them given by foreign rulers for political "goodwill" reasons and some even given by commercial firms.

Buckingham Palace, when questioned on the subject of gifts, will cite a quite bewildering set of royal rules, which cloud the issue somewhat, and then they will add that most of the presents "usually end up going to some charity or other anyway," which, to put it delicately, is not quite accurate. The rules are often bent. For example:

- The costly jewelry and other presents given to Princess Margaret by that delightfully rich couple, Imelda and Ferdinand Marcos, not counting the two large pearls set in a brooch Margaret accepted when she visited the Philippines in 1980.
- The three-strand choker of fabulous pearls given to the Queen by the Emir of Kuwait.
- The priceless jewels given to the Queen by the Sultan of Oman.
- The $1½-million worth of gifts received by the Queen and Prince Philip during their tour of the Gulf in the late 1970s.
- The $124,000 sports car given to Prince Charles by an oil-rich Arab ruler in 1987.
- The fantastic matching set of diamond and sapphire jewelry given to Princess Diana by the Sultan of Oman.

Not all the gifts are big. The Sultan of Oman gave Prince Charles a beautiful dovecot in 1988 and, in the same year, the American oil tycoon Armand Hammer gave Charles and Di a

"Baby Jogger" pram worth $234 for their younger son, Prince Harry. Another little but rather more expensive present was a cute toy car given by the state-owned Jaguar company to Charles and Di's other son, Prince William, for his second birthday. This was a two-fifths lifesize replica of a car which was then on sale to the public for £20,000. But Prince William's special mini-version, which had a 15 mph electric motor, real leather seats, walnut fascia, and plush carpets, cost more than double that to design and make.

When Princess Michael was also criticized for accepting free holidays from rich Americans, she must have wondered why, on two occasions, Princess Margaret had been allowed to accept free deluxe holidays on Sardinia's Emerald Coast from Karim Aga Khan—who used her royal presence to gain publicity for his $136 million holiday complex there. Prince Charles and Princess Di have also stayed at that millionaire's paradise. And, as recently as 1987, John Smith, columnist of the British newspaper, *The People*, hit out at Prince Andrew and his wife, "Freebie" Fergie, for "bumming free holidays" when they accepted a vacation on the Indian Ocean island of Mauritius.

Another criticism leveled against Princess Michael was that she overstepped the mark by accepting free or trade-price designer clothing in return for giving publicity to the people who made them. This criticism was decidedly strange because Fergie and Di have often done just that.

On being forced to reduce her profitable public appearances and other perks, Princess Michael reacted by saying: "I am deeply in love with my prince and I am working to help boost our income." Then, explaining why she loved accepting public invitations, she said: "I genuinely believe that service [to the public] is the rent you pay for living." This was a below-the-belt jab at the Queen's octogenarian mum, the Queen Mother, whose favorite quote (aimed at the working classes) had long been "work is the rent you pay for life."

At about this time, Princess Michael coined a famous quote

of her own by stating that she and her husband would "go anywhere for a hot meal" because they were so short of money. This was seen to be her way of complaining that she and her prince received no money from the Civil List and had to finance all their public engagements out of personal income, whereas the widowed Queen Mother was given a vast amount. (In 1989 the figure was just over $13,000 a week.)

Stressing her Poor Little Rich Girl image, Princess Michael told a journalist that she and her husband could not afford to employ live-in household staff and, like most mothers, she did much of the cooking in their apartment at Kensington Palace and also at their $2 million country home near Stroud in Gloucestershire. Buckingham Palace saw this as another snipe at the Queen Mum, who then employed a staff of more than fifty.

Another royal who dislikes Princess Michael is Princess Margaret, one of her neighbors at Kensington Palace. Margaret has said she would rather "drink poison" than pop in and have a drink with Princess Michael. Margaret's famous high-class carpenter son, Lord Linley (born in 1961), is also not particularly enamoured of the lady in question. When he was asked what he would give his worst enemy for Christmas, he replied: "Dinner with Princess Michael." On hearing of this snide crack, Prince Michael is said to have told young Linley: "Don't ever speak to me again until you apologize, you disgusting boy."

Another royal who steers clear of Princess Michael is Prince Philip. Although he respects her "spirit and cheek," he can't be seen to be too friendly with her in public as this would smack of disloyalty to his wife, the Queen.

Prince Philip certainly sympathized with Princess Michael in 1985 when it was publicly disclosed that her father, Baron Gunter von Reibnitz, had been a major in Hitler's feared SS. He had won the Iron Cross and been honored with the SS "Death's Head" ring. Prince Philip knew the press could have tarred him with the same "royal Nazi" brush had it wished, as his sister, Sophie of Greece, had married Prince Christopher of Hesse and this handsome young prince (who was a brigadier-general in the SS) had been a far more important Nazi than Princess Michael's father.

Prince Christopher escaped being tried as a war criminal because he was killed in a plane accident in 1943 while on a secret assignment for Adolf Hitler, although the palace publicity experts prefer you to believe he was murdered by Goering "after he had spoken out against the Third Reich."

Equally embarrassing is the fact that Prince Philip's other brother-in-law, Prince Phillip of Hesse, had also been a top SS man—yet Buckingham Palace believes he also "changed his mind about being a Nazi" (toward the end of the war) and ended up in a prison camp.

Princess Michael found it strange that although many senior British journalists knew about the Nazi skeletons in Prince Philip's family, they never made a big song and dance about them—as they did with her. Another surprising aspect of this whole affair was that Buckingham Palace had known all about Princess Michael's father being a Nazi long before she married into the royal family. This was confirmed by the publishers of *Debrett's Peerage* (the 212-year-old Who's Who of the aristocracy) when their publicity director, Harold Brooks-Baker said: "I did not know it was a secret. I have heard it mentioned many times."

When the news broke on April 16, 1985, in a front page story headlined: "Princess Michael's Father in German SS," British and European members of parliament demanded an inquiry and leading American Jews condemned "the royal cover-up." The fuss was such that Buckingham Palace ordered Princess Michael to sit tight and make no further comment, saying, quite rightly, that "the public memory is very short" and that the story would soon blow over and be forgotten.

But she ignored the royal command by appearing on TV the next day to explain her point of view. Speaking for just over seven minutes, she said the news had come as a terrible blow because she had loved her father. She won tremendous public sympathy by looking helplessly at the camera and, with tears in her eyes, uttered the brilliantly innocent line: "I wasn't even alive when all this happened."

Although Princess Michael had scored a superb publicity victory on behalf of the whole royal family as well as for herself, the Queen was furious that she had disobeyed orders and gone on TV. Even worse, from the Queen's point of view, was the disgraceful fact that the princess had shed tears in front of millions of viewers. Disgraceful, because the Queen believes that members of the royal family must never be seen to cry in public. Not even at funerals. There seems to be some discrimination here.

- The Queen herself was seen to have tears in her eyes when she visited the Welsh coal-mining village of Aberfan in 1966 after a landslide had killed 116 children and 28 adults.
- Press photographers have seen the Queen's son, Prince Charles, shed tears in public on at least three occasions—at the funeral of the Duke of Windsor in 1972; at the funeral of Lord Louis Mountbatten in 1979; and as recently as March 1988 when his equerry Major Hugh Lindsay was killed in an avalanche of snow while skiing with Charles at Klosters in the Alps.
- Fergie burst into tears waving goodbye to her husband, Prince Andrew, when he joined his ship, HMS *Edinburgh*, for a two-month spell in Australia.

In 1986 Princess Michael hit the headlines again when she wrote a book entitled *Crowned in a Far Country* (Weidenfeld)—the story of eight princesses crowned in countries other than their own. It was a good book, but the princess was proved to have swiped whole passages from other books. Denying she had stolen the passages deliberately, Princess Michael said she had merely forgotten to place quotation marks around notes she had made while researching information from those books.

In the eyes of those who know little about writing, this must have sounded a rather weak excuse. But many professional writers must have sympathized with the princess. Some of them probably muttering "There, but for the grace of God, go I," because plagiarism is a subject riddled with moral ambiguity —even hypocrisy. There isn't a journalist in the world who has not lifted stuff written by another writer. Every newspaper has its own library stocked with books, files, and clippings from other newspapers to which all reporters rush when they need quick information. You can lift facts and clever phrases with impunity, but be careful not to lift long whole paragraphs. Though if you do, make sure you reword them—even if only slightly. This makes your writing "original."

These rules also apply to anyone writing nonfiction books, particularly in the field of biography and history. Plunder other books and manuscripts cleverly and you can easily end up becoming a respected historian. America's piano-playing lecturer Tom Lehrer put it more succinctly when he sang that highly original song on the subject of the unoriginal sin: "Plagiarize, plagiarize, let no one's work evade your eyes . . . only be sure always, to call it—research."

Yet another hazard is that every really professional journalist or author cribs subconsciously while reading great works written by others. In the writing world, we call this "experience"—but because she was inexperienced in the game (of plagiarism), Princess Michael did not fully understand the subtle rules.

That's why she ended up paying costs and damages of nearly $20,000 to Daphne Bennett, one of the authors whose work she had purloined. The princess had also lifted about two hundred recognizable words from a book written by the late Harold Kurtz, but the publisher of that book, Christopher Sinclair-Stevenson, then the managing director of Hamish Hamilton, is a really splendid fellow.

Instead of attacking Princess Michael, he defended her by saying: "Writers 'borrow' from other people's books all the time. I have done it myself." He also accepted Princess Michael's explanation that she had mixed up her research notes. On this subject he said: "The easiest thing in the world, when you are taking notes over perhaps six months or more, is that when you read something you have written you think it was in your own words. It's perfectly understandable."

Another gentlemanly writer is Kenneth Rose, famous in Britain for his frequent and fair-minded articles about royalty in the *Sunday Telegraph*. Bringing some refreshing honesty into the subject of research, he bravely broke new ground in his book *Kings, Queens & Courtiers* (Weidenfeld, 1985) by admitting in the introduction: "I am grateful to those fellow writers whose labours I have pillaged: works of reference and newspapers, memoirs and biographies."

Having been set that admirable example, we wish to place on record our gratitude to the former Australian journalist Barry Everingham whose book *Adventures of a Maverick Princess* (Bantam, 1985) was, for us, a fabulous assessment of Princess Michael and her volatile character. This chapter was greatly improved by some of the facts and clues we pillaged from that invaluable work (and then researched further, of course).

The most interesting clue we found revolved around the biggest mystery of all in Princess Michael's adult life. This was her marriage to, and divorce from, the charming New York banker Tom Troubridge, who married Marie-Christine von Reibnitz in 1971. They were separated in 1973 and divorced by mutual consent in 1977.

Later in that year, when she was planning to marry Prince Michael, Marie-Christine applied to the Roman Catholic Church Courts asking them to annul her marriage. The grounds she gave were that she had wanted children but he had allegedly refused to make her pregnant. The laws of the Catholic church insist that both parties must be invited to give evidence at any annulment tribunal, yet Mr. Troubridge was never asked to give evidence and he was not officially told that an annulment had been applied for. In spite of this strange lapse the Catholic Court granted Marie-Christine her annulment in April 1978!

One month later Queen Elizabeth publicly gave her consent to the marriage between Prince Michael and Marie-Christine. Equally surprising, the Queen gave this divorced Roman Catholic lady the style and title of "Her Royal Highness"—which must have caused the Duchess of Windsor to turn sour in her grave.

Having magically obtained the annulment of her previous marriage, Marie-Christine was confident she would be able to marry Prince Michael in a Catholic ceremony. But just two weeks before the wedding, the Vatican said she couldn't. Pope Paul the Sixth made this decision because Marie-Christine had said that if she had children by Prince Michael, they would be raised as Anglicans.

For those who might think that was a strange decision for a staunch Catholic to take, it is only fair to point out why Marie-Christine wanted to have her cake and eat it. At the time she decided to bring up her children as Anglicans, her thinking processes were probably as follows:

> (1.) My husband is an Anglican and it will obviously please him.
>
> (2.) My husband is the first cousin of Queen Elizabeth and she, of course, is the "Defender of the Faith" (Anglican).
>
> (3.) If my children are brought up as Anglicans, they will not lose their royal rights and they will also retain their place in succession to the English throne.

So, instead of being married in a Catholic ceremony, Princess Michael had to make do with a civil one—after which she set up an aisle-altar-hymn type of campaign against the pope to force him to relax his ban on her church wedding. It took her five years but she won. On July 27, 1983, Pope John Paul the Second agreed to recognize her marriage. Three days later, Princess Michael had her church service, her marriage ring was blessed, and she was accepted back into her own church.

This caused consternation to many who felt such favoritism was unfair to the thousands of Catholics who had remained loyal to their church by turning down marriage chances in cases where their prospective partner had refused to bring up children as Catholics.

Faced with this tricky problem, the Catholic Information Office issued a balancing-act press statement indicating that the princess had promised the church authorities that although her two children (Lord Frederick Windsor, born in 1979, and Lady Gabriella Windsor, born in 1981) would be brought up as Anglicans, she would do "all in her power" to inculcate a love of the Catholic faith in them. Which just goes to show that the formidable royal lady does not lose all her battles.

Princess Michael is not carrying out so many public engagements these days. She has decided to return to writing as a way of making pin money. Her latest venture is a "sensational book about royal prostitutes" (we think she means mistresses)—for which she is said to have been paid a $136,000 advance. Entitled *Kings and Courtesans*, it is being published by Michael Joseph, and we are assured that it will "tell all" about the sexual misdemeanors of various British kings, including the Queen's recent ancestor, King Edward the Seventh and his mistresses Lillie Langtry and Sarah Bernhardt—those ladies you have already met in our chapter "Sexy Modern Royals."

According to the British press, Princess Michael's book is certain to "infuriate" the Queen, who believes that digging the dirt about royal sexual activities is terribly down-market and that such naughty goings-on between the regal bedsheets should remain forever buried under a blanket of silence. Shame, it looks as though the rebel princess, who is proud of her high I.Q. and has often indicated that she finds the Queen not the brightest of personalities, will always be jumping in and out of trouble.

# 17

## *Andy and Fergie*

When Prince Andrew married fun-loving Fergie at Westminster Abbey in July 1986, an American radio commentator told his listeners: "The Archbishop of Canterbury has consummated the marriage."

The Duke and Duchess of York—better known as Andy and Fergie—are accustomed to ribald jokes and ridicule being aimed at them. In fact, they are the British royal family's most criticized couple.

He has been slated for being badly-behaved, arrogant, lazy, spoiled, selfish, fat, and over-sexed. She has been called Her Royal Idleness, Freeloading Fergie and is regularly faulted for being fat, greedy, lazy, having a dreadful dress sense, and behaving in a very un-royal fashion, such as sticking the tip of her umbrella up people's backsides.

In spite of all that, millions of Britons have a sneaking regard for the rogue couple as they are a great double act who keep everyone wondering what they are going to get up to next.

Princess Di—who also stuck umbrellas up where she

shouldn't—can be thanked for bringing Fergie and Andy together. The two girls had moved in the same social circles for years (and it is said they both received their very first "grown-up" kiss from James Boughey, the Old Etonian son of a baronet). In the summer of 1985, Di suggested that Fergie should be one of the Queen's house guests at Windsor during Royal Ascot week. Andy had met Fergie before, but he only realized she had something special when Di threw them together.

The Queen was delighted when Andrew decided Fergie was the kind of girl he could settle down with. Pedigree-wise, Fergie was "suitable." Her father, Ron Ferguson, a former Life Guards major, was not only a close friend of Prince Philip but also his polo manager—and later, Prince Charles's.

The only problem was that Fergie had a "past" that Buckingham Palace knew could not be hidden from the tiresome tabloids. But, after making "discreet inquiries," the Intelligence boys reported back that the two men Fergie had known would, quite definitely, never sell their stories to the press. Apart from not needing that kind of publicity, both were rich men who didn't need media money anyway.

Her first love was the rich Old Etonian Kim Smith-Bingham, who met her when she was nineteen and they spent three happy years together. Her second fling was with the former reporter Paddy McNally, then the manager of racing driver Niki Lauder. Although Paddy was a widower and twenty-two years older, Fergie lived with him for more than two years and even cooked and cared for his two teenage sons. Today millionaire McNally still admires Fergie and they remain good friends— which indicates that Prince Andrew is a wise and tolerant husband.

The prince knows all about newspapers paying big money for kiss-and-tell stories. In 1984 a tall, leggy blonde dish named Vicki Hodge did more than kiss and tell about her love affair with the prince. She wrote it all down for posterity (and prosperity), and *The News of the World* obliged by paying her £40,000 for it. The Queen was most displeased to read how her second son had crushed Vicki in his strong manly arms and made love to her by moonlight in a tropical garden.

Prince Andrew was called a "mug" and a "chump" for having the bad taste to choose a girl like Vicki, but having interviewed Vicki Hodge, we don't think there was anything wrong with the prince's taste: She was definitely one of the most attractive dolly-birds of her day.

Another delectable lady who disclosed intimate details of her love affair with Prince Andrew was a Canadian girl named Sandi Jones. When she was paid an estimated £25,000 for telling a Sunday newspaper how Randy Andy laid his hands around her, other newspapers tried to diminish her social standing somewhat by describing her as a "model." When they put quotation marks around that word, they want you to believe she's something else. In Sandi's case this was not true. She's attractive, brainy, and also a thoroughbred whose father is the popular Canadian Olympic yachting organizer, Colonel Campbell Jones.

Shapely Sandi met Prince Andrew in 1976 when he was a sixteen-year-old student at Lakefield College, Ontario. While the prince courted her, she escorted him to the Montreal Olympic Games. During their "seven months of passion" he was so lovestruck that he suggested they should elope and get married at Scotland's famous Gretna Green—where underage couples can get married without parental consent. Oh, Sandi, you really should have done it. Just for the giggle, quite apart from the fortune you would have made from that spectacular story!

One girl who is definitely sitting on a million is the pretty and petite Koo Stark. That's what she was offered if she would tell all about her famous friendship with Prince Andrew. One million. Not dollars—pounds sterling. An American by birth, Koo knew the prince for about three years. As well as being one of the most beautiful girls in Britain, she was intelligent and well-mannered. This really must be so because she was a welcome guest at Buckingham Palace and also met the royal family at Balmoral. The Queen liked her—and so did Prince Philip.

The Falklands war intervened so Prince Andrew went off and did his duty for Queen and country by serving as a chopper pilot in that highly publicized campaign. The British public never really believed all those Hollywood films in which Errol Flynn single-handedly won World War II against the Nazis, but when Prince Andrew returned from the Falklands, some rather enthusiastic London newspapers tried to suggest he had out-Flynned Errol by winning the Falklands war all on his own. To his credit, the prince brushed some of this flattery aside by modestly pointing out that a few other chaps had fought along-side him and had helped just a little.

Not content with lazing around in London and resting on his laurels, Andy then flew Koo Stark off for a holiday on Prin-cess Margaret's favorite Caribbean island, Mustique. Unluckily for Andy, *Daily Express* cameraman Steve Wood was on the same plane by complete coincidence. Although Prince Andrew and Koo were casually dressed and traveling as "Mr. and Mrs. Cambridge," the photographer recognized them and sent back a scoop of a story in which he described how "Mrs. Cambridge" had curled up in her seat and snuggled her head on the shoul-der of "Mr. Cambridge" during the seven-hour flight.

It really was a humdinger of a story, which became an even bigger sensation when it emerged that at the age of seventeen, Koo Stark had appeared in various soft-porn movies in which she had a sex scene with a very deep-voiced woman artist who wore a square-faced wristwatch, flat shoes, a masculine haircut, and who, judging from all those clues, might just have been a lesbian; had sex in a forest with a young college student (male); and, as a schoolgirl, lost her virginity, full-frontal, to an actor named Andrews.

Prince Andrew was not at all perturbed by these revelations. But the British newspapers, particularly those that regard them-selves as the guardians of public morals, really got their knick-ers in a twist about a royal prince going off with such a naughty little girl. To illustrate just how naughty she was (not to sell more copies, you understand), many papers published steamy film stills of Koo on their front pages.

The sexcitement reached such a feverish pitch that one mass-circulation tabloid even ran an exclusive interview with Koo Stark's cleaning lady who, of course, told all (the little nothings) she knew "about the love affair with Prince Andrew that startled the whole world." Some idea of how the media lost its cool can be judged from the fact that the BBC television's *News at Nine* actually concluded its normally up-market show with a film clip of Koo Stark naked. But, as the cameras traveled down that ravishing lithe little lusty body, they stopped at her waist, presumably in order not to waste film.

Koo's father, Wilbur Stark, tried to take the heat out of the red-hot story by telling the press that his wife, Kathy, had gone on holiday with Koo and Prince Andrew. This was true. But Mr. Stark then added that his wife had gone with the couple to act as a chaperone "under express orders from the Queen."

We don't know whether this was true or not because the Queen speedily denied it through one of her spokesmen. On second thoughts, Her Majesty was probably telling the truth because where was "chaperone" Kathy when "Mr. and Mrs. Cambridge" slept entwined together during that seven-hour flight?

Prince Andrew was ordered back to London and was heart-broken when his mum told him that, for the sake of appearances, he must drop Koo. Being ditched so abruptly in such a nonroyal manner would have made most girls go cuckoo. But not Koo Koo. She behaved like a complete lady and earned the respect and gratitude of the entire royal family when she refused to accept that million for her story. She was astute enough to realize it was not her life story the journalists were after, but the life in Prince Andrew.

In April 1984 Andy made world headlines again when he sprayed paint over newsmen in Los Angeles. For this he was labeled "a spoiled brat" by James Bacon of the *L.A. Herald-Examiner*, who described the incident as "a deliberate act of vandalism." Prince Andrew denied doing it on purpose and said his finger had "slipped." Pouring scorn on that, the newsmen pointed out that immediately after spraying the paint, the prince had grinned hugely and said: "I enjoyed that."

A little-known aspect of this story is that the Queen read the riot act to her son by telephone and ordered him to make a *public* apology to placate the American media. Prince Andrew was aghast. It was unheard of. A member of the British royal family actually having to say "I'm sorry" to a bunch of commoners. And newshounds at that!

The prince must be given full marks for the cunning way he solved his humiliating problem. He made his apology to just one TV crew—in a hurried exchange on a very noisy aircraft apron. There was little meat on that contemptuously thrown bone. He didn't get away with it altogether though. Back home he was called "a yob" by *Daily Express* columnist Jon Akass. Even worse, he also made history by being the first member of the British royal family forced to pay compensation ($1,800) to members of the public—for damaging the newsmen's clothing and cameras.

Seasoned American writers lectured Prince Andrew on his hooliganism, but back in Britain some journalists almost broke their spinal cords leaning backward to defend the royal image. One newspaper said the prince's behavior had been "misinterpreted and overplayed" and that he most certainly did not "overstep the mark in America." Translated into plain English, that meant those American newsmen were liars.

Another paper, realizing that Andrew really *had* been a naughty little boy, but not wishing to print ascertainable lies, merely patted him on the head paternally and said that although his mother knew he had acted "rather foolishly," her main concern now was "to comfort him and restore his shattered confidence." Poor little sausage.

In Wales, that famous land of poets, they have a wise old saying that sums up the paint-spraying incident to perfection. It is: "When a working-class man knocks a policeman's helmet off, it's hooliganism, but if an aristocrat does the same thing, it's horseplay."

One year later Prince Andrew indulged in horseplay again

when he attended the wedding of Carolyn Herbert, the daughter of the Queen's racing manager. As the bride and groom were leaving the church, Andy was seen to sneak up behind Princess Di and pinch her bottom. According to witnesses, Di squealed, jumped forward, and her face turned bright red. Later Andy was told to keep his randy handies to himself in future.

After those worrying years of reckless bachelorhood during which Andy had enjoyed a variety of look-alike plastic blondes, models, sexy starlets and harlots, the Queen must have breathed a huge sigh of relief when her wayward son settled for a girl from a bigger and much more conservative mold. A perfect female equivalent—which seemed to indicate that he had some sense.

Fergie (real name Sarah Ferguson) not only has brains but is a whole bundle of bubbling fun. She's a girl who has a jolly-hockey-sticks approach to life and doesn't feel the need to put on a false act for the press cameramen.

Most people who know about the deceptive and distorting hall of mirrors that is the public relations and advertising world are well aware that with expert grooming, the right clothes—and the full support of the media—any one of a thousand pretty factory girls could be transformed into a Princess Di. But not a Fergie. She's an original. If she would only lose weight and dress properly, she could beat Di into a cocked hat. Fergie has real charisma. She also has a unique sense of humor. Proof of this came when she had a conversation with a public weighing machine in 1989. After it spoke ill of her she screamed: "Oh, you rotter."

The most subtle joke cracked about Fergie's large frame came in September 1987 when a really bitchy female journalist working for Scotland's *Sunday Mail* described Fergie's attendance at a function by stating: "She put everyone around her in the shade."

America's female journalists can also be bitchy. One gave Fergie a thrashing by describing an evening dress she wore in Los Angeles as "something quickly run up from her family's heavily embroidered velvet dining room curtains." On returning to Mother England, Fergie blamed her "bloody melons." This was her way of describing her 38-inch, C-cup breasts, which she said "get in the way a lot" and spoiled her attempts to look slimmer.

The name she gave to her bust was hardly regal, but many British women sympathized with her. They knew full well that those vicious American writers were just jealous because they don't have a wonderful royal family like ours, or wonderfully big tits like ours—so they were just looking for any old excuse to criticize. That's why they picked on our wonderfully old-fashioned British curtains.

Fergie also hit trouble when she made a short speech at a Hollywood dinner and a man at the back of the audience shouted, "I love you, Fergie." She shouted back, "I'll see you later then." This highly suggestive quip delighted the people present but not Buckingham Palace. They pointed out that the Queen would never have said *that*!

Fergie was also criticized in 1987 when she and her husband attended a special viewing of *Beverly Hills Cop II* and she giggled loudly at the forty major four-letter swear words in the 103-minute film. To make things worse, Fergie and Andy were said to have "demeaned the royal family" by seeing that film in the company of Cynthia Payne, a London housewife who had earlier embarrassed the British Establishment by being found not guilty of running a brothel at her home for members of Parliament and other VIPs.

In February 1987 a writer described Fergie as "mesmerizingly vulgar." Commenting on this, Britain's popular TV personality Ludovic Kennedy said "What a lovely phrase." One month later Mr. Kennedy followed this up by stating in a magazine article: "Isn't she awful, isn't she dreadful?"

Fleet Street's women writers have also attacked Fergie for not being a "caring" mother because she usually leaves her baby, Beatrice, at home when she flits off to different parts of the world for one or two weeks. They claim that baby Bea will grow up "feeling unloved and insecure."

If that's the case, then the Queen must certainly feel unloved and insecure because when she was one year old, her parents left her at home and went off on a royal tour overseas—for *six months*.

Also in 1987, several newspapers criticized the fact that the Queen had decided to give Andy and Fergie a $4½ million Southfork-style dream house on five acres (worth $3 million) at Sunninghill Park in leafy Berkshire. Commenting on this, *The Sun* columnist Fiona Macdonald Hull said Britain could do without "pampered Princes"—and that if the monarchy wanted to survive into the next century, it should also do without them.

Another regular criticism about Andy and Fergie is that they are "lazy royal layabouts" who always seem to be on holiday and neglect their royal duties. Here is a list of the public appearances made by each royal during the year 1988:

| | |
|---|---|
| Princess Anne | 665 |
| Prince Philip | 556 |
| The Queen | 548 |
| Prince Charles | 484 |
| Princess Di | 249 |
| Prince Edward | 176 |
| Fergie | 153 |
| Princess Margaret | 145 |
| The Queen Mum | 120 |
| Prince Andrew | 111 |

Buckingham Palace is guilty of cooking the books a little in regard to these figures. Attending glitzy film premieres, first nights at the theater, and delightful evenings at the opera have all been included as "jobs." So have many gala dinners, charity banquets, and champagne and smoked salmon cocktail parties. But, to be fair, having to do those things on a regular basis must be very wearing. Particularly on the liver.

In an attempt to clean up his lazy "clown prince" image,

Buckingham Palace wants you to know that Prince Andrew is now a very hard-working photographer. And to help him start right from the bottom of the ladder, the British Post Office gave him a plum job, taking pictures for a special issue of postage stamps. After watching the prince carry out his first big assignment—taking snaps of the twelfth-century Carrickfergus Castle in County Antrim, Northern Ireland—Fleet Street's tough press camera boys couldn't resist a little smile.

At a cost of about $150,000 to the British taxpayer, hundreds of police and troops were put on full alert as the prince arrived by helicopter. Explosives experts with sniffer dogs combed the castle looking for possible IRA bombs, and the pier below was surrounded by commando patrol boats with frogmen searching underwater for possible mines. Prince Andrew's American photographic guru, Gene Nocan, walked along the pier and set up Andy's $15,000 hassle-free camera on a tripod, measured the light and distance, and double-checked that the camera was loaded with film. Then came the moment we had all been waiting for.

The prince nonchalantly strolled along the pier to his camera and, looking very professional in a natty city slicker's double-breasted suit, tested the light with the palm of his hand, looked up at the sky, glanced nervously at the sea several times (in case an IRA frogman was there to splash water on his lens), pressed the shutter several times and then went off to have lunch with all the local VIPs in another castle while his assistant packed away the camera, tripod, and all the other accessories.

When it comes to photography, some members of the British public harbor positively negative thoughts about Prince Andrew and his wife. In 1987 Fergie asked people to send in snapshots depicting a typical day in the life of Britain—as part of a campaign to raise money for medical research. Buckingham Palace was outraged when hundreds of people sent in disgustingly pornographic photographs. These were hidden away to spare Fergie possible blushes—which she thought was a bit prissy because she would have loved to take them home and show Andy.

On October 4, 1987, a newspaper disclosed that computers had been installed in the private cars owned by Andy and Fergie, at a cost of $15,000. These switched on a warning light if police were operating radar speed traps in the vicinity and Andy was quoted as bragging that the police "can't catch me" (speeding). Describing Prince Andrew as a "roadhog," the newspaper pointed out that such devices were illegal—which is probably why the Queen quickly ordered her fast-living son to get rid of them.

Just four days later Andy took another public beating when he and Fergie returned from a freebie holiday on the fabulous Indian Ocean island of Mauritius. The Boeing 747 they traveled in was supposed to end its sixteen-hour flight at Paris but, as a special little treat for the royal couple, the plane ignored Paris and flew straight on to London, which was a terribly kind thing for Air Mauritius to do.

There was just one little snag. The other forty-nine passengers on that plane were not terribly thrilled. Instead of disembarking at Paris as they had planned, they found themselves landing at London Airport. Not only that. The plane needed refueling, so they had to sit in it for an extra hour. Only then were they flown all the way back to Paris.

The unhappiest aspect of this scandal is that Andy and Fergie must have known that this huge deviation would inconvenience those other passengers. So why didn't they refuse? The fact that they did not does rather support those critics who have repeatedly called them "the selfish royals."

# 18

## Charles and I

When PRINCE CHARLES emerged into this wonderful world at fourteen minutes past nine on the evening of November 14, 1948, the bells of Westminster Abbey were pealed five thousand times, 21-gun salutes were fired by the Royal Navy—and the fountains in Trafalgar Square spurted blue-tinted water for a week.

When Charles was one year old, an official Buckingham Palace press release told us, without tongue in cheek, that he already had six teeth.

In 1954 a British fashion industry magazine decided he was the "Best Dressed Man of the Year," but five-year-old Charles was not particularly impressed by this minor award. One year earlier, he had been named as one of the "Top Ten Best-Dressed Men in the World"—alongside such other notables as Charlie Chaplin, Fred Astaire, Billy Graham, Adlai Stevenson, and (as a shrewdly chosen political "balancer") Marshal Nikolai Aleksandrovich Bulganin of the Soviet Union.

When Charles was sixteen, a classmate at the top snob

Gordonstoun school stole one of his exercise books, and it was sold to a Scottish journalist. A swarm of British Intelligence operatives was sent out to snatch it back, but a German newspaper managed to obtain a photocopy and gleefully published an essay in which Charles described democracy as: "Giving equal voting power to people having unequal ability to think"—which gave a good insight into the royal way of thinking.

Prince Charles got his first taste of down-under democracy in 1966 when his father wisely sent him for a two-term stint at Timbertop, the country annex of Australia's up-market Geelong Grammar School. There he enjoyed the strange experiences of making his own bed, helping with the chores, felling trees, shearing sheep, and swilling out pigsties.

He also experienced his first taste of typical Aussy plain speaking when two or three of the crassly crude and stupid students who disliked Charles described him as that "pompous pommie prince." This came as a tremendous shock to us Brits back home but our wonderfully loyal media softened the blow by assuring us that this outrageously unfair, false, and totally ridiculous insult "gave more value to his acceptance by the majority of the students" who, much more accurately, described him as "a right cobber and a good old sport."

Prince Charles was just a boy on arriving at Timbertop, but he returned to England a man. In October 1967 he went on to Cambridge, where he enjoyed his first real love affair. This was with Lucia Santa Cruz, the tall, dark, and highly intelligent daughter of the Chilean ambassador to London. We are told he loved Lucia a lot but marriage was never discussed. This may have been because she was a Catholic.

After that, Buckingham Palace never stopped leaking regular little snippets that indicated that the prince loved the company of pretty young girls. We even have the evidence of Lord Louis Mountbatten that he had a right royal ball bonking around as a bachelor. Mountbatten told *Time* Magazine that Charles enjoyed "popping in and out of bed with girls." On a royal level, this comment was astonishingly indiscreet, but we presume the wily Mountbatten had an extremely good reason for making it.

Another indiscreet comment came from one of Charles's former girlfriends. A voluptuous blonde, she made the astonishing allegation that even when she was being "extremely passionate" with the prince, she "still had to call him sir."

Although Charles clearly believed in keeping his women servile, he remained the most eligible man in the world. He had everything he wanted: a good home, the best-laid table in the land, a host of servants to look after him, one hundred uniforms, lots of other lovely clothes, and a doting mother who told him what to do and how to do it—without getting into trouble.

In his spare time, he had loads of fun, huntin', shootin', fishin', deer-stalkin', playin' polo, and, on top of all this he was enjoyin' his own company, readin' good literature and listenin' to classical music. Yes, it was the good life, full of fun and fancy free, so why should he get himself lumbered with a wife?

In 1970 he heard that President Richard Nixon hoped to pair him off with his daughter Tricia, but Charles quickly knocked that on the head by unkindly describing Tricia as "artificial and plastic."

In 1972 Prince Charles was linked romantically with Grace Kelly's daughter, Princess Caroline of Monaco. Although Caroline was only fifteen at the time, Princess Grace thought it was a fantastic idea. Charles didn't.

In the late 1970s, attempts were made to match him with Lady Amanda Knatchbull, granddaughter of Lord Mountbatten. They were even packed off on holidays together, but Charles didn't fall for it—or Amanda.

As Charles entered his thirties, the royal family really started giving him a hard time. He was told that he was now "getting on in years." It was time he found a nice girl and settled down. You won't be young forever, you know. You should find a Nice Young Lovable White Protestant Virgin as quickly as you can before it's too late, you know. There are not many left, you know. It's a dying breed, and if you don't make your mind up quickly there won't be any at all, you know. Oh yes, we nearly forgot, you also have a duty to provide an heir to the throne and guarantee the succession. You do realize that, don't you son? Nag, nag, nag.

When Charles played for time by saying he did not know any girls who matched up to their rather rigid requirements, they decided to find him one ("they" being the senior female royals). The male royals had nothing to do with it. Throughout royal history, marriage arrangements were usually left to the ladies, for the simple reason that it takes a woman to sort the good girls from the bad. Men are notoriously blind in this area.

We do not know the names of all the females who took part in the sophisticated plot to find Prince Charles a wife. Our palace mole says that although the Queen and Princess Margaret were in on the secret, the actual ringleaders were Prince Charles's grandmother, the Queen Mum—and her lady-in-waiting, Lady Fermoy.

For those who have never heard of Ruth Fermoy, she was a former concert pianist and the Queen Mum's best friend. More important, Lady Fermoy was the mother of Frances, who just happened to have a delightful daughter named Sarah. She was thought to be a perfect girl for Prince Charles because her father, "Johnny" Spencer, had not only been an equerry to King George the Sixth, but also to the Queen.

At the time of King James the First, the Spencers were already the richest family in England, and their $75 million (1989 figure) family estate, taking in 15,000 acres of Britain's finest farmland and a 480-year-old Northamptonshire mansion, is famed for its antiques and fabulous art collection also worth millions.

Added to all that—in case all that was not enough—Sarah was desirable in other ways. An attractive, long-legged redhead, she was an all-around athlete who was shapely and had a good brain. Just the kind of girl Charles might go for (thought the Queen Mum and Lady Fermoy). And so the alluring Sarah was artfully cast into the social stream frequented by Charles and his best friends. Success. He took the bait because he liked everything about Sarah, particularly her fierce streak of independence, and they enjoyed a warm relationship.

When Prince Charles failed to propose, the thwarted royal romance arrangers tried to push him into a corner by the time-honored method of leaking it to the press that "marriage might be in the air." Charles and Lady Sarah were enjoying a skiing holiday with other friends at the time and an enterprising journalist managed to buttonhole Sarah and ask her if she loved the prince and was she going to marry him?

Sarah answered: "No, I am not in love with him, and I would not marry anyone I didn't love, whether it was the dustman or the King of England. If he asked me, I would turn him down." That was the end of that. So the Queen Mum and Sarah's grandmother, Lady Fermoy, had to go looking for another girl who would fit the royal bill.

They obviously didn't look far because their next choice was Sarah's younger sister, Diana. Just like Sarah, Diana was no stranger to the royal family. In fact, she was born at Park House—a mansion her parents had rented on the royal family's estate at Sandringham. Di had still been wearing diapers when twelve-year-old Charles first set eyes on her in July 1961, a few days after she was born. Di was close to the royals in another way. As a youngster she had often attended children's tea parties with Charles's younger brothers, Prince Andrew and Prince Edward, and on at least one occasion Di had played hide and seek with the Queen in the vast corridors of Sandringham.

When the Queen Mum and Lady Fermoy launched their plan to bring Prince Charles and Di together, they had a problem. Charles had always regarded Di as something of a baby sister and hadn't noticed the good legs and curvy other parts she had developed. Some books say Charles first really "noticed" Di in 1977 when she was sixteen and fell at his feet (accidentally) in a plowed field during a shooting party. This is hardly convincing. At the time, Di was wearing heavy, baggy clothing over her thermal underwear to protect her against the cold winds. Hardly feminine and definitely not glamorous.

The romance actually started in 1980 when the Queen Mum and Lady Fermoy (with the help of Princess Margaret) arranged for nineteen-year-old Di to spend a few days as a guest on board the royal yacht *Britannia*, which was berthed at the English yachting center of Cowes. Di was was taken on board by Princess Margaret's teenage daughter, Lady Sarah Armstrong-Jones.

It was a good psychological moment for Lady Di because Charles did not have a regular girlfriend at the time. He had just terminated a close friendship with Anna Wallace, the beautiful blonde daughter of a Scottish landowner. Why their relationship ended is not clear, but Ingrid Seward discloses in her excellent book *Diana* (Weidenfeld & Nicolson, 1988) that the Scotland Yard police officers assigned to look after Prince Charles "saw it as part of their duties to check into the backgrounds of the young women Charles took an interest in" and they noticed that Anna Wallace had "other boyfriends" at the time she was friendly with Prince Charles!

As well as being a good journalist, Ingrid Seward is also the editor of the extremely well-informed *Majesty* magazine, so there's a very strong chance that her information is correct. That being so, there must be a good political scandal still to be unearthed because:

- If those policemen had not been given official permission to spy on Miss Wallace's private life, their activities were improper if not illegal.
- If they were given official sanction, who gave it? And under which act?
- Did those police officers submit written reports? If so, to whom?
- Did British Intelligence have any involvement in the spying activities? If so, would they please explain how on earth they thought the security of the state was potentially in danger in this regard? They can't say Reds-under-the-bed. Can they?

In actual fact, they can. In November 1973 the *Western Daily Press* disclosed that the Intelligence boys had a secret set-up known as the Blue File, which checked the political views of any girl in whom Prince Charles took more than a passing interest. An in-depth dig was made into all her friends, and even her employer and parents were monitored or discreetly quizzed. In 1971, for instance, Charles was warned to drop all personal contact with the daughter of an aristocrat who had tickled his fancy. Why? Because she was known to have "violent left-wing leanings."

Lady Diana Spencer certainly caught the eye of Prince Charles when she spent that holiday on board *Britannia*. Later that year he invited her to join his party of friends at Balmoral. Di stayed with the Queen Mum on the royal estate—and Di's grandma, Lady Fermoy, was also there.

Back in London later, Prince Charles invited Di to have dinner with him in Buckingham Palace and also took her to see Highgrove, the million-dollar mansion he had just bought on 347 prime acres in Gloucestershire. Although Charles enjoyed Di's company, he still avoided the subject of marriage. So someone decided it was time to give him a gentle push—by judiciously leaking to the media that a serious romance was in the air.

Di became a hot property who was besieged by packs of reporters and cameramen night and day. Prince Charles gave her strict instructions not to say one word to any journalist, but some other person she trusted must have given her opposite instructions because she most definitely did leak regular information about her royal romance to several trusted reporters.

Whoever advised Di to do this was extremely well versed in the ways of the media because, in return for her secret cooperation, those trusted newsmen helped to build Di up as the most fabulous girl in the world. The kind of girl who would make a most desirable wife for Charles and a wonderful queen when he became king. It was also made abundantly clear, by various unsubtle hints, that vivacious Di was the purest of pure-white virgins—though what that had to do with the price of cloth is puzzling in view of the fact that Lord Louis Mountbatten had assured the world, via *Time* magazine, that Charles most certainly wasn't.

When Prince Charles still dithered about tying himself up in any marital knot, the press started running (possibly planted) stories alleging there was "growing public concern" about the prince's reluctance to find a wife. The various female royals then used this so-called public concern to pressure Charles. Even the Queen told him: "The idea of this going on for another year is intolerable for everyone concerned."

Being a boy who always went out of his way to please Mum, Charles capitulated and proposed marriage to Di. But he did so—according to gossip columnist, Nigel Dempster—in the firm belief that Fleet Street had "forced him into it."

Another man who did not believe all the hyped tripe about Prince Charles finding the Cinderella of his dreams—and thought it was yet another of those arranged royal marriages —was the Labour MP and veteran royal critic, Willie Hamilton. On hearing of Charles's engagement to Di, he said: "The British people, deferential as always, will wallow in it. The winter of discontent [unemployment and strikes] is now being replaced by the winter of phoney romance."

Later, Charles and Di agreed to be interviewed together on a special TV program during which they answered carefully prearranged questions. The most interesting was: "Are you in love?" Lifting his chin in a perceptibly defensive gesture, Charles cagily replied: "Yes, whatever 'in love' may mean."

To indicate what Prince Charles meant on the subject of royal love, here is one of his earlier quotes about marriage: "Creating a secure family unit in which to bring up children, to give them a happy, secure upbringing—that is what marriage is all about. Marriage is more important than just falling in love."

Instead of having his marriage ceremony performed at the

usual royal venue of Westminster Abbey, Charles said he wanted it to be held in St. Paul's Cathedral. Not really liking the idea of this break with tradition, his mum pointed out that St. Paul's was nearly three times farther from Buckingham Palace than the abbey and she didn't know whether she would have enough soldiers and policemen to line the whole processional route. Charles wittily countered this argument with: "Then stand them further apart."

Oh, we wish you could have been there. It really was a lovely wedding. Nancy Reagan was there with (an admitted) one dozen bodyguards. No less than 4,000 British policemen and 2,228 soldiers lined the route, which meant there was a cop every four or five steps and a soldier (with bayonet fixed) every six or seven paces.

Crack marksmen were stationed on every available penthouse or rooftop and a motley crew of undercover agents disguised as drunkards, hippies, tramps, and ice cream, peanut, or Union Jack vendors also mingled with the crowds along the roadside, looking for the faces of known communists and other anti-monarchy types.

Belowground, all the sewers from Buckingham Palace to St. Paul's were searched by explosives experts in case the IRA had decided to liven up the proceedings with a few royal deaths. All manhole covers were sealed and guarded. So were all nearby public letter boxes—and closed circuit TV cameras monitored every inch of the processional route. Nothing was left to chance. Not even Di's fabulous wedding dress.

An elaborate billowing ocean of ivory silk paper taffeta, it was hand-embroidered with mother-of-pearl sequins and pearls. It had a neckline decorated with Taffeta bows, lace-flounced sleeves, ornate panels back and front, and a twenty-five-foot train of the same silk trimmed and edged with sparkling old lace. It really was a sight to behold and would have cost a fortune if David and Elizabeth Emmanuel had not offered to make it at a very special trade price in return for the free world publicity they knew it would bring them. Di thought this was such a good deal that she actually instructed them to make three, just in case some kind of accident—such as spilled champagne—happened to the other two.

If Princess Di ever becomes estranged from Charles, she will not have much of a legal leg to stand on when it comes to claiming any part of his vast private fortune. At the stage in the marriage ceremony where he should have told his blushing bride: "All my worldly goods with thee I share," he resolutely and clearly said: "All thy goods with thee I share." His sister, Princess Anne, thought this was so hilarious that, after the ceremony, she winked at him and asked: "Was that a deliberate mistake?"

Whether it was deliberate or not is irrelevant. Prince Charles would not have to pay Di maintenance or alimony anyway. On a strictly legal level he could break with Di any time. He wouldn't even need to apply for a divorce either because, technically speaking, Di didn't actually marry Prince Charles in St. Paul's Cathedral on that wonderful summer's day.

When she was asked if she would take this man, Charles Philip Arthur George, as her legally wedded husband, she said "Philip Charles Arthur George" by mistake. After they left the altar, Prince Charles whispered into her ear: "Do you realize that you just married my father?"

The one mistake the couple did not make was to invite Di's stepgrandmother, Barbara Cartland, to the wedding. Yes, that endearingly enduring author who, with much help from her wonderful staff of researchers, has churned out 503 (January 1990 figure) romantic novels in which the heroine always remains a virgin until the last page.

Please don't misunderstand what we are saying. Barbara's noninvitation to the wedding was not because she or her books were disliked. On the contrary, Di has read all her intellectually untaxing paperbacks to the very last page, and thinks they are far better than all the works of Shakespeare and Dickens put together.

Dear Barbara was probably not invited because Buckingham Palace feared that if the TV cameras had zoomed in on her, she would have held up placards advertising those wonderful Gev-E-tablets, B-12 vitamins, and the Bio Strath Elixir that the old lady claimed kept her so young so long.

Enough about that fairy-tale wedding. Every half-civilized person who was half-awake on July 29, 1981, vaguely knew about it anyway. According to the Buckingham Palace publicity experts, an alleged 700 million people watched it on television received by satellite in seventy nations, quite apart from an "estimated" billion radio listeners. If their guesstimates were correct, or their ratings weren't rigged, this means that nearly one-quarter of the world's population allegedly watched or listened to the wedding!

Another mind-boggling (but true in this case) figure was the $15 million worth of furniture, silver items, rare carpets, jewelry, and antiques that the happy couple received as wedding presents from admirers all over the world.

Eleven months after the wedding, at exactly three minutes past nine on the evening of June 21, 1982, Princess Di gave birth to 7 pound 1½-ounce William—which ensured the succession the senior female royals had long plotted for—and the royal reporters rushed to the telephone to tell their editors how beautiful William was.

The reporters had not actually set eyes on the royal baby said to be so beautiful. We suspect they obtained their information from a hospital caretaker who had heard it from a woman in the hospital canteen who knew an operating room cleaner who was related to a taxi driver who drove one of the royal reporters to the hospital.

Then followed a suspiciously similar gush of feature articles pointing out that Prince Charles was the first Prince of Wales in history not to have entered into an "arranged" marriage. This really was a case of overkill, and it set the doubters and cynics wondering—had it been an arranged marriage or hadn't it? Did Charles and Di really have a lot in common—as they had claimed on television before their marriage—or didn't they? The truth is that they didn't and they don't.

- Charles loves riding horses. Di has kept as far away from them as possible ever since she fell off her pet pony at the age of eight.
- He hates going out to designer restaurants and discos. She relishes them because she adores the youth and glitter of city life.
- He adores playing polo. She says even watching it bores her stiff.
- He likes fishing. She doesn't—except for compliments.
- He likes communing with nature and walking through the heather in the rain. She says it wets her hair and spoils her pretty clothes.
- He is hooked on Bach and Beethoven. She prefers Dire Straits and the Beatles.
- He reads books on philosophy and history. She would rather open a new factory than a book—unless it's a romantic novel or one of her many volumes of personal press clippings.
- He loves long and intimate dinner parties at which he can play host to highly intelligent people who enjoy discussing serious subjects. She dislikes entertaining at home and once quipped that a wife who entertains her husband's boring old friends is actually a hostage, not a hostess.

Charles is a serious-minded person who worked hard as a student. He was the first heir apparent in British history to win a university degree and he graduated from Cambridge with a BA (with honors).

Di was a total dunce at school who failed her school leaving exams, twice. She also failed to matriculate from her Swiss finishing school (Chateau d'Oex) because she hated it and returned home in tears after only six weeks.

While chatterboxing with some members of the public, Princess Di once said she had a brain "the size of a pea." She also described herself as being "as thick as a plank." Buckingham Palace was dismayed by this and quickly reassured admirers of the royal family that the future queen of England was not really as dim as she had claimed. We were told that Di had made these jocular comments only "to put nervous members of the public at their ease."

But this excellent example of verbal gymnastics was negated when the press told the public what Di's stepmother, Raine Spencer (Barbara Cartland's daughter), thought on the subject. Being sharp-tongued, Raine is known by the nickname "Acid" Raine. And it is no secret that Di loathes her guts. That is probably why Raine stuck the knife in by saying this about Di: "How can you have an intelligent conversation with someone who doesn't have a single O-level? It's a crashing bore."

Twisting the knife in the gaping wound, Acid Raine also said: "If you said Afghanistan to Diana, she would think it was a cheese."

Slowly but surely, the differences between Charles and Di became apparent, and the rumors about their arranged marriage continued until someone worth quoting eventually gave a worthwhile quote. This was Harold Brooks-Baker, editor of *Burke's Peerage*, the snob's bible, who said: "In many ways it was an arranged marriage. Prince Charles needed a lovely wife, and Lady Diana fitted the bill. Diana was an infatuated 19-year-old only too eager to marry him. It *was* an arranged marriage, and arranged marriages are different. But it was and is a very sound, sensible, working marriage."

In September 1985 the American magazine *Vanity Fair* published an article about Prince Charles and his wife. It was written by the magazine's editor, Tina Brown, who is not only a sophisticated and glamorous lady but also happens to be a first-class journalist. In her article, Tina disclosed that Charles and Di were "becoming alienated from each other by changes in their separate personalities."

Princess Di was said to be behaving like an old-fashioned 1950s film star who was becoming increasingly disenchanted by her husband and his ways, and Prince Charles was said to be "discouraged by her lack of intellect." He was also said to dislike her female buddies and the neo-Neanderthal "Hooray Henries" who escorted them. The article added that it seemed as if Prince Charles was "pussy-whipped from here to eternity" by Princess Diana.

The British *Daily Mail* of September 27 retaliated with a splash front-page story that described Tina Brown's article as "amazing and astonishing." Sir John Junor, writing in his *Sunday Express* column two days later, went quite berserk. First, he sneered at Tina Brown for "deserting these shores for the lusher pastures of the United States" which, translated into direct English, means "she's a cow."

Then he sniped at Tina's husband, Harold "Harry" Evans (presumably because he had also "deserted" England by accompanying his wife). After all that irrelevant nonsense, Sir John criticized Tina Brown's article by stating: "The nearest I imagine either of them has ever come to knowing Princess Diana is from watching her on TV. Their combined knowledge of her married life is zero, double zero."

This really was a case of incredible misleading reasoning because Tina Brown was not only the former editor of Britain's top society magazine *Tatler*, but had moved in London's highest social circles. Quite apart from that, Tina's husband is, without doubt, one of the finest campaigning journalists Britain ever produced.

Before leaving England Mr. Evans was the editor-in-chief of Britain's influential establishment newspaper *The Times*—as well as being editor-in-chief of its sister paper, *The Sunday Times*, for fourteen years. He is the author of no less than six books on the craft of journalism, including his superb and best-selling 525-page book *Good Times, Bad Times* (Coronet, 1983). He also was awarded the European Gold Medal of the Institute of Journalists, campaigning British Journalist of the Year in 1967, British Editor of the Year in 1973, and International Editor of the Year in 1976. He ended his year as editor of *The Times* by being named as the Editor of the Year by Granada TV's *What the Papers Say* program.

For Sir John Junor to suggest that Harold Evans and his wife, who was also at the apex of British journalism, only knew about Princess Di "from watching her on TV" was pathetic patriotic propaganda—and within a matter of months this was proved to be so when the British press itself was forced to confirm the accuracy of the statements Tina Brown had made about Prince Charles's shaky marriage.

An avalanche of articles "disclosed" that Charles's marriage to Di had "long been on the rocks" because their "personalities were so different." We were told they now occupied separate bedrooms, though one friendly journalist tried to downplay this by explaining that, yes, Charles does have a single bed in his private dressing room, but he uses it only "when he is working late." No, in his home. Not at the office.

This little disclosure prompted other pressmen to say they knew for a fact that Charles and Di occupied separate bedrooms when they spent weekends with friends or went on official tours together. What about that then, hey? Gotcha!

On the contrary, smirked Buckingham Palace. You ain't got us. That's a completely different story. "The reason is that when the Princess steps out of her shower in the morning she doesn't want her husband's valet in the room and the Prince doesn't want the Princess's maid there when he is putting on his underpants."

Then came another suggestive shock-horror disclosure. Charles and Di were said to be so estranged that they no longer had breakfast together. But a friendly writer explained that one away by saying it was because the couple had "different timetables," you see?

No, we don't, because it's glaringly obvious that if the royal couple really wished to enjoy their muesli and honey together with their kids, they could quite easily adjust their timetables accordingly. In any case, how many schools and factories do they open at breakfasttime?

In an attempt to cover up the rift in the marriage, the Buckingham Palace publicity experts arranged for chummy photographs to be published of Charles and Di looking deliriously happy together. But nobody was fooled. Certainly not Old Etonian Mr. Ludovic Kennedy, who is not only one of Britain's most famous broadcasters but a talented author who really knows his way around Britain's corridors of power.

"Ludo" was accorded "Quote of the Week" status in January 1989 when, on the subject of Prince Charles and Princess Di, he said: "If this had been an ordinary marriage, they would have been parted by now." This was not said maliciously. Ludo was indirectly pointing out the great sadness of Prince Charles's position. As the heir to the English throne and the future Defender of the Faith, he simply cannot be divorced.

Another man who knows what he is talking about is the award-winning English journalist Anthony Holden, who has traveled all over the world with Prince Charles as a member of the royal press pack. In 1988—to mark the Prince's fortieth birthday—Mr. Holden wrote a book entitled *Charles*, which was published by Weidenfeld & Nicolson. Although it contained a variety of well-deserved compliments about Prince Charles, it also gave inside details about his marriage.

On the subject of Princess Di, Mr. Holden wrote: "She has a husband who no longer understands her—nor even, it seems, much likes her. In turn, to be fair, she is saddled with a marriage of opposites, to a man who cannot share her youthful *joie de vivre*, and who places an emphasis on his public life which is way beyond her. Most of the time, it is all too clear, she is bored with him."

Although much the same had already been spelled out by various gossip writers, the fact that the man who was once Prince Charles's most trusted press traveling companion had said it was explosive. So some British newspapers tried to trash Mr. Holden's outstandingly entertaining book by describing it as a mixture of "tittle-tattle, half-truths, guesswork and fiction."

This is very interesting indeed because ten years earlier— with the personal cooperation of Prince Charles—Anthony Holden had written another book entitled *Charles, Prince of Wales* (Weidenfeld & Nicolson, 1979). This was extremely well disposed toward Charles and mentioned most of his great successes. Almost to a man, the British press lauded this book as: "Witty, informative, fascinating and intelligently written."

But whatever is said about Prince Charles, we know one thing for sure. He's a splendid human being. He really *does* care about the plight of the homeless, the unemployed, and the other disadvantaged. The saddest aspect is that he is a moral crusader in a gilded cage. What can he do? Nothing really, because whenever he dares to suggest that something must be done to correct these problems, the big business boys smear him as a naive or "woolly-minded do-gooder."

A good example of this came when he addressed the National Housebuilders Conference in 1986 and accused builders of allowing inner cities to decay while swallowing up vast sections of the countryside. This, he said, was causing not only decay, but poor physical and mental health and general low morale. Reacting to this, the normally elegant and diplomatic Lord Northfield (who just happens to be the head of a building consortium) lashed out furiously by alleging that Prince Charles had been "hi-jacked by the loony Green Brigade!"

When Charles spent several days camping and meditating in the Kalahari desert with his eighty-year-old author friend Sir Laurens van der Post, he was sneeringly described as "the loony hermit Prince who enjoyed soul-searching camp-fire chats with bare-breasted Kalahari bushmen."

When Charles disclosed that he talked to the plants in his garden because he found that they "responded to kindness," he was immediately labeled "Charles, the Mystic Loon." This is strange because women's magazines and gardening books catering to intelligent readers have often confirmed that talking to plants actually does produce good results.

When Charles disclosed that he preferred to eat vegetarian dishes, the meat barons complained to Buckingham Palace that he was "doing irreparable harm" to British farmers.

When he spent several days digging and planting potatoes in a remote area of the rugged Hebrides (because he needed a rest from the hectic pace of life in London), Charles was attacked for wanting to be "A Loon Again."

Slowly but surely, Prince Charles has realized that there is a reason for all this smearing and character assassination whenever he dares to adopt an "alternative" viewpoint. The big business boys are "disciplining" him. They want him to know that when he becomes king, they are the ones who will continue to rule. Not him.

# 19

---

## *Royal Insecurity*

*E*ngland's mad KING GEORGE THE THIRD was walking in a London street one morning when a young woman tried to stab him with a small knife. As plainclothed royal bodyguards (later described by newspapers as "irate members of the public") started beating her up, the king shouted: "The poor creature is mad. Do not hurt her, she has not hurt me."

The woman, Mrs. Margaret Nicholson, was locked away in an asylum for the criminally insane after being declared a lunatic.

Even today, if anyone attacks, pretends to attack, or does anything calculated to "alarm" a royal, the lunatic label is usually applied. There are good reasons for this. It not only deters sane people from showing their displeasure, but also gives the impression that all mentally well-balanced people support the monarchy and only madmen are their enemies.

The first man to officially put this on record was William Gladstone, when he was the British prime minister in 1882. After a young man named Roderick McLean had fired a shot at QUEEN VICTORIA in March of that year, Mr. Gladstone told her not to worry because although all foreign assassins had political motives, "in England, they are all madmen."

This reassured Victoria immensely. She had been attacked several times and was beginning to suspect that her adoring public wasn't. But the queen received a shock when Roderick McLean came to trial on a charge of trying to kill her. He was found not guilty on the grounds of insanity. On hearing this verdict, the queen shouted: "If that is the law, the law must be altered."

And so, in true democratic style, Parliament altered the law in the following year so that verdicts of "guilty but insane" could be handed down by the courts. Victoria's heavy-handed ruling made an ass of the law for the next eighty-two years until 1964, when the original verdict that had displeased Her Majesty so much was finally revived.

Another attack on Victoria came in May 1842 when she and her husband Albert were being driven near Buckingham Palace. They saw a man whom they later described as "a little swarthy, ill-looking rascal" point a pistol at them from a distance of "two paces." The gun failed to work, but this didn't sound "dangerous" enough, so the public was told that it "misfired." The man avoided capture by slipping away into the crowd.

The royal records tell us that Queen Victoria knew full well that the man would try again and so, without telling anyone in her royal household, she "bravely" went out in her carriage at the same time the next day, "to challenge the assassin into making a second attempt." This could be suspected of being a slight case of overwriting by the palace publicity experts.

As it happens, the man was there and he did try again. The version Victoria gave was that he aimed his gun at her from a distance of five paces, and, she specifically said, she heard the report of a gun being fired after which she saw the man being seized.

His name was John Francis, and he was found guilty and condemned to be hanged by the neck until dead. Victoria said this was "very painful" to her. But it was much more painful for poor Mr. Francis who insisted that he had not fired the gun. He said that if the queen persisted in saying she had heard the bang of a gun, she was lying—because his gun had not even been loaded.

Anyone with only half a brain knows that a royal personage would never tell a lie when a human being's life hangs in the balance. But someone took the trouble to check the ridiculous claim, and true enough, it was proved beyond doubt that the pistol had not been loaded. Mr. Francis enjoyed a dramatic last-minute reprieve from the gallows. Although Victoria was highly peeved, she made the brilliantly ambivalent quote: "Of course I'm glad" (the gun was not loaded).

Two days later Johnny Bean, a four-foot youth of retarded growth who was also crippled, brandished a pistol as Victoria's coach swept by. Loaded mostly with paper and tobacco, the gun was harmless, and even if it had been loaded properly, the queen was well out of its range. Yet, choosing to take full advantage of the "massive public concern" (which, translated, means the newspapers were making one hell of a fuss), a well-chosen judge sentenced Mr. Bean to eighteen months in jail, saying he was guilty of "the most abominable crime." The defense counsel did not ask what the judge would have said if Mr. Bean had jumped into Victoria's carriage and ravaged her.

Retarded little Johnny Bean made his mark on history. As a direct result of his "attack" on Queen Victoria, Parliament rushed through a new Act (Section Two of the Treason Act, 1842) specifically to deal with incidents in which harmless weapons were brandished in front of royalty.

In May 1849, when Victoria was planning a visit to Ireland, William Hamilton, an unemployed man from Adare, County Limerick, decided to scare the pants off Her Royal Majesty. Sitting in the kitchen of his London lodgings, he lovingly carved out a gun from a few pieces of wood and the spout of a tea kettle. As he examined his handiwork, Mr. Hamilton realized the slightly curved barrel might give some people in the crowd the impression that he was about to commit suicide, so he borrowed a pistol belonging to his landlady instead.

The records state that Willie "fired" at Victoria as she drove near Buck House (royal slang for Buckingham Palace), yet the truth is that there was no bullet in the gun. It contained a blank. All Willie did was to point it at the queen and shout "bang." That proved he was an imbecile because everyone in London's high society knew that nobody could kill insatiable old Victoria with just one bang. When this "mad brute of an Irishman" was brought to trial at London's Criminal Court, he was found guilty and transported in chains to serve seven years hard labor in Australia—where he died.

Another Irishman who pointed an unloaded pistol at Victoria was Arthur "Paddy" O'Connor, age eighteen. He did it in 1872 in an attempt to scare the queen into releasing some of the Irish rebels held in British jails. Mr. O'Connor was branded as "weak-minded" and jailed for just one year. Queen Victoria was livid about this "ridiculously lenient" sentence and said the mad Irishman should be transported to Australia, "otherwise he will try to kill me again."

When Whitehall said it was impractical to send a short-term prisoner to Aussy, the queen's voice hit the coloratura range as she screamed that they must go and do a deal with "the lunatic." The police were then sent to have a friendly little chat with Paddy O'Connor in his cell. But he was not as weak-minded as they thought. Being called Mr. by British cops—who also gave him tea and biscuits as they talked to him—made him slightly suspicious. When they finally got to the point and said Her Majesty would be most pleased if he take himself off to Australia for a long holiday, Paddy retorted: "Then she must pay my fare." And do you know something? She did.

In June 1840 Edward Oxford, the eighteen-year-old son of a black woman and a white English shopkeeper, fired two shots at Victoria from a distance of six paces as she sat in an open carriage. When police searched his hovel of a room, they found it full of left-wing literature and pamphlets criticizing the British way of life. This proved to them beyond any possible doubt that he was incurably insane, so they threw him into Hanwell criminal lunatic asylum where he stayed locked up in maximum security for twenty-seven years. Even when he was released, Victoria insisted that he be packed off to Australia "in case he tries to kill me again."

Why did they incarcerate him for twenty-seven years? And why pack him off to Australia? The answer is that the British public was never told the full story about Mr. Edward Oxford. Incredibly, although he was a half-caste who worked as a waiter in a low-class inn and lived in a filthy little room containing only a small bed, the two pistols he had used when shooting at Queen Victoria were silver-mounted and of high quality. They bore the monogram "E.R."—the insignia of "Ernestus Rex"—better known as Deadly Ernest, the hated king of Hanover.

This delightful chap was the fifth son of England's mad King George the Third, and that he was also slightly unbalanced mentally can be judged from the fact that he once lost his temper and cut his valet's throat. This is the Ernest who was said to have fathered a child by his sister Sophia.

The public never found out how the lowly waiter Edward Oxford had managed to obtain the king of Hanover's pistols. And there was another oddity in the puzzling case. When the police searched Oxford's room, they found a letter. In London's high society, this became known as "the Hanover letter." Very suspicious indeed.

We are not suggesting that Ernest, the king of Hanover, had been mad enough to write a letter commissioning the young waiter to kill Queen Victoria. On the contrary, it could have been a love letter Ernest had written to his, perhaps, one-time boyfriend. Such things do happen. But one thing is for sure. Whatever dreadful secret that letter contained, it was not read out in court during Edward Oxford's trial—and its contents were never disclosed to the public.

In 1850 there was another highly suspicious cover-up when Victoria was riding in an open carriage and a male rushed up and smashed her on the head with his heavy and fashionably gold-topped walking cane. The description of that cane is important. It indicates that the man wielding it was not a filthy, swarthy, evil-looking, mean little half-caste waiter, crippled dwarf, or mad Irishman. He was Lt. Robert Pate, formerly of that splendid group of fellows known as the 10th Hussars.

On being so viciously bashed on her head, Victoria most unregally threw herself to the floor of the carriage and lay there until her lady-in-waiting, Fanny Jocelyn, shouted: "They have got the f-f-[fiend]." The royal records tell us that Victoria then jumped to her feet and wonderfully "calmed the terribly upset crowd" by crying out "Don't worry, I am not hurt."

Yet later that day Buckingham Palace said the queen's forehead was covered with bruises, she had a black eye, she was suffering a terrible headache, and had been "too shocked" to eat her dinner that evening. This might have been a factually impressionistic account of her injuries to suck sympathy from the masses because, truth be told, the queen was seen enjoying herself at the opera that very night.

Of all the attacks made on Queen Victoria, this was the only time she was injured. Which just goes to show how right they are to say that it takes an officer and a gentleman to do a job properly. Victoria must have been dashed grateful that he didn't try to kill her.

We don't know why Lt. Pate bashed Victoria on the pate. The police couldn't obtain the usual confession a prisoner makes of his own free will because they were unfairly handicapped by the fact that toffs cannot be tortured. According to the official records, Lt. Pate refused to explain his reasons for the attack and the public was told he was "manifestly deranged." But he was not thrown into a lunatic asylum for twenty-seven years and he was not transported to Australia.

During her reign as Britain's most beloved monarch, at least twenty-eight attacks or attempts were made against Queen Victoria. But Buckingham Palace stopped counting after the seventh as they did not wish to give the public the impression that she was mightily disliked.

Only one serious attempt was made on the life of Victoria's

oversexed son, Prince Edward. This was in April 1900, just nine months before he became KING EDWARD THE SEVENTH. A Belgian youth named Jean Baptiste Sipido jumped on the footboard of the royal train as it steamed out of the Gare du Nord in Brussels. Firing through the open window at point-blank range, he somehow managed to miss Prince Edward and his wife.

On being captured, Mr. Sipido said he had tried to kill the hated English prince because he and his mother, Queen Victoria, were responsible for thousands of Afrikaners (Boers) suffering under British rule in South Africa. Mr. Sipido was described by the English press as "an insane anarchist." But he never came to trial because he had brain enough to escape from custody and was never recaptured.

One of the craziest royal security scares came in June 1939 when the DUKE OF WINDSOR threw a large party in the restaurant on the Eiffel Tower's first platform. Halfway through the party, a woman guest screamed and pointed to one of the massive windows. It was just like one of those silent Charlie Chaplin movies. There, peering through a patch he had wiped on the misted glass, was a man kneeling precariously on one of the massive metal beams. Wearing dark glasses and a military-style raincoat, the heavily mustached man was so shocked at being seen that he jerked backward involuntarily, slipped off the beam, and fell to his death. It was never disclosed whether he was a would-be assassin or just a hopeful gatecrasher. All we know is that he was identified as Bedrich Benes, military attaché (and spy runner) for the Czechoslovak government in exile. A loaded gun was found in his raincoat pocket.

Another odd thing happened to the Duke of Windsor when he was the handsome and immensely popular Prince of Wales. As he walked through the crowd at Melton Racecourse in the twenties, an elderly woman wearing a shawl whipped out a six-inch-long hat pin and plunged it deep into his right arm.

The woman, who was described as "a lunatic," told the police that, in the same way some people pinched themselves to discover whether they were dreaming, she had "pricked" the fabulously glamorous prince "to see whether he was real or not." As he had shouted "Oh, shit" and tears had flooded into his eyes, she had gathered he was real. Although her explanation sounded ridiculous, the prince confirmed that other members of the public must have felt the way she did because, on at least a dozen occasions, he had been stabbed by women wielding hat pins or painfully pinched by them when his back was turned.

In July 1936, during the Duke of Windsor's ten-month reign as KING EDWARD THE EIGHTH, an Irishman threw a loaded pistol under his horse as he rode round Hyde Park Corner. Normally, an Irishman doing such a thing would be labeled as insane or a terrorist—or both. But Jerome Bannigan was a journalist of editor status who wrote under the pen name George McMahon, and one thing the British royals dare not do is call journalists loonies in public—although privately, they insist that many are.

Mr. Bannigan was grabbed by a policeman whose name was A. Dick. (We kid you not) Constable Dick denied Bannigan had thrown the gun at the king's horse. He said he had knocked it from the Irishman's hand just as he was taking aim at the king.

Mr. Bannigan's attitude was that the dick would say that, wouldn't he? Being seen to save the king's life would get his name in the newspapers. He would be a national hero. He would get promotion and more money, apart from having a big English medal stuck on his chest.

The truth, said the Irish journalist, was that he had not intended to harm the king. He had merely thrown the gun under his horse to cause a scene because he wished to obtain publicity for his claim that there was a top-level conspiracy to stop him publishing a magazine in London entitled *The Human Gazette*. The court was clearly impressed with Mr. Bannigan's logic, and he received the surprisingly light sentence of twelve months in jail after being found guilty of "intent to alarm the king."

It was the only time in modern British history that someone menaced a royal with a gun and was not labeled a maniac by either the press or doctors—which again indicates how the British Establishment treads warily when dealing with journalists.

When Edward the Eighth abdicated, his brother Bertie came to the Throne as KING GEORGE THE SIXTH. This is the monarch who was afflicted with a terrible stammer. And, in keeping with his timid personality, he was extremely security-conscious. So much so that he kept a fully loaded machine gun in his bedroom, so that he could spray bullets at any intruder. T-t-t-take th-th-that, you s-s-swine . . .

Some of the security measures taken to protect the British royal family are mind-boggling.

Should any of them be badly injured in an air crash, terrorist attack, or polo match, doctors will not have to go looking for true-blue blood because the royals are great donors. But they give only to themselves. The Queen and Prince Charles for instance, have blood taken from them every few months. This is carefully stored away in special containers bearing their names, for use in an emergency. Each major royal has at least twelve pints of his or her own blood stockpiled, and whenever they travel long distances, several pints go with them. This is not a new security measure. The royals have been doing it for more than twenty-five years—long before AIDS started making headlines.

When the royals travel by rail in Britain, they have a royal train that is a fortress on wheels. Costing more than $15 million, it is packed with space-age electronic devices and has its own air supply in case of a gas attack. During the last two years its fourteen carriages have been fitted with rocket- and bullet-proof twelve-ton armored steel plating. The royals need fourteen carriages because they are usually accompanied by a large entourage. In addition to the royal sleeping quarters, the train has beds and bunks for fifty-four staff.

In the unlikely event of a foreign invasion, civil unrest, or some other serious emergency, a secret plan exists whereby the Queen can be rushed to the Broad Walk in Kensington Gardens where an aircraft with short take-off ability would fly her off to safety. Other members of the royal family could make their escape in helicopters if necessary, but not the Queen. She is forbidden to travel in helicopters, as Whitehall says they are more dangerous than conventional aircraft.

The royal family has its own little airline. Known as the Queen's Flight, it costs nearly $5 million a year to run. In late 1988 a British Intelligence agent in the United States reported that pro-IRA elements in New York were planning to supply the IRA with heat-seeking shoulder-held rockets. So all the aircraft in the Queen's Flight were speedily fitted with cowling masks on their engines to minimize their "heat signature."

To be on the safe side, British Air Force fighters or heli-copters fly above and alongside royal aircraft for added security. In addition to this, all civil aircraft are warned to stay clear of royal flights (code-named Purple) so that a "sanitized" security zone surrounds them at all times. The warnings to other aircraft are given in "Notams" (telexed memoranda to air traffic con-trols).

But in January 1989 British Intelligence was shocked when Ireland's extremely well-informed satirical magazine *Phoenix* disclosed that the IRA had started monitoring the movements of all royal flights—by intercepting the Notams messages—and that there was no way of stopping them. This is an extremely vexing problem for the British because, in its New Year Dec-laration of Intent, the IRA specifically warned Britain's royal family to expect attacks.

Scotland Yard experts believe that Prince Charles, as the heir to the throne, is the most likely IRA target, but we suspect that Prince Andrew is a more logical target. Apart from being the most controversial male royal, he also took an active part, on Her Majesty's Service, in the Falklands war, which makes him a "legitimate target" in the eyes of the IRA.

Prince Charles is the most security-conscious of all the royals. This is probably because he suffered a frightening attack while serving as a lieutenant in the Royal Navy in the seventies. He was sleeping in his private quarters at the naval barracks in Portland, Dorset, when a knife-wielding fellow lieutenant broke in. Charles was trying to calm the intruder, who picked up a chair and was trying to bash the prince's brains out when a royal bodyguard, Chief Inspector Paul Officer, raced in and put him out of action.

The lieutenant was not jailed. When sparse details of his attack leaked out, Buckingham Palace predictably slapped the lid down on this can of worms by saying the attacker was "demented" and had a "long history of mental illness." How odd that this was not noticed before.

One of the least-known facts about Prince Charles is that he possesses a phenomenal sixth sense. When he is doing one of his walkabouts, his eyes scan the crowd and in some strange way he tunes into the vibes even at long distance and instantly identifies people who dislike him—even if they are smiling! Charles has often spotted an antiroyal agitator long before that person started to chant or cause trouble. The prince uses a secret body-language code to alert his official minders, and they never cease to marvel at his accuracy.

When Prince Charles goes out fishing or hunting on one of the vast and bushy royal estates, he wears a tiny radio transmitter so that his minders know exactly where he is. He also wears it in case he gets lost or covered in a snowfall while on his annual skiing holiday at the fashionable Swiss resort, Klosters.

At Prince Charles's country home, Highgrove, there is a police post in the farm buildings and TV cameras scan the entire area. Inside the main house, which has bulletproof windows, there is an unusual room with no windows at all. The door and walls are lined with thick steel, and only Charles and Di know how to open that door. The couple have made several practice runs into this room, which is to be used in case of a terrorist attack. The door is so strong that it will resist any kind of assault made during the short period it would take for police reinforcements and elite army backup men to arrive.

The Queen has a similar assault-proof room in the royal

apartments at Buckingham Palace. And in the lovely centrally heated swimming pool in the palace basement, discreetly hidden TV monitors (linked to a nearby police post) scan the pool in case one of the royals experiences a problem in the water. These are switched off when Princess Di takes one of her regular swims in the nude.

Nuclear fallout shelters are also available for the royals. Buckingham Palace and Kensington Palace each have a small one, and Windsor Castle has a large underground complex capable of housing several dozen people and even has its own secret water supply. Some political journalists have said the royal family and a skeleton staff of about fifty would take refuge there in the event of a nuclear attack. Others say they would be flown to Canada. But the most surprising rumor in Whitehall is that a secret "city," which is one-quarter of a mile wide, has been created underground near Dartmouth where the royal family, generals, admirals, intelligence chiefs, top law enforcers, and leading opinion formers would shelter during and after any nuclear attack.

Windsor Castle has been fitted with $2 million worth of the latest security devices including surveillance monitors, invisible light beam alerts, and panic buttons hidden in every room. Similar devices have also been installed at the royal family's 247-room holiday home at Sandringham, which also has a vast electronic "ditch" barrier set into the lawn.

In September 1987 Michelle Humes, a homeless girl of twenty-four, made a mockery of the security measures there. She managed to break in. Not once, but twice! When she was sent to a psychiatric unit, Prince Philip upset Scotland Yard's Royal Protection Squad by snapping: "I'm beginning to wonder who is bloody sane round here."

The bloodiest attack on a royal in modern times came just before 8 P.M. on March 20, 1974, when Princess Anne and her husband, Captain Mark Phillips, were being driven along The Mall just one minute away from Buckingham Palace. Their Rolls-Royce was forced to stop when a Ford Escort driven by a young man named Ian Ball swerved in front of them. Ball jumped out and shot Princess Anne's bodyguard, Inspector Jim Beaton, in the chest. The inspector managed to draw his gun, but it misfired. Lifting the gun with both hands, he pulled the trigger again but the shell from the previous shot had jammed in the slide mechanism and nothing happened.

Ian Ball grabbed hold of Princess Anne and tried to pull her out of the car. Acting as an anchor, Anne's husband held on to her other arm, and a lengthy tug of war took place. The tugging was so fierce that the entire sleeve of Anne's blue velvet dress split at the shoulder and Ian Ball fell backward as the sleeve came away.

To witness such a royal drama is the kind of thing every front-page-hungry news reporter dreams of. But it turned out to be a nightmare for freelance journalist Brian McConnell, who happened to be in a passing taxi. Realizing what was happening, he jumped out to help, but ended up lying in the gutter—shot in the chest by Ian Ball.

Inspector Jim Beaton, still bleeding profusely, returned to the fray when Ball threatened to shoot Princess Anne if she didn't get out of the car. She refused and, as Ball raised his gun to fire, Anne's bodyguard lurched forward and a bullet hit him in the hand.

At this moment, Police Constable Michael Hills arrived on the scene but was immediately put out of action when Ball shot him in the stomach. Princess Anne's chauffeur, Alexander Callendar, then decided to try his luck, but also ended up in the gutter with a bullet in his chest. Inspector Beaton then kicked out at Ball, who wounded him for the third time by shooting him in the stomach. Ball tried to drag Princess Anne out of the car again, but she still resisted him strongly.

Two members of the public, Glenmore Martin and Ronald Russell, then bravely came to the rescue and, as they distracted Ian Ball, Princess Anne tumbled out of the car, did a back somersault, and ended up landing on the road with her legs flailing in the air.

The incredible saga ended when Ian Ball was pinned to the ground by several people after a chase. In his pocket was a note demanding a ransom of £3 million from the Queen in return for Princess Anne. Ball later pleaded guilty to attempted murder and other charges. He was ordered to be detained for an indefinite period under the Mental Health Act.

This story contains all the basic details of the attack but, as any practiced journalist will spot, there is something missing. What did Princess Anne say during her lengthy ordeal? Did she scream? Did she swear? Did she cry? What did her husband say, and, even more important, what did he do, apart from hang on to Anne's arm? Did Princess Anne's bodyguard utter any words? If so, what?

We do not know and it's unlikely that we ever will because, even today, the royal family strongly discourages any attempt to enlarge on the attack. Brian McConnell, the journalist who was shot when he rushed to Princess Anne's aid, found himself smothered by a blanket of silence when he contacted Buckingham Palace and told them he wished to write a factual account of what happened.

"I didn't ask for permission [to write the story], I just mentioned it as a courtesy and was advised against it," he said. This strongly suggests that something is being hidden from public scrutiny and raises many questions. But the only questions we would like to pose are: Did one of the four people in the royal car do something wrong? And had any of them had any prior contact with the attacker, Ian Ball?

About seventy male and female bodyguards are engaged in routine royal protection. Their wages, expenses, and overtime cost the British taxpayer about $15 million a year. Many of them are unmarried because they are required to travel widely and be away from home often, plus having to work on night and overnight duties.

The cream of the British police force, they have all been highly trained in the use of firearms and unarmed combat. Chosen for their intelligence and tact, they have strict instructions to be as unobtrusive as possible at all times because the Queen strongly dislikes what she describes as "unsubtle security" as it tends to remind the public that the royal family is actually disliked by some nasty people—even if they *are* all "lunatics."

Members of the general public do not often realize that those men walking behind the royals in posh morning dress or black tails and bow tie are policemen. But sometimes they do stick out like sore thumbs—as on the day in August 1988 when Fergie, the Duchess of York, left hospital carrying her newborn baby, Bea. Standing discreetly in the background was a tall, well-built chappie. No, he couldn't possibly be a cop. He was wearing an immaculately cut and extremely expensive Savile Row suit. But those eagle-eyed press cameramen spotted that he was a royal bodyguard. How? Because he had a large safety pin stuck in his lapel—in case baby Bea did a pee and needed her diaper changed.

Some of those big burly police bodyguards even end up acting as part-time nannies for the royal children. Countless pictures have been seen of royal kids sitting on their knees or having their snotty little noses wiped. Prince Charles's son William even had a police bodyguard sitting in class with him all day when he was at nursery school, the windows of which were fitted with bulletproof glass. Known as "the Royal Brat," the badly behaved and spoiled little William once rained apples, bananas, and grapes on the head of a bodyguard standing under his bedroom window.

The bodyguards have often been seen performing quite menial tasks for their royal masters and mistresses. The Queen's male bodyguards regularly carry her car rug, her umbrella, huge bundles of her flowers, and even her handbag.

The journalist and author Andrew Duncan summed all this bodyguard business up in one splendid sentence when he wrote: "A Special Branch man, in morning dress, holding a couple of polo sticks for Prince Philip, is an unforgettable sight."

The most worrying time for the bodyguards is during the walkabouts performed by the royals that not only cement admiration in the public mind by way of press photographic coverage but also recruit hundreds of admirers on every appearance due to the "I've actually seen them in the flesh" syndrome.

Members of the public go home and brag to neighbors: "She was as near as I am to you (almost) . . . you know . . . and if I had reached out (over the ubiquitous barriers) I could have nearly touched her/him/them, you know . . . and then he looked right at me and smiled, you know . . . the woman next to me was really jealous, you know . . . I can't tell you how exciting it all was . . ."

On big occasions, electronic eavesdropping microphones sweep the crowds lining the royal route. These are programmed to pick up certain key words, such as gun, shoot, kill, swine, parasite, and so on. Helicopters with heatseeking equipment can pinpoint humans hiding on rooftops. Other radiation or "sniffer" devices are also used to scan crowds and balconies to detect explosives and loaded guns or rifles in case IRA men are lying in wait.

One alleged IRA marksman is Patrick Sheehy, who has been named by Scotland Yard as a lone IRA sniper who is said to be (in late 1989) "lurking in Britain with a mission to assassinate a member of the royal family."

If any attempt is made against a royal in the future, the odds are that it will be within half a mile of Buckingham Palace, as statistics show that 70 percent of all the attacks on royals during the last 150 years have been attempted as they were leaving or returning to the palace.

When the royals visit tricky places, such as Scotland and Wales—where some people regard them as "foreign royals"—they often use the "local angle" ploy. In Scotland the male royals will wear kilts. In Wales they incorporate the colors of the Welsh flag in their clothing.

Princess Di, when she was still an amateur at the game of walkabout chat, once asked a woman in a Welsh crowd the rather condescending question: "Did you notice how patriotic I am by wearing your colors?" Prince Charles later told her that his mother didn't like that kind of careless talk and would she try to avoid disclosing royal tactics in future.

In 1969 hundreds of Welsh students mounted demonstrations against the idea of an English prince named Charles being officially "foisted upon them" as the Prince of Wales. Prior to the investiture on July 1, a Welsh-speaking Special Branch contingent was posted from England and told to spend all day drinking in pubs and hotels frequented by known Welsh nationalists.

More than five-thousand policemen and soldiers were also posted in and around the area. Just before the investiture, ten sticks of explosives were found on a beach. As a result, scores of students were rounded up and held overnight without charge until the ceremony was over. In Wales today, many nationalists still insist that British Intelligence planted the explosives, so they could use the "bomb scare" excuse to detain all those students. Whatever the truth, Her Majesty the Queen was "very relieved" when her son's investiture went off without a hitch.

Protecting the Queen is the highest priority. She has been threatened more than any other royal. In September 1963 a massive police hunt was mounted in the north of England when someone wrote four letters threatening to throw acid in her face. This person, believed to be a woman, was very shrewd. She not only wore gloves when composing the letters but was smart enough not to touch the backs of the wet stamps when she stuck them on the envelopes.

Even more astutely, she did not use her tongue to wet the stamp or the adhesive flap of the envelope but used a sponge so that Scotland Yard's forensic boys would have no sample of her saliva—a most useful clue for the police, particularly now, when they have the added help of DNA genetic techniques, which can identify suspects from their blood, semen, saliva, or other tissue samples.

The woman who sent those acid threats was never traced, but she was judged to be such a potential danger that British Intelligence was called in and security arrangements were tripled for Her Majesty.

Some other problems the Queen encountered were:

- In November 1963 George Mead, a common laborer age forty-five, wrote a letter threatening to kill her. He was arrested and declared insane.
- July 1965: A vast security sweep was made in Northamptonshire after letters threatened to "destroy" the Queen. A boy of seventeen was later sent for psychiatric examination and corrective training.
- In 1966 a forty-three-year-old chambermaid threw a bottle at the Queen's Rolls-Royce. First she was charged under the Treason Act and then committed to a mental hospital.
- May 1981: When the Queen visited an oil terminal on the Shetland Islands, a bomb exploded there. She was not near the blast but would have been if her program had not been altered at the last moment. The British press said the bomb must have been planted by madmen, but this did not stop the IRA from admitting responsibility.
- The IRA was also responsible for an attempt on the Queen's person when she inspected a guard of honor in Norway in the same year. A large group of IRA supporters also attended, and one of them threw tomato ketchup, which missed Her Majesty by a matter of inches. Later, an IRA man said this was a great pity because: "Press photographs of the Queen covered in ketchup would have been almost as good publicity as if we had killed her."
- June 1981: Ronald Zen, aged forty-two, was sent for a psychiatric report after posting a hoax explosive device to the Queen.
- December 1989: London housewife Mary Nelson, aged thirty-five, was arrested outside Margaret Thatcher's home at 10 Downing Street and sent for a psychiatric examination after she produced an 8 inch knife and said she wanted to kill the Queen.

The most publicized gun attack on Her Majesty happened in June 1981 when Marcus Sarjeant, a baby-faced seventeen-year-old from a respectable family, fired six shots at Her Majesty as she rode past him on her way to the Trooping the Colour ceremony. A little-known fact is that the Queen was wearing a finely meshed bulletproof vest costing about $4,500 under her military uniform that day. Not that she needed it. Sarjeant's gun was loaded only with noisy blanks.

During his trial, the court was told that the boy was influenced by the shooting of President Reagan. He had been struck by the ease with which an unknown young man had become famous all around the world. And in a note found in his home, Marcus had written: "I may become the most famous teenager in the world. I will remain famous or infamous for the rest of my life." He was found guilty of intent to alarm the Queen, was jailed for five years and served most of his sentence in a psychiatric prison.

British Intelligence keeps a massive "Suspects List" on its computers. This contains the names of all persons known to be hostile towards the British royal family. The "Letters to the Editor" columns of all newspapers are monitored, and the name of anyone writing anything critical about the royals is also entered. Just in case.

Suspects rated as having high danger potential are placed on a "Hot List." People on this list have their mail monitored and their telephones tapped. In most cases, the listening-in is done by the government's top secret communications head-quarters, GCHQ, at Oakley, near Cheltenham, or through one of its twenty-two listening posts throughout Britain. Some 5,000 telephone conversations can be monitored simultaneously by computers which listen for not only obvious key "recognition" words such as palace, royal, H.M. or H.R.H., gun, ammunition, explosives and bomb, but also left-wing verbals such as fraternal, comrade, brother, sister, solidarity, the struggle, and the cause.

If the computer hears a suspect use one of those words, it

retains a full transcript of the conversation. Should three or more key words be mentioned, the computer lights up a warning system to alert one of its human operators and starts spitting out the transcript. Not generally known is that in really high-risk cases, a room can be bugged by a telephone even when the telephone is not being used. And, incredibly, GCHQ has highly sophisticated eavesdropping equipment which—through that dormant telephone—can pick up the impulses of an electric typewriter or computer being used in the room and computers back at GCHQ simultaneously type out exactly what the suspect is typing!

Another brilliant invention (Japanese) is the Tone Scanner. In the same way that no two fingerprints are the same, no two telephone tones are identical. So, when British Intelligence believe a suspect is making calls from public telephone boxes in a particular part of a city (such as areas in London and Liverpool well populated by the Irish), they register the tone of every call box in that area in the brain of a computer. If any of those call boxes are used by a known suspect, the computer states exactly which one it is—within seconds.

Yet another sophisticated electronic device stores the voices of all persons who have made anonymous telephone calls (recorded by the police or by businesspeople who use answering machines). This is of immense value to British Intelligence because if the computer hears that voice again, during any routine tap on a known suspect, it will immediately relate the two voices, identify the person, and spit out the number of the telephone he or she is using.

One of the names on the computer hot list is that of Alvada "Cookie" Kooken, an American-born widow who was declared insane after committing a murder. Sixty-six years old, she has threatened to kill various VIPs, including the queen's gynecologist, George Pinker.

Although regarded as dangerous and housed in Britain's top-security prison/hospital, Broadmoor, Mrs. Kooken was allowed to accompany several other inmates when they were taken for a day's outing at the seaside in 1986. On reaching the beach, she vanished. The big scandal here was that she did not escape. She just walked away from the other mental patients. Scotland Yard pressed the royal panic button and a bevy of Special Branch men rushed to patrol outside such places as Buckingham Palace. But Cookie Kooken was not there. She was recaptured in a hotel, just ninety yards away from Scotland Yard.

Buckingham Palace has the most sophisticated security devices. One is a security fence known as a perimeter intrusion detection sensor system. At a cost of over £1 million, this was bought from Israel's state-owned Israel Aircraft Industries in 1983.

There was a very good reason the normally patriotic royal family did not "buy British" in this instance. One year earlier, an unemployed painter and decorator had made a laughing-stock of all the security devices then used by Buckingham Palace. His name was Michael Fagan.

Early on the morning of Friday, July 9, he decided to pop in and have a chat with the Queen at the palace. As he climbed over the high, spiked wrought-iron railings of the palace at 6:45, he was spotted by an off-duty policeman who immediately telephoned the police control room inside the palace. They looked out of the window, saw nothing, and went back to reading their cowboy books, playing poker, sleeping, or whatever else it was that they were not supposed to be doing.

Michael then climbed through an open window and found himself in the "Stamp Room," which contains the most valuable private stamp collection in Britain. It is worth millions and Michael could have lived the rest of his life in luxury if he had taken just one volume of those stamps. Being an honest and law-abiding citizen, however, Michael did not bother with them. In any case, the reason for his visit was to speak to the Queen, not rob her home. So he walked over to the door of the room and turned the handle, hoping to gain access to the corridor. But, as the royal stamp collection is so immensely valuable, the door to it was kept locked. This was to stop unauthorized people getting in, you see.

Why did the palace security experts make sure the door was locked yet leave that window open? The answer to that is very simple yet also complicated. The simple aspect is that they didn't have to worry about the window, even though it was open, because it was fully protected by one of those highly sophisticated and invisible electronic radar-type beam devices that signals an alarm in the police control room should anyone be daft enough to climb through it.

Oh yeah, so why didn't the alarm go off when Michael Fagan clambered through? The complicated bit is that it *did*. But the inefficient officials in the police control room ignored it, presuming it was the unofficial and self-appointed palace rat catcher. This was a cat kept by the housekeeper of a nearby hotel who had ideas above his station and liked to pop into the palace now and again.

Frustrated at being unable to get out of the stamp room by the door, Michael Fagan climbed out of the window to look for another way into the palace. As he did so, the alarm in the police control room sounded again. The sergeant in charge there said, "There's that bloody alarm again," and ignored it.

Left to his own devices, and being unaware of those newfangled ones, Michael climbed up a drainpipe and found another open window. This led him into the office of Vice-Admiral Sir Peter Ashmore, the master of the queen's household. There was no alarm on his window because the doddering old palace security experts knew that it was impossible for anyone to climb so high. Impossible for them, that is.

Michael was delighted to discover that the door of this room was unlocked and let himself into one of the main palace corridors. That's when he realized his sandals were making a flip-flopping noise. Not wishing to disturb any of the sleeping royals, he considerately removed his sandals and socks and padded around the corridors admiring all the priceless portraits adorning the walls. As he did so, Michael set off at least three warning devices. The public was later told that all these alarms had "malfunctioned because they had been badly adjusted."

While making his private little tour of the palace, Michael was seen by several of the 400-odd staff who work there. One maid said she thought the barefoot man, wearing a scruffy T-shirt, faded blue jeans, and carrying a pair of sandals was "just a workman who had arrived early."

But, to get to the juicier part of the story, after breaking a glass ashtray and cutting his thumb as he tried to tidy up the mess, Michael Fagan finally found his way to the bedroom of Her Majesty Queen Elizabeth.

He made a noise closing the door behind him, which disturbed the Queen from a deep sleep. As she said later, "I realized immediately that it wasn't a servant because they don't slam doors." She could not see Michael because the room was in total darkness. Rather shocked, she did not switch on her bedside light but just lay there wondering who was in her room. The time was 7:15, so it couldn't be the maid, who had strict instructions not to wake her until 7:45.

As Michael pulled open the large curtains by the window, the Queen sat up in astonishment. She told detectives later: "Our eyes met and both of us looked dumbfounded." But Her Majesty recovered first. She could tell at a glance that he was not the class of gentleman who should be in the palace and her first words were: "Who in heavens are you?" Michael answered: "Queen . . ." which confused her somewhat, until she realized she was being addressed, not being told something.

Her Majesty then said, "How dare you? Get out of here at once!" Ignoring this royal command, Michael walked over and, without being presented (one is never "introduced" to Her Majesty), he sat on her bed. But, knowing his place, he sat at her feet. The Queen was shocked to see blood dripping on to her counterpane from the cut on his right thumb. But she played it cool and, instead of jumping out of bed, which she thought might "drive him into a frenzy," she just sat there waiting for him to speak.

Secretly, however, she slid her hand under the pillow and pressed a "panic" night alarm button behind the bedhead. Downstairs, a policeman who heard the alarm, said to himself, "That bloody thing hasn't worked for years" and switched it off. The Queen pressed it again. He switched it off again. She pressed it again and he switched it off again. This went on and on until the Queen gave up in exasperation and rang the servant's bell by her bedside. Nothing happened. (The maid who should have answered was cleaning a nearby room and didn't hear it.)

At this stage, Michael Fagan explained his presence by saying he was having trouble with the social welfare people. Smiling sweetly, but inwardly fuming, Her Majesty told him: "That's hardly my department." A brilliant answer whichever way you look at it.

Queen Elizabeth then lifted the telephone next to her bed and dialed the palace switchboard. The operator said: "Good morning, your Majesty." The Queen, quite deliberately not returning the greeting, calmly said: "I want a police officer here at once." The operator rang the police control room. We know this because the cop who took the call dutifully recorded it in the official log book. And then forgot all about it.

Meanwhile, Michael Fagan and the Queen were enjoying a nice little chat. He told her some of his personal problems. That he had a wife and four children. That he was short of money because he could not find a job, even though he was a good decorator. Although she is the richest woman in the world, the Queen did not offer to help him out of his financial problems, nor did she offer him a job—yet by this stage, she must surely have realized that she needed a new security advisor.

Instead, she calmed Michael by saying "What a coincidence, we both have four children." She also said, "And I have a son who is the same age as you." (Prince Charles, then thirty-three.) These comments might seem rather inane considering the astonishing circumstances, but Her Majesty is an extremely astute lady and she probably said those things as a "put-off," to distract the young man from possibly turning his mind to other things.

After some six minutes of polite tension-breaking conversation, at which she is adept, Her Majesty decided the police were taking rather a long time to race to her rescue and telephoned the switchboard again to ask why there was never a policeman around when One needed one. The British public was never told the answer to that royal question. All we know is what a police officer ruefully confided to one of the palace staff later: "The whole thing was a bizarre cock-up."

In the end, after ten agonizingly long minutes of Michael Fagan's hardly scintillating company, the Queen managed to make her own escape when he asked her for a cigarette. She replied that she didn't smoke but if he waited a second, she would pop out and get one for him. So saying, Her Majesty, who was wearing a pretty shortie nightie, slipped out of bed daintly and went into the corridor where she found Elizabeth Andrew, a young chambermaid.

On being told about the intruder, Elizabeth (the maid) popped her head around Elizabeth's bedroom door and saw Michael Fagan still sitting on the bed wondering why it was taking Her Majesty so long to fetch him that cigarette. Later, the Queen entertained her friends by imitating the chambermaid's reaction: "Oh, bloody 'ell, ma'am, wot's 'ee doin' 'ere?"

The Queen and the chambermaid lured Michael out to a nearby pantry by saying he would find some cigarettes there. Paul Wybrew, a senior footman (age twenty-three) then arrived, took Michael kindly by the arm, and gave him a cigarette and a glass of whiskey. As all this was going on, Her Majesty made it obvious that she was mightily displeased about the police not rushing to her aid.

Finally, a full *eight minutes* after the queen had first called them, half a dozen Keystone Kops, wearing those heavy and highly polished black boots, came galumphing up the Grand Staircase. The first to reach the top of the stairs saw his Queen peeping apprehensively around a pantry door and, being respectful, stood to attention and started straightening his tie. But this standing on ceremony annoyed the Queen and she bellowed: "Oh, come on, get a bloody move on." The bevy of cops then grabbed Michael and carted him off to the lockup.

Many British were shocked when it was disclosed that the Queen and her husband occupied separate bedrooms. But then again, the lower classes have never really understood this upper-class practice, which became popular centuries ago when the gentry started allocating separate bedrooms for married couples at weekend house parties—so that husbands sexually bored with their wives could slip into other women's bedrooms and bore them.

The fact that the Queen and her husband did not share the same bedroom became apparent when Her Majesty commented on Michael Fagan's visit to her bedroom by saying "If the Duke of Edinburgh had been sleeping here, it would have been a different story." This caused a tremendous amount of rather prurient speculation in the press. "Separate beds," pondered the *Daily Mirror*. "How important is it to cuddle up together?"

When Michael Fagan was questioned by high-ranking police officers, they were shattered to discover he had visited the palace before. This had been one month earlier, on the night of June 7. On that occasion he had climbed through yet another open window and strolled through various palace corridors.

"I walked past a couple of rooms. One said 'Princess Anne' and the other said 'Mark Phillips.' I thought they were asleep so I did not disturb them." Passing another door marked "Prince Philip," he entered the room of Prince Charles's private secretary where he found a bottle of white wine bearing the label Johannisburger Reisling 1981. After satisfying himself that it was not from South Africa, Michael opened the bottle and drank half of it.

He sat in that room for more than twenty-five minutes and then, thinking "Sod this, there's nobody here to arrest me," walked around the palace corridors again, climbed out of a window, and went home.

When he appeared in court at a preliminary hearing, charged with stealing that half bottle of wine, he caused many a laugh. Taking off his shoes, he put his feet up on the front of the dock. Later, when the Queen's name was mentioned, he glowered at his solicitor and said: "I told you not to fetch her name up. I would rather plead guilty than have Her Majesty's name dragged into this."

On coming to trial, Michael continued his comedian act. Smiling and winking at the adoring people in the press box, he made them giggle by wagging his eyebrows up and down. Then he removed his upper set of dentures and started picking his prison breakfast of porridge and bread from them.

When he was asked to take the oath, he told the judge: "I'm not religious, your worship." On being handed the oath for atheists, he even made the judge smile by saying loudly: "Please read your name clearly"—giving the instructions at the very top of the card.

Speaking confidently and with no signs of strain or mock humility, he said he had done the Queen a favor by breaking into the palace twice: "Her security was no good and I proved it. I wanted to show the Queen was not too safe.... I could have been a rapist."

The police had not squeezed this out of him during questioning, so it can safely be presumed he had been given "headline-making" advice by one of those shrewd amateur legal eagles that exist in every prison.

He said he had drunk the half bottle of wine during his first visit to the palace because he was thirsty after doing "a hard day's work for the Queen." The jury was mightily impressed by Michael Fagan. Rightly deciding that the charge of stealing that wine was a petty attempt by the police to get revenge because his antics in the palace had caused half the cops based there to be fired, they found him not guilty.

Michael was not charged with breaking into the palace on the second occasion. Neither was he charged with intent to alarm the Queen—of which he was certainly guilty. Some legal experts say there was a very good reason for this. If he had been charged with anything relating to that visit, Michael Fagan could have asked for Her Majesty the Queen to be called to give evidence that he had behaved himself while in her presence.

It's unthinkable, and could never have happened, of course. But if Michael had made that demand in open court—and some complicated technical reason had been given to explain why the Queen who, as the Fountain of all Justice, could not appear before men who are, after all, "Her Majesty's judges" —it would have left a very nasty taste in the minds of millions who believe in British fair play.

Be that as it may, although Michael was acquitted on the charge of stealing the wine and should have been released at once, he was not. The authorities let it be known that he would be kept in custody because "his state of mind" was such that he must be protected from himself. He was "quite obviously mentally unbalanced" because the police had claimed that Michael had considered committing suicide in front of the Queen. How? With that ashtray he broke while on his way to Her Majesty's bedchamber!

While Michael Fagan was safely locked up, a flock of detectives scoured his past trying to find anything they could pin on him. Eventually they discovered he had once taken away and driven a car without permission.

Michael didn't think it was fair play when he was brought to trial on this charge and was so infuriated that he behaved badly in court. At one stage he shouted, "This is a fascist country" and was removed from the court for the duration of the hearing. As he was led down into the cells he repeatedly shouted: "Sieg Heil, Sieg Heil."

The upshot was that Michael Fagan was sent to a high-security mental hospital/prison for an indefinite period. His solicitor poured scorn on this. He pointed out that his client, who had admitted entering Buckingham Palace illegally on two occasions, yet had gone unpunished, was the first person in British history to have been committed to a mental hospital—*for taking away a motor car.*

# 20

---

## *Regal Mortis*

*B*eing a ruler has its perks, but in the old days it could be a dangerous job. Of the 5,250 accepted rulers we know by name and date, at least 1,476 experienced serious problems. Of those:

- 340 were assassinated or murdered.
- 300 vanished or suffered an unknown or uncertain fate.
- 381 were deposed (including 16 who were deposed and blinded).
- 149 were forced to abdicate.
- 101 were killed in battle.
- 52 were exiled or fled in fear of their lives.
- 49 had serious mental problems or were totally insane.
- 40 died in accidents (9 of which were suspicious).

- 37 were officially executed.
- 26 committed suicide.

One ruler does not fit into any of these categories. This was MITHRADATES THE SIXTH, who reigned as the great warrior king of Pontus (northern Turkey) for forty-three years until 72 B.C. when a Roman invasion caused him to flee to the Crimea, where he set himself up as the king of Bosporus.

He reigned there for nine years until his son, Pharnaces, mounted a revolt against him. This broke the sixty-five-year-old monarch's heart, and he ordered one of his bodyguards to kill him. The obedient guard plunged a dagger into his heart. Was that suicide or murder?

The French king CHARLES THE SEVENTH, didn't want to live either. In 1461, at the age of fifty-eight, he developed an incurable abscess in his mouth that gave him horrendous pain when eating. As if he didn't have enough on his plate, Charles was convinced that a plot was afoot to poison him. So he decided it would be sensible to stop eating altogether and within five weeks starved himself to death. His French subjects were later told, quite truthfully, that their beloved monarch had died as a result of an unusual vitamin deficiency.

Another abscess stopped an English royal from becoming king. This was FREDERICK, who, as the eldest son of King George the Second, was the next in line to the throne and, as such, was the PRINCE OF WALES. In 1751, at the age of forty-four, he developed a small abscess on his body. Although it was full of yellow-green pus, it was not too painful, so he went out into the garden to play cricket with his children.

To ensure they would not be hurt, he wisely used a soft tennis ball instead of the conventional hard leather-bound cricket type. But one of his sons hit the ball hard and it smacked into Dad's abscess and burst it, which caused pain to stop play. This, as any Englishman will confirm, is a nice change from rain. Blood poisoning set in and Frederick became the first and only royal to gain the distinction of being killed by a tennis ball while playing cricket.

Today's PRINCE OF WALES is, of course, Prince Charles, and if he gets killed playing games it will most likely be polo, which, as any pukka chukka sahib will confirm, is a fast and dangerous sport. The first royal to die on a polo field was QUTB-ud-DIN AYBAK, who ruled as the sultan of Delhi from 1208 to 1210. He wasn't born with genuine royal blue blood in his veins. Actually, old chap, he was a slave with delusions of grandeur who raised an army that conquered the Upper Ganges Valley and the Punjab. In keeping with his new royal role, this cheeky upstart took up polo. But his low breeding showed when he leaned too low in the saddle and someone accidentally belted him on the head with the thick end of a polo mallet. He died instantly.

KING TAMERLANE, the Mongol ruler of Samarkand, who conquered Persia, southern Russia, and much of India, also loved polo. To make the game more interesting, he and his noblemen used the decapitated heads of their enemies instead of a ball. Tamerlane, who ruled from 1369 until he died of a brainstorm in 1405, was quite kinky about skulls. As testament to his savage victories he built massive and unforgettable pyramids—using the heads of his victims: 70,000 at Isfahan, 90,000 in Baghdad, and one containing more than 100,000 skulls after his invasion of Delhi.

In the old days, when popes sat on thrones and ruled in the manner of kings, POPE CLEMENT THE SIXTH built himself a beautiful palace overlooking the river Rhône. When he died in 1352, the Huguenots showed a total lack of respect by using his skull as a football. Even worse, the marquis de Courton later drank wine from it.

QUEEN ARTEMISIA, the Queen of Caria, indulged in a rather more elegant case of macabre drinking. She was so distraught when her husband, King Mausolus, died that she ordered her subjects to build the biggest and most splendid memorial ever at Halicarnassus (now Bodrum, Turkey). The result, in 353 B.C., was the massive Tomb of Mausolus—from which the word mausoleum derives. It became one of the Seven Wonders of the World, and although it was later destroyed by an earthquake, bits of the sepulcher are now in the British Museum. The strangest part of this story, is that Artemisia did not bury her husband's body in that incredible tomb. Instead, she had him cremated. Then she poured his ashes into a goblet of fine wine and drank the lot. Dry wine, no doubt.

Another drink-related death is said to have been arranged when that notorious king, RICHARD THE THIRD, had his brother George, the Duke of Clarence, arrested and tried for treason. On being found guilty, Clarence was executed in the Tower of London in February 1478 in a highly original way. Being a no-good drunkard, he was drowned in a large barrel of Malmsey wine. As a reminder of this, his daughter Margaret, the countess of Salisbury, wore a miniature barrel of gold on her wrist until she died in 1541.

Two other English royals also drank too much. KING GEORGE THE FOURTH died of alcoholic cirrhosis in 1830 and so did KING WILLIAM THE FOURTH, seven years later.

Muslims are not supposed to allow liquor to sully their lips. Yet MUHAMMAD THE THIRD, a Bahmani sultan in India, died in 1482 of severe liver damage caused by alcohol. He must have used a funnel.

Four rulers who ate unwisely were:

- ALEXANDER THE GREAT, who gorged himself and died at a feast in 323 B.C.
- KING HARTHACNUT (son of King Canute) collapsed and died after eating a fifteen-course meal washed down by huge jugs of wine at an English wedding feast in 1042. He was twenty-four.
- KING HENRY THE FIRST died after eating a vast amount of lampreys—an eellike fish—at a banquet in 1135.

- FAROUK, the obese and debauched king of Egypt who was exiled in 1952, choked to death in a Rome restaurant in 1965 at the age of forty-four.

England's KING JOHN, of Magna Carta fame, was responsible for a most gruesome case of starvation. He had a "favorite" boyfriend named Sir William de Braose and naturally disliked William's wife, Maud, and her young son. So he had them thrown in a dungeon. When the cell was opened eleven days later, both were dead. The son had died first and Maud, in her last desperate moments of hunger, had gnawed at the boy's cheeks in an attempt to suck blood from him.

Even ordinary eating was hazardous for royals in the old days when poison was a popular method of putting them down. For that reason, human guinea pigs were usually employed to taste all their food beforehand. This was a life time job—if the royal in question had no enemies.

EMPEROR NAPOLEON BONAPARTE did not have a taster when he was imprisoned on St. Helena by the British—which is probably why he died of chronic arsenic poisoning in 1821 (not cancer of the stomach as is often claimed).

ALEXANDROS, the twenty-seven-year-old king of Greece, died of a different kind of poisoning in 1920. Blood poisoning—after being bitten by his pet monkey.

The most romantic case of royal poisoning happened in Nottinghamshire, England. This was in 1290 when King Edward the First was suffering from poison in a battle wound and his fifty-year-old wife, QUEEN ELEANOR, not trusting doctors, sucked all the poison from the wound. It saved his life but killed her. King Edward was so impressed by her devotion to the crown that he had large crosses erected at each of the twelve places her coffin stopped during its coach journey to London. These memorials were named the "Eleanor Crosses." Three of them still stand at Geddington, Northampton, and Waltham.

The most astonishing poisoning case was that of Gregory

Rasputin, the mad, bad monk who wielded a mystic power over the Russian EMPRESS ALEXANDRA after saving the life of her son. Resenting Rasputin's power and the change he was bringing to the old court, the transvestite homosexual Prince Felix Yusupov decided to poison him. Being too frightened to do it alone, he enlisted the aid of three noblemen.

On the night of December 17, 1916, they gave Rasputin a cup of coffee laced with enough arsenic to kill all the men in the room—and an elephant. They expected Rasputin to topple to the floor within seconds of gulping it down. Instead he licked his lips with great relish and then sat down to listen to some music for an hour.

Dumbfounded, the conspirators then pumped three bullets into his chest and shoulder. After that he was stabbed in the back. As he attempted to get to his feet, the noblemen kicked and battered him and then used strong ropes to tie his hands and feet. Dragging him to a car, they drove him to the Neva River where they broke a hole in the ice and pushed him into the freezing water, which should have sapped his strength within minutes. It did not. Rasputin bellowed curses at them and, although his hands were still bound, made repeated attempts to wriggle out of the hole with his elbows. Stamping on his arms and beating him about the head, they finally managed to grab hold of his long hair and hold his head under water until he drowned.

A rather more poetic death was suffered by MAELGWYN THE TALL, the brave Welsh warrior king of Gwynedd. When the Black Plague swept through Wales in the year 547, Maelgwyn was so determined not to catch the disease that he barricaded himself inside the church of Ros, near Conway Bay, and ordered his troops to guard the doorway twenty-four hours a day to stop anyone from getting in. Eventually the guards started to worry about his failure to take in trays of food. Venturing in, they found their monarch dead. Of the plague.

Another ruler who died of plague was LOUIS THE NINTH of France. That is both true and untrue. He died of plague in 1244 when he was thirty but, during the funeral service, he frightened the life out of the mourners by sitting bolt upright in his coffin and demanding to know what the hell they were doing because he wasn't ready for that place yet. He continued to live until 1270 when he really did die—of the plague. He lives on in history, however, as he was made a saint twenty-seven years later.

Not quite so saintly was the death of JAMES, THE DUKE OF MONMOUTH, the bastard son of the "Casanova king" Charles the Second by his first full-time mistress, the loose little Lucy Walter. When Charles died in 1685, Monmouth was angry that Charles's brother James was given the throne. Although he was born illegitimate, Monmouth felt that, as the first son of King Charles, he was far more entitled. So he raised an army and tried to have the crown placed on his head. Without success. He was captured and sentenced to death. His demise was a dreadful mess because somebody apparently forgot to sharpen the axe. The executioner (Jack Ketch) had to take four swings at the neck before Monmouth's head was parted from his body and eyewitnesses tell us that he suffered horribly. The executioner, that is.

The keeper of the king's pictures then discovered the blunt fact that the palace did not have a portrait of Monmouth. They solved the problem cleverly though—by stitching the decapitated head back on. Placing the "reformed" Monmouth in a posh chair, they assigned German-born artist Sir Godfrey Kneller (real name Gottfried Kniller, until he was given his title) to paint a reasonable likeness.

Scotland's KING ROBERT THE THIRD was definitely the saddest royal bastard. No disrespect meant, it's just that he was born ten years before his parents were married. A gentle and kindly youngster, he was brain-damaged when a horse kicked his head in. His so-called nobleman took advantage of this by misruling in his name. They enjoyed their power so much that they imprisoned his son and heir and deliberately starved him to death so that their nominee, James the First, could take the throne. Poor King Robert, he may have been mentally lacking but he could not have been totally daft. Just before he died at sixty-nine in 1406, he wrote this epitaph for his gravestone: "Here lies the worst of kings—and the most miserable of men."

Other royals who suffered were:

- BRUNHILDA, the warrior queen of Eastern France. She was about sixty when overthrown by her own noblemen in the year 613. This did not stop them killing her cruelly though. They caught a wild stallion, tied its legs together, and ill treated it until its mouth was frothing with pain. Then, after tying Brunhilda to its tail, they released the horse from its bonds and off it raced, with the queen bouncing behind. End of reign.
- Scotland's KING JAMES THE SECOND died in battle at thirty in 1460 when one of his own cannons exploded and a metal splinter sliced off the top of his head.
- ALEXANDER THE SECOND became the emperor of Russia in 1855 when he was thirty-seven. He died in 1881 when a bomb was thrown at him near his palace.
- CHANG TSO-LIN, a former bandit leader, was fifty-three when he became the de facto ruler of northern China in 1926, but he died from multiple injuries when blown up in a train two years later.

A different kind of explosion happened when Queen Mary's eldest brother, Prince "Dolly," died in 1927 of peritonitis. During the grand funeral procession toward the royal vaults at Windsor, hundreds of spectators heard his body explode in its coffin. Since then the bodies of British royals are usually embalmed before being laid to rest in peace, instead of pieces.

WILLIAM THE CONQUEROR suffered a similar explosion. Many history books claim he died of injuries sustained in battle in the town of Mantes, near Paris, in July 1087. The less romantic but true story is that he was not actually fighting at the time. He had ordered his troops to set fire to Mantes, and as he rode through the burning town his horse stumbled. As man and mount crashed to the ground, two of the king's three most private parts were crushed excruciatingly against the pommel of his saddle. He also suffered an abdominal injury and, in an attempt to alleviate the agonizing pain, he ate and drank to excess until he died on September 9.

After the sixty-year-old monarch had lain in state for a while, they trundled his body by horse and carriage all the way to the Abbey of Saint Stephen at Caen where it was to be entombed in a beautiful coffin carved out of marble. But the stonemasons who had chipped it out to size had been working on old measurements and the body was just too big to fit inside. When two soldiers were ordered to stand on the body in an attempt to squeeze it in, they became rather enthusiastic and irreverently jumped up and down on it. This broke the king's spine—which tore a hole in the front of his distended stomach and caused it to explode with a fearful bang. The stench was so disgusting that everyone had to race out of the building.

The coffins used for British royals have been known to weigh over one ton because they are lead-lined, to stop worms and similar creepy-crawlies getting at their regal bodies. But humans sometimes still get at them. It happened to the above-mentioned William the Conqueror. Nearly five-hundred years after he was finally squeezed into that marble coffin, thieves looking for valuables smashed it open and stole everything except his thigh bone. Just over two-hundred years later, during the French Revolution, some souvenir hunter even took that. Some peasants simply have no respect.

In 1813 the British royal family asked their royal surgeon, Sir Henry Halford, to go to the royal vaults at Windsor and examine the body of King Charles the First, the monarch who was beheaded by Oliver Cromwell. While carrying out his macabre assignment, Sir Henry noticed that in the area of the neck where Charles's head had been parted from his body there was a rather pretty little chunk of backbone. He liked this fourth neck vertebra so much that he took it home, filled it with salt, and placed it on his dining-room table. He found it was a terrific conversation piece when he entertained guests to lunch or dinner and that right royal salt cellar stayed on his table for thirty years until 1843.

This was when some spoilsport ran around to tell the then reigning monarch, Queen Victoria, all about it. She, not at all amused, said it was unbelievable bad taste that any part of a king's body should be used in such a common (salt of the earth) way and angrily ordered Dr. Sir Henry to replace it in King Charles's tomb.

The most hilarious aspect of this story is that while Sir Henry Halford was examining the cadaver of King Charles, several workmen were repairing the walls to the royal vault. It is probable that one worker saw Sir Henry steal that bit of backbone, because he also swiped something—a finger bone belonging to King Henry the Eighth, whose tomb had also been opened. The workman didn't make a salt cellar out of it though. He used it to make a knife handle! The royal archives do not disclose what happened to the workman when his naughtiness was discovered, but we can guess.

Some royal deaths were not at all exciting:

- MARGARET, the "Maid of Norway," sailed from Norway in 1290 at the age of seven to become the queen of Scotland, but died of severe seasickness on the way.
- CHARLES THE EIGHTH of France was terribly polite. As he was entering a tennis court at the Chateau d'Amboise in 1498, he bowed courteously to his wife and allowed her to precede him. But as he brought his head up again, it banged against a low wooden beam, which fractured his skull and killed him.

- QUEEN ELIZABETH THE FIRST died of septic tonsils in 1603.
- KING HAAKON THE SEVENTH of Norway died in September 1957 when he slipped on the soap in his marble bath and bashed his head on one of the taps.
- SIR MADHO RAO SCINDHIA BAHADUR SRINATH, the millionaire maharajah of Gwalior, died of diabetic carbuncles in Paris in 1925, at the age of fifty-one.
- FRIEDRICH-AUGUST THE SECOND, the king of Germany, died at fifty-seven in August 1854 when he missed his step getting out of a horse-drawn carriage and bashed his head on the edge of the pavement. Some negligent minion forget to lay the red carpet over that disgracefully dangerous obstacle.
- ALBERT, the king of Belgium, rose to great heights and was acclaimed as "the best constitutional monarch who ever reigned in Europe" but in February 1934, at the age of fifty-nine, he lost his grip and fell to his death while climbing a sheer cliff.
- HERCULE became the ruler of the tiny principality of Monaco in 1589 when he was twenty-seven. Although he was a handsome man, his subjects turned ugly and in 1604 threw him to his death over a cliff.
- Scotland's KING ALEXANDER THE THIRD died in 1286 when he fell off his horse. Normally, that wouldn't have been so bad, but he happened to be on the edge of the cliffs at Kinghorn, Fife, and plunged over.

Some rulers really plumbed the depths in their determination to climb to power. When Ariarathes the Fifth, the king of Cappadocia (Asia Minor), died in circa 130 B.C., his widow

QUEEN NYASA murdered all five of her sons to ensure she ascended to the throne. And in the year 940, ERIK "THE BLOOD-AXE" murdered all seven of his brothers so that he could co-rule as the king of Norway with his half-brother, HAAKON.

Problems with relatives were not uncommon. IRENE was born in Greece in 752 and became an orphan who had to fend for herself in the back streets of Athens. Being very beautiful, she realized that sex was her greatest weapon and used it to raise herself socially. At the age of seventeen she caught the eye of the Byzantine Emperor LEO THE FOURTH and married him in the same year. Tired old Leo died in 780, overstrained but happy, at the age of thirty-one. Impressive Irene then became EMPRESS IRENE who ruled as regent for her son Constantine the Sixth, then aged ten.

When Constantine came of age in 790, he ungratefully banished his mother but, being streetwise, she raised an army and returned to blind and depose him two years later. As he disappeared without trace, it is presumed he was murdered. In order to remain empress, Irene also imprisoned her late husband's five brothers. They apparently still had many supporters though, because in 802 she was deposed and banished to Lesbos, the famous Greek island of Lesbians where it was felt she would experience great difficulty in finding enough men to raise another army. She must have been quite unhappy and frustrated on the island, as she died within a year.

Of the sexy royal deaths, the most piquant was that of ATTILA, THE KING OF THE HUNS who, at the age of forty-seven married the dazzlingly beautiful Ildeco in 453. After the ceremony they enjoyed a great feast which went on until late that night. Then the bridal couple repaired to the beautifully silk-cushioned royal tent, where they remained until the sun started to go down next day. Only then did a servant pop his head around the tent flap to ask what they wanted as the first course for their breakfast. Cornflakes or soup, sire? Negative. Poor old Attila was dead and his ravishingly beautiful bride lay weeping beside him, totally unaware that her late husband had pioneered a sexual position that even the Kama Sutra missed—one foot in the grave.

Although Johan Ankarstrom was a former palace page boy, sex was apparently not the motive when he shot and killed forty-six-year-old KING GUSTAV THE THIRD of Sweden at a lavish masked ball in 1792. Ankarstrom was viciously flogged in public for three days and then executed.

Very few royals have died penniless.

- CHARLES THE SECOND, king of the French Carolingian dynasty, was such a wretched ruler that he was deposed in 877 and died in total poverty ten years later at the age of sixty-five.
- Another Charlie was CHARLES EDWARD, the grandson of England's King James the Second. The royal propaganda machine has conned the world into knowing him by the name "Bonnie Prince Charlie," but he was far from bonnie. The cold truth is that he was a miserable, bad-tempered, wife-bashing, and womanizing drunkard who died stone broke in 1788 at the age of sixty-eight while exiled in Rome.
- QUEEN MARIE de MEDICI was the wife of King Henry the Fourth of France. In 1601 she gave birth to the boy who became Louis the Thirteenth. She was also the regent of France from 1610 until 1617. But everyone, including her son Louis, disliked her oversexed and obstinate behavior, and she was thrown into jail. After managing to escape in 1631—allegedly by using her feminine charms on a guard—she fled to Belgium and spent her last eleven years living like a tramp. Although it was hushed up at the time, she is said to have died while sleeping in the hayloft of a farm near Cologne, Germany, at the age of sixty-nine.

- The most recent impecunious ruler was Sir Edward Mutesa, better known as KING FREDDIE, THE KABAKA OF BUGANDA. Born in 1924, he was overthrown by Dr. Milton Obote. Fleeing to England, Freddie eventually became so short of money that he humbly applied for social security handouts—the only modern king known to have done that! This inoffensive fellow who once ruled Uganda was penniless when he died in 1969. But God surely did not mind because, as the proverb says: "It's better to go to heaven in rags than to hell in embroidery."

It would be interesting to know how many of the royal rogues mentioned in this book actually did make it to heaven. Six-year-old Princess Margaret was convinced that her grandfather, GEORGE THE FIFTH, had somehow managed to get there after he left us in 1936, because she made this most revealing remark: "Grandpa has gone to heaven and I'm sure God is finding him very useful."

That great sexual athlete, King Edward the Seventh, had a much more cynical attitude. When he was asked by one of the young royals whether his mother, QUEEN VICTORIA, would be happy in heaven, he replied: "I don't know. She will have to walk behind the angels—and she definitely won't like that!"

# 21

---

## Fascinating Facts

### A Short Tale

EMPEROR NAPOLEON BONAPARTE, born in 1769, died in captivity on the island of St. Helena in 1821. His greatest defeat was at Waterloo in 1815, but his worst humiliation actually came 157 years later when his penis, pickled in a jar, came up for auction at Christie's London showrooms in 1972. The embarrassment was twofold because it was prematurely withdrawn when nobody raised a bid and, shock, horror, it was only one inch long. Napoleon's force drive was cut off by his confessor priest. Although we are not told why, it was almost certainly because the great little fellow had syphilis when he died (of arsenic poisoning).

# Big Bloomers

Another unusual item offered for auction in London was a pair of QUEEN VICTORIA'S king-size silk knickers beautifully embroidered with the Victoria Regina monogram, which raised eyebrows and $225. We can disclose that they were bought by Malcolm Forbes, of *Forbes* business magazine fame who not only collected art, motorbikes, castles, and hot air balloons but also Fabergé eggs (he owned twelve, each worth well over $1 million).

There is no doubt that Mr. Forbes had a rich sense of humor. On buying himself a private jet in the seventies, he had it painted gold and named it *Capitalist Tool*. So what did he do with Victoria's knickers? He had them framed and today they hang opposite the giant double bed in the master bedroom of his London mansion, Battersea Lodge, which gave Ronald Reagan and his wife Nancy a big giggle when they slept in that room as Malcolm's guests in June 1989.

# Double Breasted

KING HENRY THE EIGHTH'S second wife, Anne Boleyn, was born with a small extra finger on her left hand—which helped Henry to claim she was a witch. He also alleged she had three breasts and brought her to trial on charges that she was "the biggest whore in the realm" who had committed adultery with one thousand lovers, allegedly including her brother, George. Sexy Anne lost her head completely in 1536 when it was chopped off, but she will always be remembered in royal history, for being the mother of that little girl named Elizabeth—who became the Queen of England in 1558.

## Merry Lies

QUEEN ELIZABETH THE FIRST didn't appreciate some of the
ugly truths about British history, so she ordered William Shakespeare to redraft it up to and including her own time. She
even censored his comedy *The Merry Wives of Windsor*. Not
liking the idea of Sir John Falstaff being depicted as a dirty old
sod who lusted after two married women, she demanded he
be portrayed as being deeply in love.

## Footloose

KING CHARLES THE EIGHTH of France was born in 1470 with
six toes on his left foot. His descendant LOUIS THE FOUR-
TEENTH had a different problem. Toward the end of his sev-
enty-two-year reign, his toes started rotting. He discovered this
only when his valet found a toe in one of the royal bedsocks.
Louis died of syphilis in 1715 and his heart was embalmed.

## Eat Your Heart Out

Nearly 150 years later that embalmed heart came into the
possession of William Buckland, the dean of Westminster. William was a brilliant man, but he worked so hard that he suffered
a mental breakdown during which he had the heart of King
Louis served to him for dinner one night. And he ate it.

## Have a Heart

England's KING HENRY THE THIRD offered his heart to the
abbess of Fontevraud while visiting her home in 1254. After

his death someone remembered the promise so Henry's heart was cut out and sent to her by special courier. We don't know her reaction.

## Now Hear This

A cynical Italian politician once said that if an Englishman "of any importance" gets scratched in a foreign land, the whole of the British Establishment bleeds.

This was certainly true in 1739 when Britain's KING GEORGE THE SECOND entered into a war with Spain because a Spaniard had chopped off an English sea captain's ear. The captain was Robert Jenkins, and the conflict he caused became known as The War of Jenkins' Ear. Some history books do mention the subject but, more often than not, they leave you with the impression that the man who cut off the ear was barbaric and the Englishman was an innocent man done wrong. Not quite so. At the time, British ships made a regular practice of visiting various Spanish colonies to conduct illicit (tax-free) trade with the local natives. This annoyed the Spanish king, FELIPE THE FIFTH so much that he ordered Spanish ships to stop and search any suspect British vessel sailing near his foreign possessions. Captain Jenkins found himself in trouble as he sailed his British brig *Rebecca* past Cuba on his way to London from Jamaica in 1731. Just off Havana he was stopped by a Spanish customs and excise vessel commanded by Captain Fandino.

Jenkins later alleged that the Spanish captain had "plundered" the cargo he had bought legally in Jamaica and had then cut off his ear. Answering this claim, Captain Fandino said Jenkins was a lying tax evader who had pompously talked about defending his cargo "with his life" until one swish of a sword had shut him up.

Seven years later, in 1738, King George somehow heard about Jenkins losing his ear and called him in to give evidence in the British House of Commons. When a member of Parliament asked Jenkins if he could prove his story, he produced a jar containing his ear—pickled in alcohol. That little piece of pickled evidence, and the wide publicity given to the story told by Captain Jenkins, caused extreme indignation against Spain and was an important factor in rousing hostility between the two countries.

At first, it was just a long war of words. When the Spaniards insisted that Jenkins was a liar, the British replied that it was ridiculous for anyone to suggest that an Englishman would cut off his ear to save his face (for losing some of his cargo). The Spaniards countered by alleging that the Brits were just looking for any excuse to start hostilities and that the case of Robert Jenkins and his pickled ear was just a propaganda ruse to whip up hatred against Spain in the eyes of the British public.

When the British asked why they should do such a thing, the Spaniards said Whitehall obviously did it to condition their gullible masses into being willing to pay the extra taxes necessary for such a war. When King George the Second called this tommyrot, pure bunkum, and absolute balderdash, the Spanish king goaded the British by asking them to explain why on earth they were making such a big fuss in 1738 about an incident that had happened in 1731. That did it. In early 1739 the British declared war on Spain. It lasted for nine years.

## *Submariner*

The first royal to travel in a submarine was that gay Scots king of England, JAMES THE FIRST. He did it in 1624 when he voyaged underwater from Westminster pier to Greenwich in a submerged wooden boat totally covered with leak-proof leather. Invented by the Englishman William Bourne, it was constructed by the Dutchman Cornelius van Drebbel, but the first mechanical (hand-propelled screw) submarine was invented in 1776 by the American David Bushnell of Connecticut.

# Able Alf

KING ALFRED THE GREAT is remembered by all British school-children for being foolish enough to burn some cakes after being told to watch them carefully, but this doubtful legend has overshadowed his real achievements.

- Although a backward student in his youth who only learned to read when he was an adult, Alfred mastered Latin and ordered that important books be translated so that more of his subjects could read and understand them. He also worked on the translations himself.
- In the year 886 he ordered pennies to be struck for the economic convenience of his people and became the first English king to have his face on a coin.
- Alfred invented the first "clock." This was a candle, bearing hourly markings, which was encased in a transparent animal horn. The candle burned down at a regular rate because it was completely protected from wind and drafts.
- Having fought off the invading Danes, Alfred decided that England's coasts should be patrolled by large boats manned by seventy to one hundred rowers so that warning could be given of future invaders. Thus was born the British Royal Navy.

# Ruling the Waves

The Dane CANUTE, who became king of England in 1016, is remembered as the megalomaniac who tried to stop the incoming tide by lashing at the waves with a whip. In fact, he was a wise old monarch. He took his courtiers down to the beach to watch as he tried to whip the waves into submission because he wished to demonstrate that although he was a mighty king, like all other men, he was powerless against nature.

## Seaworthy

When the famous diarist Samuel Pepys told KING CHARLES THE SECOND that there was such a thing as a flying fish, the king and his courtiers were most skeptical until an officer of the King's Maritime Regiment confirmed that he had personally seen such fish flying high above the water to escape from bigger fish.

Accepting this firsthand evidence, King Charles said: "From the very nature of their calling, no class of our subjects can have so wide a knowledge of the seas as the officers and men of our loyal Maritime Regiment and henceforth, should we ever cast doubts upon a tale that lacks likelihood, we will first 'Tell It To The Marines' and let them judge."

## Unable Seamen

KING JOHN of Magna Carta fame had an unusual servant. This was Solomon Attefeld, who was known as The Royal Head Holder. He was rewarded with large tracts of land for holding the king's head when he went to sea to stop him being seasick. Sixty years later KING EDWARD THE FIRST adopted this idea by also hiring a head holder when he sailed. (Source: *Relics of Literature* by Stephen Collet, London, 1825.)

# No See

In 1865, when General Mariano Melgarejo became president of Bolivia, he held a great feast to which he invited the recently appointed British minister. During the meal General Melgarejo introduced his mistress to the guests and ordered them all to stand up and salute her. When the British minister refused, Melgarejo had him stripped naked, tied him facing backward on a donkey, and had him drummed out of the capital as thousands lined the streets to watch.

On hearing of this diabolical insult to her British Empire, Queen Victoria ordered her Royal Navy to send half a dozen gunboats to Bolivia and bombard the hell out of it after sinking all its ships. When her highly embarrassed admirals timidly pointed out that Bolivia had no sea-coast as it was bounded by Brazil, Paraguay, Argentina, Chile, and Peru, Queen Victoria was even more livid. Calling for a map, she used a pair of scissors to cut out the highly undesirable republic.

She also ordered her prime minister to strike Bolivia from the maps for all time. Thereafter, on the huge map of the world hanging in the House of Commons, the area once representing Bolivia was completely blacked out. Geographies made no reference to the country and as far as England was concerned it ceased to exist—until June 1871, when General Melgarejo was deposed and assassinated.

# Sore Eye

In 1892 PRINCE CHRISTIAN OF SCHLESWIG-HOLSTEIN went out hunting and was blinded in one eye when Queen Victoria's son Prince Arthur shot him by accident. To make up for this, Victoria bought him several glass eyes of different colors. His favorite was one that was deliberately bloodshot, and until he died in 1917, he wore it to match the other whenever he had a cold.

## Eyesore!

Britain's QUEEN MARY once opened a door she shouldn't have in the 1930s and walked in on an officer lying stark naked on his bunk. Later, when introduced to him during a military parade, she quipped: "I believe we have met before." This just goes to prove that Buckingham Palace really is telling the truth when they say the royals have a great memory for faces.

## Blind Loyalty

After the Spanish Armada was beaten (mainly by bad weather) in 1588, QUEEN ELIZABETH THE FIRST agreed to attend a huge naval tournament put on for the valiant and victorious British seamen. Some gigantic flatterer in charge of the arrangements issued orders that: "On account of the dazzling loveliness of Her Majesty, all seamen, on receiving their prizes, should shield their eyes with the right hand." That is how the naval and military salute was born. (Source: British Naval Records, 1589.)

## Tricky Dicky

Britain's most controversial monarch is RICHARD THE THIRD, who ruled from 1483 to 1485. He is said to have been a blood-thirsty tyrant who had his brother drowned in a barrel of wine; murdered Henry the Sixth and his son; deposed his two nephews and ordered them to be slain in the Tower of London and was himself murdered after losing his horse at the battle of Bosworth Field where he shouted: "A horse! A horse, my Kingdom for a horse."

In 1924 a group of gallant royalists founded the Fellowship of the White Boar which was renamed the Richard III Society in 1959. With a membership of four thousand today, its aim is to secure a reassessment of Richard's role and reputation in English history.

The society claims that far from being a monster, Richard was "a noble, upright, courageous, tender-hearted and most conscientious King." The society conducts historical research, installs plaques and church windows in his name and commemorates his death by inserting memorial notices in newspapers every August 22. Although it has done a lot to whitewash Richard's tarnished royal image, the society still has not been able to disprove his involvement in the murder of the two princes in the Tower.

His Royal Highness the Duke of Gloucester (who just happens to be a descendant of Richard the Third) is the proud patron of the society and anyone wishing to join can write to the General Secretary, Mrs. Elizabeth Nokes, at 4 Oakley Street, Chelsea, London SW3.

## *Beat This*

Like most boys, KING EDWARD THE SIXTH did not always learn his lessons when at school. But, being a royal, he could not be caned by his teacher so, whenever His Royal Highness hadn't done his homework, someone else had to take the rap. This was a boy named Barnaby Fitzpatrick—who was whipped as Edward watched. When KING CHARLES THE FIRST flunked his lessons, a boy named Mungo Murray was whipped on his behalf. Hence the term whipping boy.

# Go Fly a Kite

The sixth-century Chinese emperor GAO YANG had a novel way of punishing condemned prisoners. He used them to test man-flying kites—an early form of hang gliding. The prisoners were thrown from a tall tower, clinging to the bamboo and silk contraptions. The luckiest victim flew for two miles before crash landing and breaking his neck.

# Call Me Pedro

PEDRO THE SECOND became the emperor of Brazil in 1831 and, being a scholarly man ahead of his time, decided to back a young American who had the seemingly crazy idea of inventing a machine that would enable people to talk to each other at long distance—through wires. The man was Alexander Graham Bell, and after his telephone was patented in 1876, he allowed Pedro to make the very first royal phone call. Pedro was deposed in the 1889 revolution and died exiled in Paris two years later, but Bell went on to fame and fortune.

# Royal Birdie

The first royal female known to have played golf was MARY QUEEN OF SCOTS. She was certainly the first golf widow because she merrily played several holes in public a few days after allegedly having her husband, Lord Darnley, murdered in 1567. After being imprisoned for nineteen years, Mary was beheaded on the orders of her cousin, Queen Elizabeth the First.

## Premarital Sex

Dozens of books have been written about HENRY THE EIGHTH and his six wives, but we think the best little-known fact about him is the excuse he used to get rid of his fifth wife, Catherine Howard. Breaking all the rules in the adultery game, he charged her with having had intercourse before his marriage to her. This was with Thomas Culpeper, a handsome musician. That is why, by a special Act of Parliament, what's more, poor Catherine was beheaded in 1542.

## Well Hung?

KING JOHN reigned over England from 1199 to 1216 and is usually discreetly described as the monarch who "often invaded the honor of the female nobility." But although he was a ram himself, he was furious when he discovered that his wife, Isabella, had bedded a younger, more handsome, and better endowed fellow. In revenge, he had the man murdered and hung the corpse over Isabella's bed.

## A Right Royal Pickle

When the Russian emperor PETER, the so-called Great, found out that his wife, Catherine, had been unfaithful, he had the guilty man's head chopped off and placed in a large jar of alcohol. This was put on Catherine's bedside table and kept there as a constant reminder of her unfaithfulness.

## Pillow Talk

The French King LOUIS THE TENTH was much crueler to his twenty-five-year-old wife, Queen Margaret. In 1315, after ten years of marriage, he discovered she had entertained another in her bed. After having her tried and convicted of adultery, he had her smothered to death with a pillow—on that same bed.

## What a Bastard!

HENRY THE FIRST, who reigned from 1100 to 1135, sired twenty known bastards by six mistresses. But that astonishing British record was beaten into a cocked hat by the German prince Frederick August who, by becoming a Catholic for purely political reasons, hustled himself into being crowned AUGUST THE SECOND, KING OF POLAND. When he died at sixty-three in 1733, he left more than 350 illegitimate children cluttered about Europe—and he acknowledged them all. A world record.

## Royal Pimps

KING CHARLES THE SECOND had a royal pimp named Sir Charles Berkeley who went around all London's theaters looking for pretty young actresses who would be willing to perform for the king privately—in bed.

When he was Prince of Wales, EDWARD THE SEVENTH had an equerry named Harry Tyrrwhitt-Wilson who acted as his pimp. Known as The Smiler, Tyrrwhitt-Wilson asked the prince which women he fancied and then set up assignations for him by informing the ladies to prepare for the royal coming.

GEORGE THE FOURTH had a personal pimp while he was

prince regent. The bastard son of an Irish butler and a chambermaid, Sir John MacMahon was paid £2,000 a year and was described as George's "private secretary." But his main duty was to procure pretty young girls for His Majesty.

## Virgin on the Ridiculous

The old MAHARAJAH OF PATIALIA had a squadron of royal pimps who scoured the villages of the Punjab to find young virgins for him to deflower because he insisted on having sex with a virgin every day. (His enemies sneered that he only did this because he couldn't bear the criticism an experienced woman would have given him.)

When the old rogue visited London, he was welcomed as a friend and ally by the British royals. This raises some interesting questions: How did His Highness manage while in England? Did his British Special Branch bodyguards close their eyes when he recruited local talent? Or was he allowed to bring a planeload of young Indian virgins with him?

KING CAROL THE SECOND of Rumania was another royal who liked virgins. He was so well-endowed that several young girls are said to have died after he had ruptured their perinea. He also had a royal surgeon who performed abortions on any underage girls who fell pregnant. King Carol used taxpayers' money to silence all the mothers of those young girls and his sexual exploits only became known to the public after the Rumanian government kicked him out in 1940 after he had ruled for ten years.

He was reduced to lying on the floor of a train as angry members of the public fired bullets at him. Even then, being a royal, he managed to survive regally in exile with his mistress, Magda Lupescu, until 1953 when he died in Portugal.

# Nuptial Mass

KING HENRY THE EIGHTH of England had six wives but was no great shakes when compared with the following:

- Israel's wise KING SOLOMON had seven hundred wives.
- KING MUTESA OF UGANDA had seven thousand.
- KING MONGUT OF SIAM (of "King and I" fame) had nine thousand wives and concubines.
- Men didn't have the monopoly on multiple marriage. QUEEN KAHENA OF NIGERIA had four hundred husbands. She never had to pretend a headache.

# Wedding Belles

MARY, the daughter of King Charles the First, was nine years old when she married the Dutch prince WILLEM THE SECOND. He was then fourteen. It took them nearly nine years to produce their first and only child, WILLEM THE THIRD, who became king of England in 1689.

ISABELLE, the daughter of Charles the Sixth of France, was only seven years old when she became the second wife of twenty-nine-year-old KING RICHARD THE SECOND of England in 1396. Three years later she was a widow at the age of ten.

# Court Short

The least known of England's queens is MATILDA, an arrogant little madam who had little happiness in her life. At the age of twelve she was married off to Heinrich the Fifth, the twenty-eight-year-old emperor of the Holy Roman Empire. He made her a widow when she was twenty-three and five years later her family forced her to marry seventeen-year-old Geoffrey the Fifth of Anjou. The only daughter of Henry the First, Matilda became Queen of England in April 1141 but fled from her throne eight months later to escape the wrath of her overtaxed subjects. She was one of the shortest reigning queens in two senses as she was only four foot two inches tall.

## Cut Short

The shortest reign of an English monarch was that of Lady Jane Grey, who was officially proclaimed QUEEN JANE OF ENGLAND in July 1553 when she was fifteen. She was deposed after nine days by QUEEN MARY ("Bloody Mary") and beheaded seven months later.

## Long Life

The longest reign of all time was that of KING PEPI THE SECOND, alias Phiops II, who ruled Egypt for ninety years. He came to the throne at the age of six but there were no flies on him. He made sure of that by keeping naked slaves near him, their bodies smeared with honey.

## Dirty Life

One of the longest reigning European rulers was LOUIS THE FOURTEENTH. Known as the "Sun King," he was the vainest monarch in French history and his coronation robe was the most expensive ever known. Encrusted with diamonds and pearls, it cost one-sixth of the value of the Palace of Versailles.

Louis hated washing and took only three baths in the whole of his adult life. But he loved beds and owned 413.

## Butter Fingers

Britain's longest reigning monarch was QUEEN VICTORIA, who ruled for sixty-four years. Toward the end of her reign she was so fragile and senile that when photographed holding one of her many grandchildren, it was feared that she would drop the infant. To avoid this, a servant (presumably female) hid under her skirts and held up the baby.

## Manic Cure

During World War II the British *Daily Sketch* went just a little over the top when it published a lengthy article suggesting that workers were not working hard enough. Headlined "Do Your Bit To Help Win The War," the madly patriotic article stated that lazy (factory) girls should take particular note of the fact that the Duchess of Kent was "now manicuring her own fingernails." No wonder Hitler was beaten hands down.

## Born Again Royal

QUEEN ELIZABETH celebrates two birthdays each year. One on April 21, the day she was really born, and an official birthday, which is celebrated on the second Saturday in June.

Why? Because Queen Victoria, once she was married, absolutely refused to leave her home on her birthday and preferred to spend it with her many relatives, counting the thousands of birthday presents sent to her from all over the world. So Parliament had to invent a birthday on which soldiers, sailors, and airmen and so on, could take part in heavily rehearsed, square-bashing military and ceremonial parades, commemorating the fact that their beloved queen had not been born on that day.

## Phil-The-Lip

The only son of Prince Andrew of Greece was born on a dining room table in a house called Mon Repos on the island of Corfu in 1921. His first name was PHILOPPOS and his family name was SCHLESWIG-HOLSTEIN-SONDERBURG-GLUCKSBURG.

The infant prince, a great-great-grandson of Queen Victoria, was carried aboard the British cruiser HMS *Calypso* in a cot made from an orange box when his family was forced to flee from Greece into exile.

At eighteen he was attending Dartmouth Naval College where the thirteen-year-old Princess Elizabeth first set eyes on him. We are told that she was impressed by how high he could jump, and that it was love at first sight.

On February 28, 1947, Philoppos of Greece became a naturalized British subject and changed his name to Philip Mountbatten. He and Elizabeth officially announced their engagement five months later on July 10, 1947. At the time, Philip was earning less than £9 a week and possessed only one suit, three naval uniforms, and a pile of darned socks.

On the eve of his wedding, however, Philip was created His Royal Highness and given a £10,000 a year state salary plus some grand titles (fit for a future queen): Baron of Greenwich, Earl of Merioneth, Duke of Edinburgh, and a Knight of the Most Noble Order of the Garter. "It was a great deal to give a man all at once," drily commented his father-in-law, King George the Sixth.

When Philip wed on November 20, 1947, his three sisters, Margarita, Theodora, and Sophie, were deliberately not invited.

They had married Germans (two were members of Hitler's Nazi SS) and Whitehall thought it would be "unwise" to invite them because the war against Germany had ended only two years earlier. It was felt the British public would resent Buckingham Palace entertaining such honored guests.

"Phil the Lip" is famous for his outrageous remarks. His daughter, Anne, says he suffers from "donto-pedology"—the art of opening his mouth and putting his foot in it.

- In the early sixties, Pope John the Twenty-third granted the Queen an audience. When it was over Prince Philip, noticing that one of the guards of honor had a black eye, asked him: "What happened to you then? Did you meet a Protestant?"
- In 1968 the prince described the American Apollo space program as a "waste of money." One month later the astronauts Frank Borman, Jim Lovell, and Bill Anders made their historic circumnavigation of the moon in Apollo 8.
- In 1969 during a trip to Canada Philip said: "We don't come here for our health. We can think of better ways of enjoying ourselves." Canadians were so annoyed that the government removed Queen Elizabeth's face from some of its coins.
- In the same year, while visiting Paraguay, he told its dictator president, Alfredo Stroessner: "It's a pleasant change to be in a country that isn't ruled by its people."
- In 1986 Philip and his wife made a state visit to the People's Republic of China. Chatting with some British students there, he described Peking as "ghastly" and warned them, "If you stay here much longer you'll go back with slitty eyes." This made world headlines. The next day, as Philip emerged from a Buddhist temple, two American journalists teased him by slanting their eyes with their fingers.

"What's your problem?" he snapped. "Is the sun too strong for you?"

- Many pet shop owners must have wondered if the sun had affected Prince Philip's reasoning when he stated that one should be "Very, very careful of people who keep tropical fish in their homes." Explaining, he added: "Such people are usually suffering from some psychiatric problem." Piranhoia, no doubt.

His Royal Highness Prince Philip, the Duke of Edinburgh, Baron of Greenwich, Earl of Merioneth, Lord High Steward of Plymouth, Ranger of Windsor Great Park, Honorary Colonel of the University of Edinburgh Training Corps, Colonel-in-Chief of the Royal Corps of Australian Electrical and Mechanical Engineers, Air Commander-in-Chief of the Royal Canadian Air Cadets, Admiral of the Fleet of the Royal New Zealand Navy, also holds the honorary ranks of colonel in Kentucky, deputy sheriff in Harris County, Texas, and honorary admiral in the "Great Navy of the State of Nebraska". This is all very interesting because Phil-the-Lip once said: "Anyone with a title is a more or less likeable halfwit."

## Eyes Off!

PRINCESS ANNE was the only female competitor to be excused a sex test when she represented Britain in the horse jumping contests at the 1976 Montreal Olympics.

## 'Cor Blimey!

The Queen's English (that is English as she is "supposed" to be spoke) is actually only spoken by 3 percent of the British people.

## Codswallop

PRINCE CHARLES and his wife, DIANA, never use fish knives and forks when eating fish dishes at home because Charles hates them. Why? He says they are "so middle class!"

## Eye Spy

Britain's biggest gathering of spies takes place in Buckingham Palace at the end of November every year when about twelve hundred members of the diplomatic corps in London join QUEEN ELIZABETH and other members of her family for cocktails and canapes from 9:30 P.M. until midnight. At least 30 percent of them are accredited intelligence agents plus a few dozen who, for political reasons, are "nonadmitted" agents—although many of them are known as such by British Intelligence. Or so they say.

## Relax Folks!

Once a month QUEEN ELIZABETH invites six or eight "high achievers" to enjoy an informal lunch with her in Buckingham Palace. They can be musicians, bankers, writers, film stars, TV or radio personalities, and even comedians. They are taken to the 1844 Room—so named because Emperor Nicholas the First of Russia used it when he visited Queen Victoria in that year. There they are offered drinks and cigarettes until the big moment when Her Majesty arrives. The door opens and half a dozen corgis charge in followed by their mistress—who is carrying a handful of dog biscuits. This is the Queen's standard ploy to make everybody feel "at home."

# *Home Truths*

When QUEEN ELIZABETH holds a big do at the six-hundred-room Buckingham Palace, she gets out her best "crockery." Made of solid gold and including twenty-four dozen plates, the whole collection weighs about five tons and is estimated to be worth more than $15 million. All her butter pats have the royal monogram on them—and so do the royal milk bottles.

She loves grilled haddock, chicken, roast beef, saddle of lamb and Dover sole, but dislikes oysters, olives, egg-plants, garlic, milk puddings, shrimps, octopus, and lobsters ("What awful-looking creatures"). Her favorite tipple is a nice double gin and tonic followed by white German wine for dinner.

Her guests get champagne (Mumm de Mumm 1982) and caviar but, as Sigmund Freud so rightly observed, the primary burden of a ruler is to ward off envy, so Her Majesty regularly lets the press know how economical she is. For instance, we are assured that she uses only one bar of the electric fire in her private study. And every year, some British newspaper tells us how the world's richest woman earns "a few extra pennies" by allowing members of the public to pick blackberries (at 35 pence a pound) and raspberries (40 pence) on her Sandringham estate. That's interesting. Isn't it the taxpayer who finances the growing of those berries in the first place?

# *Life's Just One Great Picnic*

PRINCESS MARGARET once said, quite seriously, that the only way to run a successful picnic was to take your own butler along. This reminds us of the unnamed princeling at Eton who was told to write an essay on poverty. In it, he stated: "They were a very poor family. The father was poor, the mother was poor, and even the chauffeur and the butlers were poor ..."

# The Poor Royals

In 1969, when the British economy was in poor shape, PRINCE PHILIP appeared on an American television program. He said things were so bad back home that the royal family was "about to go into the red." He then added: "We may have to move from Buckingham Palace to smaller premises." Philip said it in jest of course. But hundreds of viewers in the United States felt so sorry for him and poor wife that they actually sent donations to help the poor royals make ends meet and Buckingham Palace had the embarrassing task of returning all the money! Convincing, aren't they?

# Purely Voluntary!

The biggest financial embarrassment for Buckingham Palace came just before PRINCESS ANNE married Mark Phillips in 1973. Some total idiot in the corridors of power sent out an instruction that members of the British Armed Forces might wish to contribute toward a wedding present or two for the happy couple. It was suggested that each officer should give 30 pence and each soldier 5 pence. Then came the crunch. The memo stated that anyone not wishing to donate must state so in writing "within 48 hours"! When this vicious little bit of blackmail was leaked to the press, the Ministry of Defence quickly backtracked by saying "all donations would be purely voluntary, of course." No need to put it in writing, old chap.

# Praying For Page One

In 1924, when the DUKE OF WINDSOR was the Prince of Wales, he traveled on the liner Berengaria. With him was his private secretary Alan Lascelles, who made him promise to attend the ship's church service next day. Lascelles then sat down and wrote a letter to his wife, Joan. In it he told her that His Royal Highness's attendance at church "will be excellent propaganda." (Source: *In Royal Service: The Letters and Journals of Sir Alan Lascelles* [Hamish Hamilton, 1989].)

## Dirty Linen

When KING EDWARD THE EIGHTH went into exile and became the DUKE OF WINDSOR in 1936, he ended up in Austria and, feeling a little homesick, popped in to see Sir Walford Selby at the British Legation in Vienna.

The duke was delighted when Selby invited him to stay for lunch with his wife and daughter. But, during the meal, the duke asked: "What are those odd little silver rings for?" Lady Selby explained that as their linen table napkins did not always get dirty, they were used for two or three meals and, for identification purposes, each member of the family had their own napkin ring.

The forty-three-year-old duke was incredulous. With eyes popping and mouth agape, he said: "Do you really mean to tell me that people don't get a fresh napkin for every meal?"

## GREAT!

Queen Elizabeth's great-great-great-great-great-great-great-great-grandfather, Colonel Augustine Warner of Virginia, was George Washington's great-grandad. This is how:

Colonel Augustine Warner of Virginia

Mildred Warner
wed
Laurence Washington

Augustine Washington

George Washington

Mary Warner
wed
Major John Smith of Virginia

Mildred Smith
wed
Robert Porteus of Virginia

The Rev Robert Porteus of Virginia

Mildred Porteus
wed
Robert Hodgson

The Rev Robert Hodgson

Henrietta Mildred Hodgson
wed
Oswald Smith

Frances Dora Smith
wed
13th Earl of Strathmore

14th Earl of Strathmore

Elizabeth Bowes-Lyon
(The Queen Mother)

Elizabeth II

# The Family Reigns

QUEEN ELIZABETH II (1952–) is the daughter of
GEORGE VI (1936–1952), who was the brother of
EDWARD VIII (Jan. 1936–Dec. 1936), who was the son of
GEORGE V (1910–1936), who was the son of
EDWARD VII (1901–1910), who was the son of
QUEEN VICTORIA (1837–1901), who was the niece of
WILLIAM IV (1830–1837), who was the brother of
GEORGE IV (1820–1830), who was the son of
GEORGE III (1760–1820), who was the grandson of
GEORGE II (1727–1760), who was the son of
GEORGE I (1714–1727), who was the cousin of
ANNE (1702–1714), who was the sister-in-law of
WILLIAM III (1689–1702), who was the son-in-law of
JAMES II (1685–1688), who was the brother of
CHARLES II (1660–1685), who was the son of
CHARLES I (1625–1649), who was the son of
JAMES I (1603–1625), who was the cousin of
ELIZABETH I (1558–1603), who was the half-sister of
MARY I (1553–1558), who was the second cousin of
JANE (10–19 July 1553), who was the first cousin of
EDWARD VI (1547–1553), who was the son of
HENRY VIII (1509–1547), who was the son of
HENRY VII (1485–1509), who was the cousin of
RICHARD III (1483–1485), who was the uncle of
EDWARD V (9 April–25 June 1483), who was the son of
EDWARD IV (1461–1470 and 1471–1483), who was the
  cousin of
HENRY VI (1422–1461 and 1470–1471), who was the son of
HENRY V (1413–1422), who was the son of
HENRY IV (1399–1413), who was the cousin of
RICHARD II (1377–1399), who was the grandson of
EDWARD III (1327–1377), who was the son of
EDWARD II (1307–1327), who was the son of
EDWARD I (1272–1307), who was the son of

HENRY III (1216–1272), who was the son of
JOHN (1199–1216), who was the brother of
RICHARD I (1189–1199), who was the son of
HENRY II (1154–1189), who was the cousin of
STEPHEN (1135–1141 and 1141–1154), who was the cousin
of
MATILDA (April 1141–Nov. 1141), who was the daughter of
HENRY I (1100–1135), who was the brother of
WILLIAM II (1087–1100), who was the son of
WILLIAM, that bastard (illegitimate) Frenchman, who
conquered England in 1066

# 22

## Fact and Fiction

### Puddle Piffle

Britain's most famous legalized pirate, Sir Walter Raleigh, was the not-so-secret lover of that famous Virgin Queen, ELIZABETH THE FIRST, for many years. She adored his attentions so much that she showered him with many "rewards"—including the nice little present of 42,000 acres of land in Munster, Ireland. But he fell out of favor with the Queen when she caught him having it off with Bessy Throckmorton, one of her ladies-in-waiting.

The propagandists give schoolchildren a rather different picture of Sir Walter. They present him as the chivalrous blade who saved Elizabeth from getting mud on the hem of her skirt by placing his cloak over a puddle in her path. Claiming this never happened, many historians insist that this world-famous nonact of gallantry was invented by Sir Walter Scott in 1821 when he wrote his novel *Kenilworth*.

## *Sign Here*

Legend has it that KING JOHN signed the Magna Carta in 1215. Not so. He was illiterate. He is also said to have affixed his seal to it. Not so. He delegated the job to one of his courtiers because he hated the idea of having to sign away much of his royal power to the barons who disliked him. The Magna Carta has been vaunted as a "Charter of English liberty." Not so. Those barons who forced King John into that highly publicized "signing session" actually conned the peasants out of their tiny little minds. The Magna Carta gave the people very little they did not have already. The principles of trial by jury, habeas corpus, parliamentary control of taxation, and so on already existed.

## *Landlubber*

PRINCE HENRY OF PORTUGAL was known to his subjects as the Great Navigator. In truth, he hated the sea and never sailed himself. But, to be fair, he personally provided the finance for ships and seamen who were brave enough to venture into the deep and unknown waters he dreaded. For this, he deserves his place in history as the inaugurator of the Age of Discovery. He paid for the erection of an observatory and established a school of navigation whose pupils were responsible for the discovery of the Madeiras in 1418.

## *Hanky Panky*

Some French historians claim LOUIS THE FOURTEENTH invented the handkerchief. Not so. But he did pioneer square ones by telling his valet to have some made in that shape because all the ones he had were round and he could never find the middle. Some British historians claim the hankie was "invented" in the fourteenth century by KING RICHARD THE SECOND when he was a bright little youngster. Skeptics say it is impossible to believe that no human being had ever wiped his nose or sneezed into a piece of cloth before then. They regard the royal "invention" as just another one of those "aren't our aristocrats wonderful" tales.

In the same way, the fourth earl of Sandwich is credited with having "invented" the sandwich in 1762 because he placed a portion of meat between two slices of bread rather than interrupt a twenty-four-hour gambling session to eat a proper meal. There's something wrong here. England's KING CHARLES THE SECOND placed cheese between chunks of bread (and even biscuits) when he lived in the woods while on the run from Oliver Cromwell in 1651. But as Charles was a sexy old "baddie," they could hardly name him as the inventor, and the earl of Sandwich is still the man whose name appears under the word sandwich in many dictionaries. (On the other hand, maybe they were right. Can you imagine walking into a café and asking for "a toasted cheese and tomato charles the second, please"?)

## Not So Mad?

History shows that the "good guys" often get away with it when they do something wrong. The baddies most certainly don't. KING HEROD is a good example.

They say he was totally insane. Not true. It is now believed he was suffering from a disease that gave him temporary hallucinations and crippling headaches. Today's PRINCE CHARLES is on record as saying his mad ancestor King George the Third was not really insane but "merely suffered periodic attacks of a metabolic illness not then understood." If they can cleanse mad George the Third in that way, why not Herod?

They also say Herod had his enemies killed by the score.

Yet not much of a hue and cry has been made about that "great hero of chivalry," Holy Roman emperor CHARLEMAGNE, who once had four thousand Saxon prisoners beheaded in a single day. Not because they were the enemy, but because Charlemagne felt it would have been too expensive to feed them.

History is full of lies, distortions, and mistakes. King Herod died in 4 B.C. How then could he have ordered his soldiers to kill the infant Jesus? The answer, according to the experts, is that 4 B.C. was the *true* year of the Nativity.

Another notorious madman of history is the EMPEROR NERO. Many films have shown him sitting on the balcony of his palace playing a violin as Rome burned in the valley below. Not true. The violin was not invented until some fourteen hundred years later. So he must have been playing a lyre? Nope. In fact, Nero was not even in Rome at the time. He was some fifty miles away in Antium.

Many history books ignore the fact that Nero built superb aqueducts all around Rome so that fresh water could be channeled into the city from the countryside. Nero also warned the rich property owners *not* to use lead piping in the houses they rented out. Why? Because his advisor, Vitruvius, had told him that water passing through lead pipes caused serious illness. This really is thought-provoking because it was only about nineteen hundred years later that scientists discovered that lead pipes used for the conveyance of drinking water caused brain damage in youngsters through lead poisoning.

Nero was definitely no angel though. Like most royals, he hated being beaten at anything. A little-known fact is that he was actually a contestant in the official Olympic Games and actually won gold medals! But only because he scared his opponents by making it clear they would be executed if he did not win.

He also frightened judges. Once, when he entered a chariot race, Nero fell out of his chariot halfway around the arena. He still won the race though. The judges disqualified all the other contestants on the grounds that they had cheated—by not waiting for the emperor to remount!

# Author! Author!

The book *Historia Regum Britanniae*, written in the twelfth century by Geoffrey of Monmouth, was the greatest literary hoax ever perpetrated by one man—and his lies were happily perpetuated by various British kings.

A Welshman, Monmouth became the archdeacon of Llandaff, Wales, in 1140 and was consecrated bishop of St. Asaph in 1152. He was also a respected church chronicler, which might explain why he was able to con most of the world for centuries by weaving known historical characters and events into a brilliantly tangled web of deceit.

Incredibly, he invented KING ARTHUR—that chivalrous fellow who later became world-famous for carrying a sword named Excalibur and sitting at a "democratic" Round Table at Camelot with knights in shining armor, such as the insufferably virtuous Sir Galahad.

In his book *Kings and Queens of Early Britain* (Methuen, 1982), the brilliant detective-historian Geoffrey Ashe shows that Monmouth's lies were supported by KING HENRY THE SECOND because they fabricated a royal line—unbroken by Caesar's demeaning conquest of Britain. Welcome propaganda indeed! In addition, King Henry was tickled pink at the idea of people thinking he was a descendant of such an illustrious monarch as King Arthur.

And so Monmouth's fake history went on to become the most influential tract ever written in Britain. Later writers further cemented the Big Lie so deeply into the public mind that it can never be erased:

- Frenchman Robert de Borron introduced the legend of The Grail.
- Chretien de Troyes added Lancelot and Guinevere to the hoax.

- Sir Thomas Malory's great romance, *Le Morte d'Arthur*, added to it.
- Tennyson's *Morte d'Arthur* and *Idylls of the King* were based on it.
- Edmund Spenser wove a summary of it into his renowned *Fairie Queene*.
- Shakespeare took the plot of *King Lear* from it.
- And Milton, Dryden, Pope, Wordsworth, Swinburne, Drayton, Morris, and White all helped to confirm the legend.

Although a shrewd old Yorkshire monk named William of Newburgh publicly denounced Geoffrey of Monmouth as "a shameless and saucy liar" in his own time, nobody of importance listened. But centuries later, when the truth about Monmouth's lies started to leak out, the royal genealogists desperately hunted through old tomes to back them up.

Eventually they found a great British warrior leader named RIOTHAMUS. That didn't have quite the right ring to it, but then they had a bit of luck. In another old document they found that Riothamus was described as Arty. That's it, they cried. That's him. Arty. It must be short for Arthur. (They conveniently ignored the possibility that he might have been a great lover of the arts.) And now, whenever doubt is cast upon King Arthur of Round Table fame, you can be sure someone will pull out "Arty" as proof that King Arthur really did exist.

One other thing you can be absolutely sure of: Every now and again a story will surface in a newspaper or magazine quoting some professor or antiquarian who claims that an astonishing new document, site, monument, cave, or artifact has been discovered that "*strongly indicates*" there really was a King Arthur who lived in Camelot.

# A *Burning Question*

Another world-famous legend is that JOAN OF ARC was an illiterate shepherdess of poor parents who, after hearing "voices" from heaven, led French troops against the English and was burned alive as a result.

Joan's real name was Jehanne Darc. She was not illiterate nor a shepherdess. Her parents were not poor. And powerful evidence indicates that she did *not* perish on that famous bonfire.

These claims are made in the book *Jehanne la Pucelle: l'Histoire, les Documents* (1983). The author, Florence Maquet, discloses that Joan was really of royal birth and explains what happened to Joan after she was allegedly burned. This exciting 400-pager was not written to make money. It took ten years to research and is a labor of love backed up by massive documentation and statements by Joan of Arc herself. It shows that Joan mixed with noblemen who accepted her as one who was born and bred in a royal court and showered her with expensive presents long before she started working her "miracles."

The author and other historians have uncovered strong proof that Joan was the illegitimate daughter of QUEEN ISABEAU OF FRANCE by a liaison with Louis d'Orleans—the younger brother of Charles the Sixth.

Far from being guided by the voices of angels and saints, Joan's military career was secretly planned and financed by the ambitious QUEEN YOLANDE OF ANJOU, who wanted her son-in-law, the Dauphin, to be enthroned as CHARLES THE SEVENTH. Donning a suit of armor, Joan led four thousand French troops to victory after victory against the English—who then controlled much of France.

She succeeded in having her half brother the Dauphin enthroned in July 1429, and this was when Joan's military enthusiasm and charisma made her a political liability. She undermined the new French king's delicate negotiations for peace. That is why, when the Burgundians captured Joan, no ransom was offered for her and she was sold to the English. They set her up in a rigged show trial presided over by a "neutral" judge in the pay of the British and he condemned her to death as a witch guilty of heresy.

But, knowing the truth about Joan, the class-conscious English could not stomach the idea of executing a woman who was a princess by birth. So they did a deal with her. A female prisoner who was an ordinary member of the public (that is, a commoner) was burned at the stake, and Joan was held in luxurious confinement until the hue and cry died down.

The details of Joan's fake execution tell their own story. The crowd watching it was pushed back unusually far by no less than eight hundred English soldiers, and the woman who was burned at the stake in May 1431 was so heavily cloaked and hooded that she was not recognizable.

Four years later the French king concluded a peace treaty with the duke of Burgundy, and seven months after that he triumphantly entered Paris. Just five weeks later Joan of Arc reappeared near Metz and made no attempt to hide her identity. She was positively identified, not only by her two brothers but by many other reliable witnesses who had known her.

Joan was allowed to live in peace because part of her deal with the English was that she would not resume fighting or seek nationwide acceptance from the general public (or the French king) as the famous Joan of Arc. In 1436 she married a knight from Metz named Robert des Armoises, had two children by him, and lived quietly until at least 1457.

Much later the false story that she had been burned (by the hated English) suited Napoleon, so he built her up as a cult figure who was a glowing example of the true, honorable, and patriotic French spirit. As recently as 1920, Joan's legend was finally entrenched in the mind of the world when Pope Benedict the Fifteenth made her a saint.

Anyone wishing to read Florence Maquet's book should write to: Aux Amateurs de Livres, 62 Avenue de Suffren, Paris.

Another excellent book pouring scorn on the claim that a poor, uneducated peasant girl could ever be accepted by the French aristocrats—and agrees that she had royal, not divine, support—is: *Jeanne d'Arc et la Mandragore* (Editions du Rocher, 1983). If you are interested, the address to write to is: Editions du Rocher, 28 Rue Comte Felix Gastaldi, Monte Carlo.

The author is Pierre de Sermoise, an accepted authority on the fifteenth century. Unlike Florence Maquet, however, he possibly has an ax to grind as he is a direct descendant of Robert des Armoises, the man who married the "resurrected" Joan of Arc.

Nonetheless, M. Sermoise's book presents vitally important new material on Joan's birth. By analyzing the ink and watermarks on manuscripts recording royal events, he discovered that false details had been inserted about Queen Isabeau giving birth to a son named Philippe who was stated to have died the same day. Not true, says the author. Philippe never existed. His name was never mentioned in the lists of masses at the time, nor in the inventories related to royal coffins. He says the child born was almost certainly Joan.

Even stronger evidence is that an original document giving Joan of Arc immunity from arrest (safe conduct) was drawn up in 1436—five years *after* she was allegedly burned by the English! However, nothing will eradicate the story that Joan of Arc died a martyr on that flaming pyre. Politically it's a much more desirable tale.

In the words of a conservator at the Bibliothèque Nationale: "The truth about Jeanne d'Arc is veiled behind one of the greatest acts of brainwashing in the history of the past few centuries."

# Royal Books

This is a bibliography with a difference. It lists some of the good, bad, indifferent, and even absurd books on royalty we read (often between the lines) in our relentless search for basic roguish facts, weird events, and that all-important different point of view, before doing our own in-depth research.

*The Reality of Monarchy* by Andrew Duncan (Heineman, 1970). In this well-documented study Mr. Duncan scored a mind-boggling world scoop by publishing the royal family tree of Queen Elizabeth's corgi dogs. This is not as outlandish as it might at first appear because that family tree gives us an insight into the Queen's sense of humor: The tree starts with "Susan" (died 1959) who produced "Honey." And "Honey" gave birth to "Bee," who later gave birth to "Buzz...."

*The Story of Princess Elizabeth* by Anne Ring (John Murray, 1930).

Her Majesty the Queen had such a varied and exciting life

up to the age of four that Anne Ring decided to write this biography. It doesn't have many quotes in it—apart from "Mama," "Dada," and "ga-ga"!

*The Little Princesses* by Marion Crawford (Cassell, 1950).
Written by the Queen's nanny, this book outraged the Royal Family, not so much for what it contained but because a royal servant could be so "disloyal" as to disclose intimate details about The Family. "Crawfie," as she was known at Buckingham Palace, wrote the (friendly and respectful) book because she needed the money for her retirement. If they had paid her better, she would not have done it, she said. In royal jargon, "Doing a Crawfie" means being a double-crosser.

*Theirs Is the Kingdom, the Wealth of the Windsors* by Andrew Moreton (Ambassador Books, 1989).
Describes for the first time the fabulous wealth of the British Royal Family and how Queen Elizabeth became the richest woman in the world.

*Chips: The Diaries of Sir Henry Channon* (Weidenfeld & Nicolson, 1967).

*Inside Kensington Palace* by Andrew Morton (Michael O'Mara Books, 1987).
An excellent look inside the London base of fifteen members of The Family with gossipy tidbits such as the fact that many of the staff have left because of the poor pay and that some of those remaining still accept outside work to bolster their meagre pay packets.

*Dreams about H.M. the Queen and Other Members of the Royal Family* by Brian Masters (Blond/Briggs, 1972).
This book claims that up to one third of the British population has dreamed about the Royal Family. The dominant dream for housewives is that the Queen arrives for tea unexpectedly and the house is a mess.

*The Queen* by Ann Morrow (Book Club Associates, 1983).
Full of perceptive comments and anecdotes.

*Queen Elizabeth II* by Douglas Liversage (Arthur Barker, 1974).

*The Wit of Prince Philip* by Leslie Frewin (Frewin, 1955).

*Philip* by Basil Boothroyd (Longman, 1971).

*Prince Philip* by Peter Lane (Robert Hale, 1980).

*Born Bewildered* by Helene Cordet (Peter Davies, 1961).

Miss Cordet's parents were Greek. She was born in France, married an Englishman and then a Frenchman. Her claim to fame is that she was a childhood friend of Prince Philip. He was her best man when she married the first time, and godfather to her two children, Max and Louise. Before Prince Philip married Princess Elizabeth, a French newspaper published a photograph of a "mystery blonde" in Philip's life and said she would *not* be invited to the royal wedding (by Elizabeth). The photograph was of Helene Cordet but she denies any romantic involvement with the prince. The book is a bit of a yawn and it's hard to understand why the publishers thought it was worth 191 pages. Unless, of course, they knew something we don't . . .

*The Ultimate Family* by John Pearson (Michael Joseph, 1986).

*The Royal House of Windsor* by Elizabeth Longford (Weidenfeld, 1974).

*The Royal Jewels* by Suzy Menkes (Grafton Books, 1985).

*The Windsor Style* by Suzy Menkes (Grafton Books, 1987).

*The Windsor Story* by J. Bryan & C. Murphy (Granada, 1979).

*Gone With the Windsors* by Iles Brody (John C. Winston, 1953).

A very revealing book considering it was written when the duke and duchess were still alive. It is crammed with excellent detective work and engrossing anecdotes.

*Astrology and the Royal Family* by Roger Elliot (Pan Books, 1977).

This witty paperback gives the charts and horoscopes of all the major characters in the British Royal Family. Written in a breezy style, it gives details of their not always heavenly personalities.

*Nothing to Declare* by Mike Thomas (Bozo Press, 1984).

Britain's conservative-minded book chains are not keen to have this off-beat 76-page paperback on their shelves, so it is obtainable only by post for £2 from B. M. Bozo, London WC1. Mike Thomas is an Englishman who describes his country as: "Pokey backstreet England with its flag-waving mindlessness," where the women's magazines are "packed with Royalty and recipes to help the loyal poor celebrate the rich." He doesn't think much of the Queen either: "Her furtive expression still bothers me. Doesn't she strike you as shifty? It's hard to avoid feeling that there's something more. I wouldn't trust someone like that an inch. Compared to her, Richard Nixon looks sincere."

*Diana, Princess of Wales* by Penny Junor (Sidgwick & Jackson, 1982).

*Charles and Diana* by Ralph G. Martin (Grafton Books, 1986).

*Princess Di, The National Dish* by Diana Simmonds (Pluto Press, 1984).

*The Art of Giving* by Stuart Jacobson (Weidenfeld, 1987).

A witty book with splendid snippets such as the fact that on her first visit to the Himalayas, Queen Elizabeth gave the King of Nepal the very latest stereo system—only to be told that the country had no electricity.

*The Royal Shopping Guide* by Nina Grunfeld (Pan, 1984).

A unique guided tour of over three hundred British shops and manufacturers which provide the Royal Family, by appointment, with everything from dog kennels to champagne. Each entry is illustrated and gives details of the royal providers, together with their address, history, and royal connection. A useful book for those wanting to know where Di buys her shoes, who blends Her Majesty's tea, and who makes the rompers for royal babies. A must for Yuppies.

*The Gardens of Queen Elizabeth, The Queen Mother* (Viking, 1988).

Who would think that such a book could hit a British best-seller list? It did. For at least one week. Or so they claimed.

*The Country Lifebook of Queen Elizabeth the Queen Mother* by Godfrey Talbot (Ambassador Books, 1989).

The dear old Queen Mum helped the author to compile this

rather boring 192-pager which has 254 photos and the fore-
word was written by none other than Prince Charles.
*Blood Royal* by Christopher Sinclair-Stevenson (Cape, 1979).
*Monarchs in Waiting* by Walter J. P. Curley (Hutchinson, 1975).
*A Distant Mirror* by Barbara W. Tuchman (Macmillan, 1979).
*Elizabeth I* by Monroe Stearns (Franklin Watts, 1970).
*Kings and Queens of England* by Lady Antonia Fraser (Wei-
denfeld, 1975).
*Cromwell—Our Chief of Men* by Lady Antonia Fraser (Panther,
1975).
*The Dream King—Ludwig II of Bavaria* by Wilfrid Blunt (Ham-
ish Hamilton, 1970).
   A superb book.
*Ferdinand and Isabella* by Melveena McKendrick (Cassell,
1969).
*King of Fools* by John Parker (MacDonald, 1988).
*The Myth of British Monarchy* by Edgar Wilson (Journeyman
Press, 1989).
   In this critical appraisal, Mr. Wilson says the abolition of the
   Monarchy is the great taboo in British politics. No politician
   dares to propose it and pit his own popularity against the
   mass of pro-royal propaganda continually published in the
   British media, or against an Establishment which upholds
   "a family of hereditary billionaires."
*The Royal Whore: Barbara Castlemaine* (Barbara Villiers) by
Allen Andrews (Hutchinson, 1971).
*Lucy Walter: Wife or Mistress?* by Lord George Scott (Harrap,
1947).
*Marlborough the Man* by Bryan Bevan (Robert Hale, 1975).
*Marlborough* by Correlli Barnett (Eyre Methuen, 1974).
*A Character of Charles II* by Samuel Tuke, 1660.
*Happy Death of King Charles II* by Father Huddleston, 1687.
*The Newsmen of Queen Anne* by W. B. Ewald (Houghton Mifflin,
1956).
   A look at how and why newspapers began in England. Five
   years after the restoration of Charles the Second, the English

saw their first real newspaper, the *Oxford Gazette*. Before this, only irregular news books and pamphlets had been printed. To keep a strong control over the newshawks, the "Casanova king," Charles the Second, appointed a censor named Roger L'Estrange. But he was also a Casanova who closed his eyes to unlicensed news sheets if the printer's wife was "nice" to him!

*William and Mary* by Henri and Barbara van der Zee (Macmillan, 1973).

*George the Third* by John Heneage Jesse, 1867.

*The Oxford Book Of Royal Anecdotes* by Elizabeth Longford (Oxford University Press, 1989). Yet another Longford gem.

*Victoria R.I.* by Elizabeth Longford (Pan, 1966).

*Queen Victoria* by Cecil Woodham-Smith (Hamish Hamilton, 1972).

*Queen Victoria's Other World* by Peter Underwood, 1987.

Sold by Ambassador Books, P. O. Box 756, London SW9, this is an interesting study of the largely unexplored fascination Queen Victoria had for the unseen and the paranormal. The author uncovers the conspiracy of silence concerning Victoria's macabre interest in death and its draperies.

*Highness: The Maharajas of India* by Ann Morrow (Grafton Books, 1986).

The Irish-born author is a former court correspondent of the British *Daily Telegraph*. Her splendid book tells of the luxurious life-style of the rulers of India. One studded his fridge with diamonds. Another filled his swimming pool with champagne (sweet or dry according to his guests' tastes). Another had eight hundred dogs, each with its own room, telephone and servant. And the most jealous ordered his sexy wife to wear a chastity belt. She agreed on condition that it be made by Cartier and studded with blue-white diamonds. It was!

*Sultans in Splendour* by Philip Mansel (Andre Deutsch, 1988).

*Propaganda and Empire: The Manipulation of British Public Opinion 1880 to 1960* by John MacKenzie (Manchester University Press, 1984).

Heavy, but useful.

*Edward the Rake* by John Pearson (Weidenfeld, 1975).

*Edward VII* by Giles St. Aubyn (Collins, 1979).

*The Follies of King Edward VII* by Allen Andrews (Lexington Press, 1975).

Among the more spectacular follies was the railway station King Edward had built for his use only! It was at Wolferton, two miles from his holiday home at Sandringham. He also had a special train—"The Prince's Train"—laid on for his travels between London and Wolferton.

*Edward VIII* by Frances Donaldson (Weidenfeld, 1974).

The author is the wife of the Labour Peer, Lord Donaldson, and her book is written with precision, wit, and legitimate skepticism.

*The Guinness Book of Kings, Rulers and Statesmen* by Clive Carpenter.

This fabulous book lists them all. Worldwide from 3000 B.C. to 1979. Available from Guinness Books, London Road, Enfield, Middlesex, U.K., it is an absolute *must* for every history teacher as it's the finest quick reference book to the world's rulers et cetera. Also gives brief need-to-know biographies and those all-important dates.

*Dictionary of National Biography* (Oxford University Press).

Published since 1917, these twenty-three volumes are priceless. How can any historian manage without them?

*Encyclopedia Britannica.*

*Encyclopedia Americana.*

*Webster's Biographical Dictionary* (Merriam).

*Chambers's Biographical Dictionary* (Chambers Ltd, 1938).

*Vicars of Christ* by Peter de Rosa (Bantam, 1988).

A shocking and well-documented expose of the Papacy by a "rebel" Catholic priest, it centers mainly on the time when Popes occupied thrones and were more powerful than most monarchs.

*The Catholic Encyclopedia* (Grolier, New York).

Often gives the other side of the story, as does:

*Dictionary of Catholic Biography* by J. J. Delaney and J. E. Tobin (Robert Hale, 1962).

*One Hundred Great Kings, Queens and Rulers of the World* edited by John Canning (Odhams, 1969).

*Homosexuals in History* by A. L. Rowse (Weidenfeld & Nicolson, 1977).

Gaily written and artistically researched. But not enough royal Queens.

*Happy and Glorious—An Anthology of Royalty* edited by Peter Vansittart (Collins, 1988).

*The Enchanted Glass* by Tom Nairn (Radius, 1988).

A highbrow appraisal of British royalty, its "manipulation of the media" and the "conspiracy of the Rulers against their underlings."

*World Famous Acquittals* by Charles Franklin (Odhams/Hamlyn, 1970).

*More Incredible* by Kevin McFarland (Hart, 1976).

*Strange But True* edited by Tim Healey (Octopus Books, 1987).

*Things You Thought You Thought You Knew* by Graeme Donald (Unwin, 1986).

*Cabbages and Kings* by G. Uden and R. Yglesias (Kestrel/Penguin, 1978).

*Royal Romance* by Tim Satchell (New English Library, 1986).

*Anne, the Princess Royal* by Brian Hoey (Grafton Books, 1989).

*Anne and the Princesses Royal* by Helen Cathcart (W. H. Allen, 1975).

*The Lineage and Ancestry of H.R.H. Prince Charles* by Gerald Paget (Skilton, Edinburgh, 1977).

The author produced this two-volumed life's work when he was aged ninety-two. It costs £60 and in it, he traces no less than 262,000 of the prince's ancestors, showing that he is descended from just about everybody who had been anybody, anywhere!

Some of the books we mention are out of print and may be difficult to find. But if you are particularly keen to have one tracked down, the man to write to is Britain's "King of Books."

This is Mr. Richard Booth, who is the self-appointed ruler of "the independent Book Kingdom of Hay-on-Wye" where he has more than one million secondhand books stocked on nine miles of shelving.

His address is: "The Limited," 44 Lion Street, Hay-on-Wye, via Hereford, Wales. HR3 5AA.

# Index